METHODS IN MOLECULAR BIOLOGY

For further volumes:
http://www.springer.com/series/7651

For over 35 years, biological scientists have come to rely on the research protocols and methodologies in the critically acclaimed Methods in Molecular Biology series. The series was the first to introduce the step-by-step protocols approach that has become the standard in all biomedical protocol publishing. Each protocol is provided in readily-reproducible step-by step fashion, opening with an introductory overview, a list of the materials and reagents needed to complete the experiment, and followed by a detailed procedure that is supported with a helpful notes section offering tips and tricks of the trade as well as troubleshooting advice. These hallmark features were introduced by series editor Dr. John Walker and constitute the key ingredient in each and every volume of the Methods in Molecular Biology series. Tested and trusted, comprehensive and reliable, all protocols from the series are indexed in PubMed.

Manuscript Instructions https://drive.google.com/file/d/1K4Az5vpAFVzYadJ3jKx2-QSo7Dqa_SNA/view?usp=sharing

Cellular Spatial Characterization and Analysis

Edited by

Timothy L. Frankel

Department of Surgery, University of Michigan–Ann Arbor, Ann Arbor, MI, USA

Arvind Rao

Computational Medicine and Bioinformatics, University of Michigan–Ann Arbor, Ann Arbor, MI, USA

Humana Press

Editors
Timothy L. Frankel
Department of Surgery
University of Michigan–Ann Arbor
Ann Arbor, MI, USA

Arvind Rao
Computational Medicine and Bioinformatics
University of Michigan–Ann Arbor
Ann Arbor, MI, USA

ISSN 1064-3745 ISSN 1940-6029 (electronic)
Methods in Molecular Biology
ISBN 978-1-0716-5026-4 ISBN 978-1-0716-5027-1 (eBook)
https://doi.org/10.1007/978-1-0716-5027-1

This Humana imprint is published by the registered company Springer Science+Business Media, LLC, part of Springer Nature
The registered company address is: 1 New York Plaza, New York, NY 10004, U.S.A.

Preface

The era of immunotherapy and the advanced understanding of the tumor microenvironment have necessitated the development of new methods to describe cellular phenotypes and behaviors. Previous techniques to study the tissue microenvironment often relied on examination of single cells, disregarding valuable spatial information that can provide important context. Recent technological advancements in staining and imaging have allowed for the characterization of transcriptomic and proteomic cellular profiles in situ. By pairing with more sophisticated computer-aided microscopy and signal amplification, understanding spatial relationships even at the subcellular level is now possible. The application of informatics and spatial modeling methodologies to cellular spatial data has created novel ways of understanding biologic interactions.

This methods book brings together a compendium of not only novel staining techniques but also protocols and practices to process data using various bioinformatic approaches. It is divided into broad themes covering traditional immunohistochemistry, advanced spatial proteomics, and spatial genomics.

Ann Arbor, USA *Timothy L. Frankel*
Ann Arbor, USA *Arvind Rao*

Contents

PART III SPATIAL GENOMICS

Contributors

Aadith Kumar • *Department of Surgery, University of Michigan, Ann Arbor, MI, USA*
Ahmad Makky • *Department of Pathology and Neuropathology, University Hospital and Comprehensive Cancer Center Tübingen, Tübingen, Germany*
Ahmed M. Elhossiny • *Department of Computational Medicine and Bioinformatics, University of Michigan, Ann Arbor, MI, USA; Department of Surgery, University of Michigan, Ann Arbor, MI, USA*
Alberto Olivei • *Department of Surgery, University of Michigan, Ann Arbor, MI, USA*
Alexander D. Borowsky • *Helen Diller Family Comprehensive Cancer Center, University of California, San Francisco, School of Medicine, San Francisco, CA, USA*
Alexander Rochwarger • *Department of Pathology and Neuropathology, University Hospital and Comprehensive Cancer Center Tübingen, Tübingen, Germany*
Amalie M. Grønning • *Department of Clinical Medicine, Aarhus University, Aarhus, Denmark*
Amina Nurmammadova • *Department of Pathology and Neuropathology, University Hospital and Comprehensive Cancer Center Tübingen, Tübingen, Germany; Institute for Cell Therapy Discovery and Innovation, The University of Texas MD Anderson Cancer Center, Houston, USA*
Andrea J. Radtke • *Center for Advanced Tissue Imaging, Laboratory of Immune System Biology, National Institute of Allergy and Infectious Diseases, National Institutes of Health, Bethesda, MD, USA; Leica Microsystems, Wetzlar, Germany*
Andrew Spiteri • *Department of Surgery, University of Michigan, Ann Arbor, MI, USA*
Annika Jäger • *Department of Pathology and Neuropathology, University Hospital and Comprehensive Cancer Center Tübingen, Tübingen, Germany*
Arvind Rao • *Department of Computational Medicine and Bioinformatics, University of Michigan, Ann Arbor, MI, USA; Department of Biomedical Engineering, University of Michigan, Ann Arbor, MI, USA; Department of Biostatistics, University of Michigan, Ann Arbor, MI, USA; Department of Radiation Oncology, University of Michigan, Ann Arbor, MI, USA*
Ashley P. Tsang • *Department of Computational Medicine and Bioinformatics, University of Michigan, Ann Arbor, MI, USA*
Bavani Kannan • *Cancer Discovery Hub, National Cancer Centre Singapore, Singapore, Singapore*
Benjamin B. Green • *Department of Clinical Medicine, Aarhus University, Aarhus, Denmark*
Brian D. Griffith • *Department of Surgery, University of Michigan, Ann Arbor, MI, USA*
Christian M. Schürch • *Department of Pathology and Neuropathology, University Hospital and Comprehensive Cancer Center Tübingen, Tübingen, Germany; Cluster of Excellence iFIT (EXC 2180) "Image-Guided and Functionally Instructed Tumor Therapies", University of Tübingen, Tübingen, Germany*

CHRISTINE BESCHORNER • *Department of Pathology and Neuropathology, University Hospital and Comprehensive Cancer Center Tübingen, Tübingen, Germany*
EMILY SPERANZA • *Florida Research and Innovation Center, Cleveland Clinic Lerner Research Institute, Port Saint Lucie, FL, USA*
FRÉDÉRIC H. LOGIN • *Department of Clinical Medicine, Aarhus University, Aarhus, Denmark*
GITTE A. PEDERSEN • *Department of Clinical Medicine, Aarhus University, Aarhus, Denmark*
HIDETOSHI MORI • *Center for Immunology and Infectious Diseases, University of California, Davis, CA, USA; Helen Diller Family Comprehensive Cancer Center, University of California, San Francisco, School of Medicine, San Francisco, CA, USA*
HIROSHI ICHISE • *Lymphocyte Biology Section, Laboratory of Immune System Biology, National Institute of Allergy and Infectious Diseases, National Institutes of Health, Bethesda, MD, USA; Department of Immunology and Cell Biology, Graduate School of Medicine, The University of Osaka, Suita, Japan*
IAN T. LAMBORN • *Lymphocyte Biology Section, Laboratory of Immune System Biology, National Institute of Allergy and Infectious Diseases, National Institutes of Health, Bethesda, MD, USA*
JAKE MCGUE • *Department of Surgery, University of Michigan, Ann Arbor, MI, USA*
JASON YONGSHENG CHAN • *Cancer Discovery Hub, National Cancer Centre Singapore, Singapore, Singapore; Division of Medical Oncology, National Cancer Centre Singapore, Singapore, Singapore; Oncology Academic Clinical Program, Duke-NUS Medical School, Singapore, Singapore; Singapore Translational Cancer Consortium, Singapore, Singapore*
JEFFREY CHUN TAT LIM • *Institute of Molecular and Cellular Biology, Agency for Science, Technology and Research (A*STAR), Singapore, Singapore*
JIA GUO • *Biodesign Institute and School of Molecular Sciences, Arizona State University, Tempe, AZ, USA*
JING YI LEE • *Cancer Discovery Hub, National Cancer Centre Singapore, Singapore, Singapore; Cancer Stem Cell and Biology, Duke-NUS Medical School, Singapore, Singapore*
JING ZHAO • *Department of Pathology and Neuropathology, University Hospital and Comprehensive Cancer Center Tübingen, Tübingen, Germany*
JOE POH SHENG YEONG • *Institute of Molecular and Cellular Biology, Agency for Science, Technology and Research (A*STAR), Singapore, Singapore; Singapore Translational Cancer Consortium, Singapore, Singapore*
JOSEPH NICHOLS • *Department of Pathology and Neuropathology, University Hospital and Comprehensive Cancer Center Tübingen, Tübingen, Germany*
JUAN ECHEVERRY • *Department of Physics, University of Illinois Urbana–Champaign, Urbana, IL, USA*
KAREN GREIF • *Department of Pathology and Neuropathology, University Hospital and Comprehensive Cancer Center Tübingen, Tübingen, Germany*
LANZHU LI • *Department of Pathology and Neuropathology, University Hospital and Comprehensive Cancer Center Tübingen, Tübingen, Germany; Cluster of Excellence iFIT (EXC 2180) "Image-Guided and Functionally Instructed Tumor Therapies", University of Tübingen, Tübingen, Germany*
LEANNE ARAKKAL • *Lymphocyte Biology Section, Laboratory of Immune System Biology, National Institute of Allergy and Infectious Diseases, National Institutes of Health, Bethesda, MD, USA*

Lene N. Nejsum • *Department of Clinical Medicine, Aarhus University, Aarhus, Denmark*
Lu Xiao • *Biodesign Institute and School of Molecular Sciences, Arizona State University, Tempe, AZ, USA*
Marina Pasca Di Magliano • *Department of Surgery, University of Michigan, Ann Arbor, MI, USA*
Mohammed Zidane • *Department of Pathology and Neuropathology, University Hospital and Comprehensive Cancer Center Tübingen, Tübingen, Germany*
Nastassja Lehmann • *Department of Pathology and Neuropathology, University Hospital and Comprehensive Cancer Center Tübingen, Tübingen, Germany*
Qian Kong • *Research Center for Chemical Biology and Omics Analysis, School of Science, Southern University of Science and Technology, Shenzhen, China; Department of Chemistry, School of Science, Southern University of Science and Technology, Shenzhen, China*
Rashmi Kumar • *Department of Surgery, University of Michigan, Ann Arbor, MI, USA*
Reva Kulkarni • *Department of Computational Medicine and Bioinformatics, University of Michigan, Ann Arbor, MI, USA*
Rikke Nørregaard • *Department of Clinical Medicine, Aarhus University, Aarhus, Denmark*
Ronald N. Germain • *Center for Advanced Tissue Imaging, Laboratory of Immune System Biology, National Institute of Allergy and Infectious Diseases, National Institutes of Health, Bethesda, MD, USA; Lymphocyte Biology Section, Laboratory of Immune System Biology, National Institute of Allergy and Infectious Diseases, National Institutes of Health, Bethesda, MD, USA*
Ruijun Tian • *Department of Chemistry, School of Science, Southern University of Science and Technology, Shenzhen, China; Research Center for Chemical Biology and Omics Analysis, School of Science, Southern University of Science and Technology, Shenzhen, China*
Sangjin Kim • *Center for Biophysics and Quantitative Biology, University of Illinois Urbana–Champaign, Urbana, IL, USA; Department of Physics, University of Illinois Urbana–Champaign, Urbana, IL, USA*
Saumya Manmadhan • *Department of Pathology and Neuropathology, University Hospital and Comprehensive Cancer Center Tübingen, Tübingen, Germany*
Søren H. Elsborg • *Department of Clinical Medicine, Aarhus University, Aarhus, Denmark*
Timothy L. Frankel • *Department of Surgery, University of Michigan, Ann Arbor, MI, USA*
Vibeke S. Dam • *Department of Clinical Medicine, Aarhus University, Aarhus, Denmark*
Vikneswari Rajasegaran • *Cancer Discovery Hub, National Cancer Centre Singapore, Singapore, Singapore; Singapore Translational Cancer Consortium, Singapore, Singapore*
Vivien I. Maltez • *Division of Allergy, Immunology, and Rheumatology, Department of Pediatrics, University of California San Diego, San Diego, CA, USA; Lymphocyte Biology Section, Laboratory of Immune System Biology, National Institute of Allergy and Infectious Diseases, National Institutes of Health, Bethesda, MD, USA*
Xi Wang • *The Second Clinical Medical College of Jinan University, the First Affiliated Hospital of Southern University of Science and Technology, Shenzhen People's Hospital, Shenzhen, China*

YANNICK PALMOWSKI • *Department of Pathology and Neuropathology, University Hospital and Comprehensive Cancer Center Tübingen, Tübingen, Germany*
YIZHENG ZHANG • *Department of Pathology and Neuropathology, University Hospital and Comprehensive Cancer Center Tübingen, Tübingen, Germany*
YU-HUAN WANG • *Department of Physics, University of Illinois Urbana–Champaign, Urbana, IL, USA*
ZHEN WEI NEO • *Institute of Molecular and Cellular Biology, Agency for Science, Technology and Research (A*STAR), Singapore, Singapore*
ZIV YANIV • *Office of Cyber Infrastructure and Computational Biology, National Institute of Allergy and Infectious Diseases, National Institutes of Health, Bethesda, MD, USA*

Part I

Multiplex IHC

Check for updates

Chapter 1

High-Plex Tissue Imaging with Conventional Immunofluorescence Platforms and Open-Source Software via Iterative Bleaching Extends Multiplexity (IBEX)

Ian T. Lamborn, Hiroshi Ichise, Emily Speranza, Leanne Arakkal, Vivien I. Maltez, Ziv Yaniv, Andrea J. Radtke and Ronald N. Germain

Abstract

Iterative bleaching extends multiplexity (IBEX) is an easy-to-use, highly multiplex immunofluorescent tissue imaging method that employs widely available microscopy platforms, commercial reagents, and open-source software. In this article, we describe how to implement this method in a laboratory that has minimal experience with immunohistochemistry.

Keywords IBEX, Multiplex, Microscopy, Spatial proteomics, Optical imaging, Immunofluorescence

1 Introduction

A key tenet of biology is that "form fits function" [1], meaning that the cellular organization and 3-dimensional structure of a tissue or organ is inextricably linked to the biological activities it performs. 2D and 3D highly multiplex tissue imaging technologies can now probe the complex composition of biological tissues in detail, providing new insights into their function.

Most methods for high-complexity tissue imaging require specialized equipment and/or proprietary reagents and software [2]. To enable the larger research community to perform high-plex imaging using widely available microscopy platforms and reagents, our laboratory developed iterative bleaching extends multiplexity (IBEX), an easy-to-use, iterative, and highly multiplexed immunofluorescent staining protocol that is compatible with diverse fluorescence imaging platforms [3, 4]. Additionally, the IBEX method utilizes the Insight Segmentation and Registration Toolkit (ITK), open-source

The authors Ian T. Lamborn, Hiroshi Ichise, and Emily Speranza contributed equally.

Timothy L. Frankel and Arvind Rao (eds.), *Cellular Spatial Characterization and Analysis*, Methods in Molecular Biology, vol. 2995, https://doi.org/10.1007/978-1-0716-5027-1_1,

software with a simplified, non-command driven user interface version (SimpleITK) [5, 6], for automated alignment of iterative images. Currently, the IBEX method is compatible with >1200 commercially available antibodies and >75 commercially available fluorophores, with these numbers continually increasing as knowledge sharing of validation efforts continues [7]. Furthermore, while the IBEX method is compatible with automated handling systems that can increase speed and reduce inter-sample variability, such additional equipment and systems are not necessary to generate robust, highly multiplex spatial proteomic data sets, as demonstrated in a recent detailed protocol [3]. Since the original description of the method [4, 6], IBEX has been used by ourselves and others to characterize the spatial organization of many mouse and human tissues [8–12].

The following protocol is a simplified iteration of our previously described "manual IBEX" protocol that utilizes conventional immunofluorescence platforms without the need for automated staining equipment (hereafter referred to as "manual IBEX") [4]. This protocol is intended to be readily adopted and performed in any laboratory already performing fluorescent immunohistochemistry with a need for only a few additional reagents and the use of open-source software. For reference, we note throughout where non-essential automation platforms or other specialized equipment have been successfully integrated into the manual IBEX method. Additionally, we provide links to video tutorials on critical steps in manual IBEX, as well as additional procedural considerations for staining high-background tissues, such as those encountered in the tumor microenvironment, and highly fixed tissues (e.g., 10% formalin for 7 days), as is often required for tissues containing biohazardous infectious agents.

2 Materials

2.1 Tissue Dissection, Grossing, and Embedding

1. 0.25× BD Cytofix/Cytoperm Fixation and Permeabilization Solution (cat. no. 554722): mix 3 ml of 1× pH 7.4 phosphate-buffered saline for every 1 ml of BD Cytofix/Cytoperm solution (*see* **Note 1**).
2. Tissue-Tek O.C.T® Compound (Sakura Finetek, cat. no. 4583).
3. 30% (w/v) sucrose solution: dissolve sucrose in sterile 1× PBS and pass through 0.22 μm bottle top sterile filter (*see* **Note 2**).
4. *Optional:* Dissecting microscope (Zeiss Stemi 2000-C Stereo Microscope 6.5×–50× or comparable instrument).
5. Forceps, 13 cm, curved, standard grade.
6. Fine dissection forceps.
7. Dissection scissors.
8. Dissecting mat, flexible, polypropylene.
9. Histomolds, suggested 10 × 10 × 5 mm or 15 × 15 × 5 mm.

2.2 Tissue Sectioning

1. Glass microscopy slides.
2. Chrome alum–gelatin (Newcomer Supply, cat. no. 1033A) (*see* **Note 3**).
3. Glass coverslips.
4. Oven (Boekel Scientific, cat. no. 133001 or a comparable instrument).
5. Cryostat (Leica Biosystems, cat. no. CM1950 or a comparable instrument).
6. Low-profile microtome razor blades.
7. Paintbrushes, camelhair brush.

2.3 Tissue Blocking and Immunolabeling

1. ImmEdge® Hydrophobic Barrier PAP Pen.
2. Blocking buffer: to 1× PBS add 0.3% (v/v) Triton-X 100, 1% (w/v) bovine serum albumin (BSA), and 1% (v/v) human (BD Biosciences, cat. no. 564219 for human tissue) or mouse (BD Biosciences, cat. no. 553141 for murine tissue) Fc Block, or similar blocking buffer.
3. Vacuum aspirator.
4. Microscopy slide moisture chamber.
5. Antibodies (*see* **Note 4**).
6. *Optional:* PELCO BioWave Pro microwave (Ted Pella Inc., cat. no. 36500-230).
7. *Optional*: PELCO SteadyTemp Pro (Ted Pella Inc., cat. no. 50062).
8. Fluoromount-G Mounting Medium.

2.4 Microscopy

1. Fluorescent Microscope—protocol compatible with fluorescence microscopes including confocal and widefield microscopes as well as slide scanners.
2. Immersion oil (optional, depending on objective).

2.5 Fluorophore Inactivation

1. Kimwipes.
2. 1 mg/ml $LiBH_4$ solution: dissolve $LiBH_4$ (STREM Chemicals, cat. no. 93-0397; purchase in 1 g aliquots) into diH_2O and allow to sit at RT for 10 min until the formation of bubbles occurs. Pass the solution through a 0.22 μm syringe filter attached to a 20 ml syringe to remove any impurities prior to use (*see* **Note 5** and instructional video entitled "Demonstration of making 1 mg/ml of $LiBH_4$" on the IBEX community website at https://ibeximagingcommunity.github.io/ibex_imaging_knowledge_base/videos.html).
3. *Optional:* Ultraviolet (UV) Light Emitting Diode (LED) (OPENLUX, cat. no. B07VH3CVSF) or a comparable instrument.

2.6 Image Registration

1. *Recommended*: Computer with ≥32 GB of RAM and running Windows, Linux, or OSX. Suggested specifications for use with Imaris software or Imaris Viewer: 3.3 GHz CPU (Intel or AMD), 6 to 8 cores, NVIDA Quadro RTX 4000 8GB GPU
2. Imaris Viewer (Oxford Instruments, https://imaris.oxinst.com/imaris-viewer)
3. *Optional*: Imaris "Full Version" software package (Oxford Instruments) or comparable image processing software suite
4. SimpleITK Imaris Extensions (https://github.com/niaid/imaris_extensions)
5. Python (interpreter and core libraries), e.g., Miniconda (https://docs.conda.io/en/latest/miniconda.html) (*see* **Note 6**).

2.7 Opal-Plex: Tissue Embedding and Sectioning (FFPE)

1. Microtome for FFPE sectioning (Leica Microsystems, cat. no. 14051956472) or equivalent
2. Glassmicroscopy slides
3. Tissue flotation bath (Newcomer supply, cat. no. 6952) or similar.

2.8 Opal-Plex: Tissue Pre-Processing—Dewaxing and Re-hydration

1. Xylenes (Sigma, cat. no. XX0060-4) or equivalent
2. IHC staining stations (Newcomer supply, cat. no. 68432A) or equivalent are highly suggested
3. 100% ethanol (histology grade)
4. DiH_2O
5. 10% neutral buffered formalin
6. Tris-buffered saline with Tween (TBST): dilute 10× TBS to 1× with diH_2O and add 0.5% (v/v) Tween 20

2.9 Opal-Plex: Immunostaining

1. Opal 7 color manual detection kit (Akoya Biosciences, OP-000003)
2. Opal 480 reagent pack (Akoya Biosciences, cat. no. SKU FP1500001KT)
3. Opal 780 reagent pack (Akoya Biosciences, cat. no. SKU FP1501001KT)
4. Glass coverslips
5. 10× spectral DAPI (Akoya Biosciences, SKU FP1490) or equivalent
6. Fluoromount-G Mounting Medium

2.10 Opal-Plex: Image Acquisition

1. Widefieldmicroscope; we recommend the PhenoImager from Akoya Biosciences as it is designed for Opal fluorophores. However, any widefield scope will work as along as it is set up to detect the correct spectral range. We have also used a Leica SP8 confocal microscope with white light laser.

2.11 Opal-Plex: Fluorophore Inactivation and Restaining

1. TBST
2. 1 mg/ml $LiBH_4$ solution

2.12 Automation: Immunolabeling

1. Automated staining instrument (suggested: Leica Bond Rx or Rxm) and associated staining reagents specific to automated strainer used. For example:

   Bond Wash Solution (Leica Biosystems, cat. no. AR9590)
   Bond Titration Containers (Leica Biosystems, cat. no. OPT9049)
   Bond Small Volume Containers (Leica Biosystems, cat. no. OP79193)
   Bond Large Volume Containers (Leica Biosystems, cat. no. OP309700)
   Leica Bond universal cover tiles (Leica Biosystems, cat. no. S21.4611)
2. Glass microscopy slides
3. Blocking buffer
4. Antibodies (*see* **Note 4**)

3 Methods

The manual IBEX method (see Sects. 3.1–3.6) represents a core, simplified protocol that requires only a few additional reagents and open-source software beyond those employed in traditional fluorescent immunohistochemistry studies and without a need for automated staining equipment. This protocol is written for preparing/staining fixed-frozen tissue samples (i.e., paraformaldehyde fixed and OCT compound embedded tissues), our preferred method of tissue preservation. However, IBEX has been employed with fixed frozen, snap (fresh) frozen, and formalin-fixed paraffin-embedded (FFPE) tissues with success [13]. A modified IBEX protocol which employs Opal™ Multiplex (Opal-plex) for amplifying signals in highly fixed samples such as tissue containing biohazardous infectious agents or high background tissue such tumor is presented in Sects. 3.7–3.12. Lastly, procedural modifications for adding automaton to the manual IBEX protocol are presented in Sects. 3.13–3.14.

3.1 Tissue Dissection, Grossing, and Embedding

1. Upon obtaining a fresh tissue sample, take note of tissue landmarks that will permit anatomical re-orientation throughout processing and fixation. Be sure to preserve these features (*see* **Note 7**).

2. To ensure efficient fixation, grossly trim tissue using a scalpel so that the shortest dimension is ≤5 mm.
3. Remove excess fat and connective tissue with dissecting tools (scalpel, forceps, scissors) on a dissecting mat with or without the use of a dissecting microscope (*see* **Note 8**).
4. For optimal fixation conditions, fix samples by submerging processed samples into 0.25X BD Cytofix/Cytoperm solution in a sealed tube (e.g., 50 ml conical tube) at a fixative to tissue (v/v) ratio of 20:1. Steps 1–4 should be done as quickly as possible to preserve tissue and cell integrity.
5. Incubate samples at 4°C for 16–24 h (*see* **Note 9**) with gentle rocking.
6. Wash away excess fixative by submerging samples in 1× PBS at a PBS to tissue (v/v) ratio of 20:1 at room temperature (RT, 20–21°C) with rocking for 5 min to remove excess fixative. Repeat twice (*see* **Note 10**).
7. Dehydrate samples by submerging tissue in 30% (w/v) sucrose solution at 4°C for 16–24 h (*see* **Note 11**). Use a sucrose to tissue (v/v) ratio of 20:1.
8. Embed samples by filling Histomold with Tissue-Tek O.C.T Compound (OCT media) and submerging tissue completely in the OCT media (*see* **Note 12**).
9. Place Histomold containing submerged sample on dry ice until frozen solid and then store samples at −80°C (*see* **Note 13**).

3.2 Tissue Sectioning

1. Remove OCT media-embedded tissue block from −80°C and allow it to equilibrate to −20°C in the Cryostat.
2. Coat a glass slide by adding 15 μl chrome alum–gelatin to one side. Spread evenly using the edge of a cover slip or a separate glass slide via the blood smear technique. (*see* **Note 14** and instructional video entitled "Coating a slide with chrome alum–gelatin adhesive" on the IBEX community website at https://ibeximagingcommunity.github.io/ibex_imaging_knowledge_base/videos.html).
3. Dry-coated slide in oven at 60°C for 1 h (*see* **Note 15**).
4. Using a cryostat, section the OCT media-embedded tissue into 5–20 μm thick sections and transfer onto RT chrome alum–gelatin coated slide (*see* **Note 16**).

3.3 Tissue Blocking and Antibody Immunolabeling

1. Draw a circular boundary around the adhered sample using an ImmEdge Hydrophobic Barrier PAP Pen. Allow to dry completely at RT (5–10 min) (*see* **Note 17**).
2. Rehydrate tissue by covering adhered tissue section with 1× PBS pH 7.4 for 5 min then aspirate PBS (*see* **Note 18** and **Note 19**).

3. Block tissue section by covering tissue with blocking buffer and placing slide in slide moisture chamber containing RT water in the lower section. Incubate for 30 min at RT then aspirate blocking buffer (*see* **Notes 20** and **21**). *All subsequent steps are conducted with slide remaining in moisture chamber until coverslip mounting (i.e., Step 12).
4. Wash sample with enough 1× PBS to completely cover the sample, or by submerging the slide in PBS for 1 min. Repeat this step 2 more times (*see* **Note 18**).
5. Remove PBS and cover tissue with antibody solution (*see* **Notes 18** and **22**).
6. Incubate samples for 1 h at 37°C, or 4 h at RT, or overnight at 4°C. Be sure to use a slide humidity chamber or similar to prevent evaporation of antibody solution/drying of tissue sample as well as light exposure (*see* **Note 23**).
7. (*Optional—if PELCO BioWave Pro is available*). Place samples in PELCO BioWave Pro microwave equipped with PELCO Steady Temp Pro and run two consecutive 2-1-2-1-2-1-2-1-2 programs. Ensure slide moisture chamber contains RT water and is closed (*see* **Note 24**).
8. Wash sample three times with 1× PBS for 1 min each wash (*see* **Note 18**).
9. (*Optional—only necessary if using unconjugated primary antibodies in* Step 5) Cover tissue with secondary antibody solution. Incubate samples for 30 min at 37°C, or for 1 h at RT, or overnight at 4°C (*see* **Note 23**).
10. (*Optional—if PELCO BioWave Pro is available*). Place samples in PELCO BioWave Pro microwave equipped with PELCO Steady Temp Pro and run the 2-1-2-1-2-1-2-1-2 program once. Ensure slide moisture chamber contains RT water and is closed (*see* **Note 24**).
11. Wash sample three times with 1× PBS for 1 min each wash (*see* **Note 18**).
12. Remove as much PBS as possible without drying out tissues. Quickly add the minimum amount of Fluoromount-G mounting medium necessary to completely cover and surround each tissue section. Gently cover with a coverslip (*see* **Note 25** and instructional video entitled "Mounting tissue and applying coverslip" on the IBEX community website at https://ibeximagingcommunity.github.io/ibex_imaging_knowledge_base/videos.html).
13. Allow mounting medium to dry for at least 1 h at RT prior to imaging (*see* **Note 26**).

3.4 Image Acquisition (see Note 27)

1. *(Cycle 1)* Position the slide on the stage in a reproducible position (*see* **Note 28**).
2. *(Cycles 2 and beyond)* Position the slide on the stage exactly as was done in Step 1 (*see* **Note 28**).
3. *(Cycles 2 and beyond)* Adjust the z-plane to begin imaging at the same z-plane used to begin acquisition of the cycle 1 image (*see* **Note 29**).
4. Acquire and save image (*see* **Note 30**).

3.5 Fluorophore Inactivation and Restaining

1. If using oil immersion objective, carefully remove excess immersion oil from coverslip by gently blotting with a Kimwipe (*see* **Note 31**).
2. Submerge slide and coverslip in a container filled with enough of 1× PBS pH 7.4 to completely cover the slide when in a vertical orientation. Wait until coverslip loosens (typically 30–60 min) (*see* **Note 32**).
3. Carefully remove slide from container. Ideally coverslip will have fallen off naturally. If coverslip is loose but still attached, gently lift a corner of the coverslip with a pair of fine forceps or razor blade (*see* **Note 32** and instructional video entitled "Coverslip removal after image acquisition" on the IBEX community website at https://ibeximagingcommunity.github.io/ibex_imaging_knowledge_base/videos.html).
4. Wash sample three times with 1× PBS for 1 min per wash to thoroughly remove mounting medium (*see* **Notes 18** and **33**).
5. While washing samples, prepare 1 mg/ml $LiBH_4$ solution; wait for bubbles to appear in the solution (*see* **Note 34**, and instructional video entitled "Making 1 mg/ml of $LiBH_4$" on the IBEX community website at https://ibeximaging-community.github.io/ibex_imaging_knowledge_base/videos.html).
6. Cover tissue with enough 1 mg/ml $LiBH_4$ to completely cover the sample for 15 min (*see* **Notes 18** and **34**).
7. *(Optional)* If attempting to fluorophore inactivate Brilliant Violet 421 (BV421) or Brilliant Violet 510 (BV510) fluorophores, place the slide on UV LED while tissue is simultaneously exposed to 1 mg/ml $LiBH_4$ for 15 min. Perform this step in a cold room (4°C) to prevent overheating the tissue (*see* **Note 35** and Fig. 1).
8. Wash sample three times with 1× PBS for 1 min per wash to thoroughly remove $LiBH_4$ (*see* **Note 36**).
9. Repeat Steps 5–13 in Sect. 3.3 for each additional cycle of immunolabeling.
10. Repeat Step 2–4 in Sect. 3.4 for each additional cycle of image acquisition.

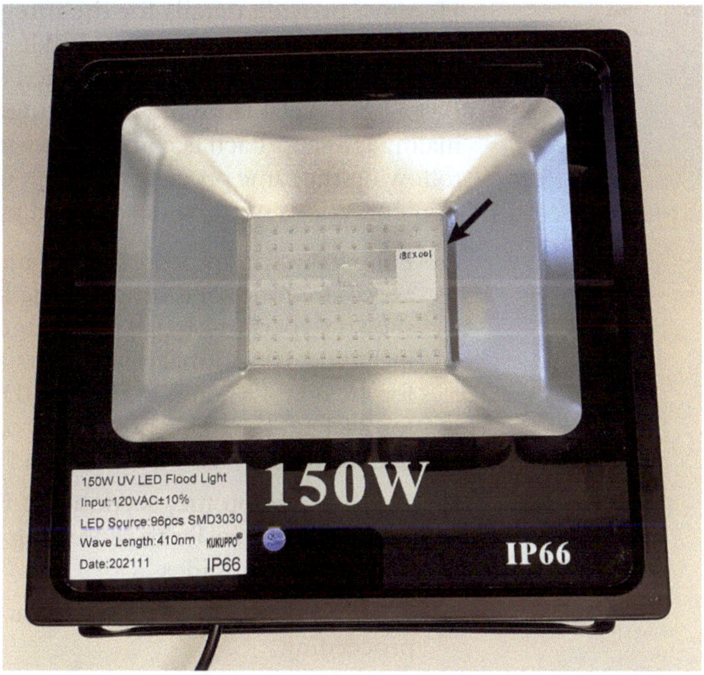

Fig. 1 Set up of a fluorophore inactivation platform with a UV LED. The arrow points to slide glass covered with $LiBH_4$. A sample slide is placed on the LED directly. LED illumination should be performed at 4°C in a box that can prevent light penetration

11. Repeat Steps 1–8 for each additional fluorophore inactivation.
12. Repeat Steps 9–12 until the desired number of cycles and markers is reached.

3.6 Image Registration

1. Regularly updated instructions for Python download/installation/setup and SimpleITK Imaris Extensions download/setup can be found at https://github.com/niaid/imaris_extensions and have been previously published [3].

3.7 Opal-Plex: Tissue Embedding and Sectioning (FFPE)

Differences in the physiologic state of a tissue (e.g. inflammation or tumor microenvironments, TME) as well as the preservation method can dramatically affect immunolabeling and image acquisition success (for technical considerations when staining tumors *see* **Notes 37–41**). Archived FFPE or very highly fixed samples (i.e., fixative concentration >4% paraformaldehyde and/or fixation times >72 h), such as samples preserved from tissue containing biohazardous infectious agents, are commonly encountered staining/imaging challenges due to harsh fixation conditions. In these situations, the use of TSA (tyramine signal amplification)-based reagents can replace traditional conjugated antibodies allowing for greater signal amplification.

Here we provide details for the integration of the manual IBEX method with Opal multiplex IHC kits [4], our TSA-based reagents of choice. This method was validated on samples generated from a Biosafety Level 4 laboratory following 7 days of fixation in 10% formalin. This approach is compatible with other TSA-based reagents following the same process; however, optimal fluorophore inactivation conditions must be determined prior to imaging.

1. Follow standard protocols for fixation and embedding of samples as required for your samples. The following procedure has been shown to perform well with a range of tissue fixation conditions, including 10% formalin for 7 days at 4°C, 4% paraformaldehyde for 48 h at 4°C, and 0.25× of BD Cytofix/Cytoperm solution for 24 h at 4°C. This protocol is optimized for samples embedded in paraffin wax (i.e., FFPE and not samples frozen in OCT).
2. Using a microtome, section the FFPE tissue into 5 μm thick sections and transfer to slide using a water bath to float sections and pick up on slides.
3. Allow sections on slides to dry at RT for at least 24 h before proceeding.

3.8 Opal-Plex: Tissue Pre-Processing—Dewaxing and Rehydration

1. Melt excess formalin off slides by incubating at 60°C for 40 min with the slides in a vertical position.
2. In a chemical safety hood, prepare xylene and 100%, 95%, and 70% of ethanol in staining jars (*see* **Note 42**). Volume depends on the staining stations used but should be enough to cover the slide.
3. Submerge slides into xylene for 10 min at RT.
4. Transfer to a new xylene for 10 min at RT.
5. Transfer slides to a solution of 100% ethanol for 10 min at RT.
6. Transfer slides to a solution of 95% ethanol for 10 min at RT.
7. Wash slides in a solution of 70% ethanol for 5 min at RT.
8. Rinse slides in water briefly.
9. Soak slides in 10% neutral-buffered formalin for 15 min.
10. Rinse slides in diH_2O.
11. Store slides in 1× TBST buffer until ready to proceed (*see* **Note 43**).

3.9 Opal-Plex: Immunostaining

1. Follow the manufacturer's protocol for immunostaining Opal Multiplex IHC kit of choice (*see* **Notes 44–47**).
2. Mount slides with a coverslip and a water-soluble mounting media (*see* Step 12 in Sect. 3.3).
3. Allow mounting media to set for at least 1 h before image acquisition.

3.10 Opal-Plex: Image Acquisition

1. Follow Sect. 3.4 for image acquisition (*see* **Note 48**).

3.11 Opal-Plex: Fluorophore Inactivation and Restaining

1. Follow Steps 1–3 in Sect. 3.5, substituting 1× TBST for 1× PBS pH 7.4 (*see* **Note 49**).
2. Once the coverslip is removed, soak the sample in TBST for at least 10 min at RT to remove excess mounting media (*see* **Note 33**).
3. While the slides soak, prepare 1 mg/ml $LiBH_4$ solution; wait for bubbles to appear in the solution (*see* **Note 34**, and instructional video entitled "Demonstration of making 1 mg/ml of $LiBH_4$" on the IBEX community website at https://ibeximagingcommunity.github.io/ibex_imaging_knowledge_base/videos.html).
4. Cover the tissue with enough 1 mg/ml $LiBH_4$ to completely cover the sample for 10 min (*see* **Notes 18 and 34**).
5. Aspirate $LiBH_4$ and repeat Step 4 two more times (*see* **Notes 50** and **51**).
6. Wash sample three times with 1× TBST for 1 min per wash to thoroughly remove $LiBH_4$ (*see* **Notes 18** and **36**).
7. Resume/follow the immunostaining with Opal Multiplex IHC reagents manufacturer protocol [14] starting at peroxidase quenching and removal of any bound antibody (*see* **Note 52**).
8. Repeat Steps 1–3 in Sect. 3.9 for each additional cycle of immunolabeling (*see* **Notes 47 and 53**).
9. Repeat Sect. 3.10 for each additional cycle of image acquisition (*see* **Note 54**)
10. Repeat Steps 1–6 for each additional cycle of Opal fluorophore inactivation.
11. Repeat Steps 7–11 until the desired number of cycles and markers is reached.

3.12 Opal-Plex: Image Registration

1. Images produced using Opal Multiplex IHC regents can be registered using the same protocol for general "Manual IBEX" produced images detailed in Sect. 3.6.

3.13 Automation: Immunolabeling with Leica Bond (or Similar Instrument)

Here, we highlight some of the automation steps that have been taken with commercially available instruments. Additional information about automation of the IBEX method can be found here [3].

1. Process, embed, and section tissue as previously discussed in Sects. 3.1 and 3.2.

2. Add Fc blocking buffer, primary antibodies, and secondary antibodies to separate staining containers (dependent on automated staining instrument) and load according to the user-defined protocol (*see* **Note 55**).
3. Set up the staining protocol by consulting the manufacturer's protocol (*see* **Note 56**). An example protocol for staining on the Leica Bond is shown below (*see* Table 1).

Table 1
Example of Leica Bond protocol for one round of IBEX staining

Step N	Wash	Reagent	Ambient	Temp. (°C)	Inc. (min)	Comment
1		Detection System Reagent	Yes		0:00	Needed to link reagents to protocol
2	Yes	Bond Wash Solution	Yes		20:00	This is the rehydration step. Can be adjusted depending on tissue
3	Yes	Bond Wash Solution	Yes		0:00	
4	Yes	Bond Wash Solution	Yes		0:00	
5		Blocking Buffer	Yes		10:00	
6		Primary Antibody Mix		37	30:00	
7	Yes	Bond Wash Solution	Yes		0:00	
8	Yes	Bond Wash Solution	Yes		0:00	
9	Yes	Bond Wash Solution	Yes		0:00	
10		Secondary Antibody Mix		37	15:00	Optional step if including a secondary antibody
11	Yes	Bond Wash Solution	Yes		0:00	Optional step if including a secondary antibody
12	Yes	Bond Wash Solution	Yes		0:00	Optional step if including a secondary antibody
13	Yes	Bond Wash Solution	Yes		0:00	Optional step if including a secondary antibody

An example staining protocol of staining with primary and secondary antibodies. Choose "Indicated volume" in the dispense type in the instrument at the individual step.

4. Perform nuclear staining manually, if desired, directly before mounting the slides with Fluoromount-G (*see* **Note 57**).
5. For image acquisition, follow Sect. 3.4.

3.14 Automation: Fluorophore Inactivation and Restaining

1. Follow the general process of fluorophore inactivation (*see* Sect. 3.5). Fluorophore inactivation with $LiBH_4$ and/or photobleaching (Steps 6–7 of Sect. 3.5) will be done manually (i.e., without the use of automation equipment). Leica Biosystems does no not recommend the use of $LiBH_4$ on the Leica Bond instruments.
2. To perform a wet start on the instrument, place slides on staining trays and quickly cover with the Bond universal cover tile from the instrument (*see* **Note 58**).
3. To prevent the slide from drying out, pipette 100 μl of PBS in between the instrument cover tile and slide at the top (since the tray is tilted, the PBS should flow down the slide against the coverslip).
4. Load samples onto the instrument as normal and run the staining protocol with the new set of primary antibodies.

4 Notes

1. Pay attention to the published expiration date on BD Cytofix/Cytoperm solution as outdated solutions can yield suboptimal results.
2. Filtered solution can be stored at 4°C for several months if kept sterile.
3. We purchase chrome alum–gelatin from Newcomer Supply, but recipes are available online if this item does not ship to your country (e.g., https://www.laboratorynotes.com/preparation-of-chrome-alum-containing-gelatin-solution-for-preparation-of-coated-slides-for-histological-tissue-sections/).
4. Unconjugated and directly conjugated antibodies are compatible with IBEX. A user-curated database of validated antibodies is available [7]. Highly multiplexed IBEX panels for human tissues have also been described and shared publicly [15, 16].
5. Always prepare $LiBH_4$ solution in a chemical fume hood with appropriate personal protective equipment (PPE). Mixing $LiBH_4$ with diH_2O will generate hydrogen gas, which is highly flammable and may ignite spontaneously. For this reason, we always work with small amounts of $LiBH_4$ relative to the amount of water initially added. We do not mix >10 mg of $LiBH_4$ with diH_2O. This amount can be quickly diluted

to 1 mg/ml with volumes handled by standard serological pipets/pipet-aids. Always wrap $LiBH_4$ stock with parafilm (suggest Bemis Company Inc., cat. no. S37440) and store in the presence of desiccant. We recommend replacing $LiBH_4$ stock every 4 weeks, as repeated exposure to moisture/air has been observed to reduce fluorophore inactivation efficacy. Be sure to follow institutional guidelines for proper disposal of hazardous chemicals.

6. Miniconda is a free/open-source, minimal installer for Conda (i.e., a bootstrap version of Anaconda) that includes Conda, Python, and necessary packages for operating these programs. The above link will provide the latest Miniconda installer links for common operating system platforms compatible with the SimpleITK Imaris Extensions.
7. While working with fresh tissue (prior to fixation), we work quickly and keep fresh tissues in chilled 1× PBS to avoid drying and minimize autolysis. If working with patient biopsy samples, clinical imaging data and operative notes of the procedure can be helpful for establishing orientation. Tissue-specific histological orientation conventions have been reviewed elsewhere [3, 17].
8. Work quickly during this step to avoid damage due to autolysis. Complete removal of fat and connective tissue does not need to occur during this step/prior to fixation, as additional fat/connective tissue removal can be done after fixation (ideally before dehydration in 30% sucrose solution), if necessary.
9. Incubations longer than 24 h can lead to over-fixation and fixation-related epitope loss in an epitope-dependent manner. Overall, in our experience, fixation up to 3 days will preserve most epitopes without appreciable fixation-related epitope loss. If more highly fixed tissues are required, we suggest following the Opal-plex protocol listed below (*see* Sects. 3.7–3.12) when epitope loss is problematic.
10. If additional fat/tissue processing is still required, it is often easier to remove fat at this stage prior to tissue dehydration in sucrose solution.
11. Samples will initially float in sucrose solution; however, after dehydration most tissues will sink if the sample is not excessively fatty. Samples can be kept in 30% sucrose solution at 4°C for up to 7 days if necessary.
12. Some users prefer to blot samples quickly on a fiber-free absorbent towel (e.g., Kimwipe) prior to placing in OCT media. Choose Histomold size such that tissue does not occupy >60% of the Histomold volume. Ensure tissue is oriented according to standard conventions [3, 17]. Use care to avoid bubbles within OCT media.

13. Always keep the top of the molds uncovered as the tissues freeze to allow excess water to escape. The OCT media will turn opaque white when frozen. Samples can be stored at −80°C for several years.

14. It may require multiple spreading passages with the slide to ensure even coating of chrome alum–gelatin without streaks. If chrome alum–gelatin pools on the slide, aspirate excess fluid and re-spread, as these accumulations can result in autofluorescence artifacts during image acquisition. Be mindful of the stated expiration date on chrome alum–gelatin.

15. For best results, prepare chrome alum–gelatin-coated slides freshly (i.e., the day of tissue sectioning) for best results or no more than 7 days prior to tissue sectioning. If chrome alum–gelatin coated slides are prepared ahead of sectioning, store at RT (do not freeze as this will compromise the adhesive properties).

16. Tissue will immediately adhere to the RT slide upon contact. Once tissue is mounted, user may proceed with subsequent steps immediately, or tissue-mounted slides may be stored at RT for ~5 days if necessary. For best results, we recommend allowing fresh sections to dry and fully adhere overnight at RT before proceeding with rehydration/blocking/staining the following day (12–24 h following sectioning). Always visually inspect sections to ensure they are completely flat on the slide (i.e., no wrinkles) for maximal adherence and best image quality. We also suggest preparing additional backup slides at this time.

17. Take care not to draw over areas of the slide covered with OCT, as this will cause the hydrophobic barrier to slough off during subsequent steps. A single, thin monolayer, evenly applied in a closed circle should dry in 5–10 min at RT and is sufficient to withstand repeated rounds of staining.

18. A typical 1 cm × 1 cm surface area will require ~200 μl of solution for rehydration, blocking, staining, washing, and fluorophore inactivation steps. Adjust volume according to surface area, ensuring the solution does not spill beyond the ImmEdge border.

19. Once tissue has been rehydrated, it must remain hydrated—either in isotonic buffered solution or coated with Fluoromount-G and a coverslip throughout the remainder of the protocol to prevent sample from drying, which can result in imaging artifacts.

20. Our standard procedure utilizes blocking buffer with species-specific Fc Block at 1:100 dilution followed by incubation at RT for 30 min. However, incubation times as short as 15 min (e.g., in non-diseased tissues) may be sufficient, or as

long as 60 min (e.g., in tumors) may be necessary. We typically include 0.3% (v/v) Triton-X 100 in our blocking buffer solution. However, if not targeting intracellular/intranuclear antigens, this may not be necessary and should be empirically tested.

21. If using biotinylated primary antibodies (typically followed by fluorophore-conjugated streptavidin or anti-biotin secondary antibodies), it is important to use avidin/biotin-specific blocking reagents, e.g., Avidin/Biotin Blocking Kit (ThermoFisher, cat. no. 004303), following an initial Fc Block. Similarly, if staining carbohydrate moieties using fluorophore-conjugated lectins, a carbohydrate/glycoprotein-free blocking buffer should be used, e.g., Carbo-Free Blocking Solution (Vector Laboratories, cat. no. SP-5040-125)

22. We typically stain by diluting primary antibodies in 1× blocking buffer at previously determined titrations. All reagents must be carefully titrated before experimental imaging acquisition. Many antibody suppliers provide suggested working concentrations/conditions in their product specifications, which can serve as a starting point for titration optimizations. Please review all datasheets before using any antibodies/reagents.

23. Please be mindful that although these incubation times/temperatures are generally sufficient, incubation times can vary based on target tissue, tissue thickness, and target antigen [3, 4].

24. The PELCO BioWave Pro is a specialized non-heating microwave that accelerates immunolabeling without tissue loss or epitope damage; however, it is not essential. For the "2-1-2-1-2-1-2-1-2 program," each "2" denotes 2 minat 100 W and each "1" denotes 1 min at 0 W. This is run consecutively two times (total 28 min) for primary antibodies. It is run one time (14 min) for secondary antibodies.

25. We typically use 10–40 μl per tissue section. Ensure there are no bubbles on or near the tissue.

26. Once Fluoromount-G begins to dry, do not reposition the coverslip, as this will cause tissue to stretch and distort on the slide and make registering multiple cycles impossible.

27. Manual IBEX is compatible with a wide range of imaging platforms, including upright and inverted confocal and widefield microscopes.

28. Because manual IBEX requires removing the sample from the microscope stage for each round of fluorophore inactivation and immunolabeling, returning it to the same position on the stage during each cycle aligns the x and y coordinates of the image and allows reproducible acquisition of the same tissue region. By convention, we typically ensure the upper left corner

of the slide is pushed snugly into the upper left corner of the stage slide mount. A tile scan is typically required to capture the regions of interest. Save those regions for the following cycles. See also the instructional video entitled "Setting focus mpa in Leica LAS X Navigator for manual IBEX: 1 of 2 videos" on the IBEX community website at https://ibeximagingcommunity.github.io/ibex_imaging_knowledge_base/videos.html).

29. We typically do this by identifying distinguishing landmarks within the tissue (e.g., distinct nuclear morphology) and adjusting the z-plane to match the cycle 1 image. If software allows (as is the case with Leica Application Suite X), we find it helpful to load and overlay the cycle 1 image on the current cycle image. This can be toggled on and off to check exact z-plane alignment. If collecting multiple z-slices (i.e., a z-stack), we find it useful to identify landmarks in the first and last z-slice and define those planes as the beginning and end of the z stack [3]. See also the instructional video entitled "Focus Map Set UP After Cycle 1 for manual IBEX: 2 of 2 videos" on the IBEX community website at https://ibeximagingcommunity.github.io/ibex_imaging_knowledge_base/videos.html).

30. A common fiducial must be included and collected in all cycles to perform image registration. Our most commonly used fiducial ($LiBH_4$-insensitive) fluorophores are Hoechst and/or Alexa Fluor 594. We typically collect images of the fiducial fluorophore using the same laser wavelength, laser power, and detector settings in each cycle. See the IBEX Imaging Community Reagent Resource page for a complete, up-to-date list of $LiBH_4$-compatible/incompatible fluorescent probes (https://ibeximagingcommunity.github.io/ibex_imaging_knowledge_base/fluorescent_probes.html). Stitch tiled images with Mosaic Merge (Leica LAS X software) or equivalent module before attempting registration.

31. This minimizes the possibility of immersion oil contacting tissue if/when the coverslip spontaneously lifts off the slide during subsequent PBS soaking.

32. Wait until the coverslip detaches from the slide naturally or, at minimum, is moving freely on the slide under the force of gravity. Attempting to remove the coverslip before it has sufficiently loosened may result in tissue deformation and/or loss.

33. Mounting medium must be completely removed to achieve effective fluorophore inactivation.

34. The formation of bubbles indicates the solution is ready for filtration and subsequent use. For best results, use the solution immediately after filtration. We have noted effective fluorophore inactivation up to 4 h after initial dissolution of $LiBH_4$.

35. We place the slide directly on the UV LED. The UV LED is kept at 4°C. Be sure a UV-opaque cover is used to prevent UV light exposure during this photobleaching process. This is effective for inactivating Brilliant Violet 421 and Brilliant Violet 510, which are resistant to $LiBH_4$ fluorophore inactivation.
36. Incomplete removal of $LiBH_4$ may result in fluorophore inactivation of subsequent antibody stains.
37. To understand the spatiotemporal changes occurring within the TME, one must have high confidence in the immunostaining protocols and antibodies used. There is no homeostatic tissue that can be used as a perfect control for solid tumor staining, as it is a diseased/altered state.
38. Some antibody-fluorophore conjugates with well-validated performance in non-diseased tissues perform suboptimally within tumor samples. Examples include anti-mouse CD3 Alexa Fluor 488 (BioLegend, cat. no. 100210), anti-mouse CD3 Brilliant Violet 510 (BioLegend, ca.t no. 100234), and anti-mouse PD-1 Brilliant Violet 421 (BioLegend, cat. no. 109121) when used in MC-38-derived tumors (common murine model of colorectal carcinoma [18]) as well as KPC-derived tumors (common murine model of pancreatic ductal adenocarcinoma [19]). Performance varies depending on the tumor type and tissue autofluorescence. We thus recommend all new antibody-fluorophore conjugates be tested first in non-diseased tissue as discussed elsewhere [20, 21], followed by an additional sequence of validation in the specific tumor samples of interest.
39. It is important to note that each antibody-fluorophore conjugate pair is a unique biochemical and will interact with tissue differently based on the fluorophore to which it is conjugated, the fluorophore-to-protein (F/P) ratio, and more.
40. In particular, phycoerythrin (PE)-conjugated antibodies are quite susceptible to non-specific binding within tumor tissues (in particular, gastrointestinal and pancreatic adenocarcinoma tumors) and other inflamed tissues, in part due to increased cell death. Instead, we recommend using alternative fluorophores with similar excitation/emission spectra to PE, such as Alexa Fluor 555 or eFluor 570.
41. Tissue flatness: Tumors are often large pieces of tissue, which generally increases the difficulty of achieving a flat z-plane to image. Use of the CryoJane tape transfer system (Leica Biosystems, cat. no. 39475205) can alleviate this issue if thin sections are required, as can the use of the Focus Map in Leica LAS-X software during image acquisition in Navigator mode or an equivalent function if available.

42. Xylenes and formalin should be handled in a chemical hood, as they produce toxic fumes. Ethanol is highly flammable and should also be handled in a chemical hood. Take precautions to avoid exposure to heat or open flame.
43. Slides should be processed shortly after storage. However, we have found them to be stable for up to three days in TBST if kept at 4°C.
44. Staining of primary antibodies can be done overnight at 4°C, 4 h at RT, or for 30 min using the Pelco BioWave (*see* Steps 7 and 10 in Sect. 3.3) [3].
45. Fluorophore sequences may be ordered in any way to achieve optimal signals. Opal 520, Opal 540, and Opal 620 do not efficiently inactivate with exposure to $LiBH_4$ and can instead be used as fiducials [3]. To ensure optimal alignment, use these fluorophores on targets that are widely expressed throughout the tissue.
46. Fluorophores should be validated individually before being added to a panel to check for optimal signal with each given primary antibody to fluorophore pairing.
47. After the final round of primary antibody staining, secondary antibody staining, and Opal fluorophore reaction, do not perform nuclear counterstaining (e.g., DAPI, Hoechst, etc.), as subsequent heating steps can cause issues with nuclear stain leakage.
48. Prior to setting up an experiment, we recommend individually validating that each Opal fluorophore is compatible with your imaging setup (i.e., proper filter cubes, spectral detectors, etc. are available). We have successfully used Opal fluorophores on confocal and widefield imaging platforms with either filter cubes or spectral detectors in inverted or upright configurations.
49. We recommend the use of TBST here because it was initially tested as recommended by the Opal Multiplex IHC kit protocols and has been consistently compatible with Opal Multiplex IHC reagents. We have not tested 1× PBS pH 7.4 in this context.
50. Alternatively, a 30-min incubation with 1 mg/ml $LiBH_4$ may be used.
51. It is not necessary to re-prep 1 mg/ml $LiBH_4$ here, as the solution has been effective for fluorophore inactivation up to four hours after preparation.
52. Removal of unbound antibody can be accomplished with any conventional microwave with adjustable power levels.
53. For second or higher rounds of staining, only Opal 480, Opal 570, Opal 650, and Opal 690 can be used.

54. Following the second round of staining, mount the slides in the same position on the stage as before and image using the same platform. When imaging, be sure to collect channels including unbleached channels (Opal 520, Opal 540, and/or Opal 640) to serve as a fiducial.
55. The total volume added to each container is the number of slides × 150 μl with an added dead volume of 300 μl.
56. According to the Leica Bond user manual (https://www.leicabiosystems.com/sites/default/files/media_product-download/2022-04/21_7707_501_a05_bond_6_0_user_manual_en-US.pdf). Primary antibodies or secondary antibodies can be incubated with sections for 30 min at 37°C or for 15 min at 37°C, respectively. We typically include three separate wash steps (Bond wash solution) following incubation with the primary and secondary antibody solutions. Pre-loaded protocols for primary antibody staining (or primary antibody staining with a secondary) can be used as provided by the company and pre-loaded onto the instrument software. No pre-treatment steps such as HIER (heat-induced epitope retrieval) or baking/de-waxing steps are needed.
57. Nuclear staining can be performed with automated instruments, but we prefer to stain manually because DAPI staining is often less consistent.
58. After fluorophore inactivation, slides can be returned to the instrument for staining of the second or subsequent panel(s). Ensure that tissues do not dry out while handling samples.

Acknowledgments

This research was supported by the Intramural Research Program of the National Institutes of Health (NIH). The contributions of the NIH author(s) were made as part of their official duties as NIH federal employees, are in compliance with agency policy requirements, and are considered Works of the United States Government. However, the findings and conclusions presented in this paper are those of the author(s) and do not necessarily reflect the views of the NIH or the U.S. Department of Health and Human Services. Z.Y. was supported by federal funds from the National Institute of Allergy and Infectious Diseases, National Institutes of Health, under Bioinformatics and Computational Biosciences Branch (BCBB) Support Services to Medical Science and Computing under Contract HHSN316201300006W/75N93022F00001. E.S. was supported by Cleveland Clinic Start-up Funds.

Conflict of Interest AJR is now an employee of Leica Microsystems. All other authors have no conflicts of interest to declare that are relevant to the content of this chapter.

References

1. Campbell NA, Reece JB (2002) Biology, 6th edn. Benjamin Cummings, San Francisco, p. 1247. xxix
2. Hickey JW et al (2022) Spatial mapping of protein composition and tissue organization: a primer for multiplexed antibody-based imaging. Nat Methods 19(3):284–295
3. Radtke AJ et al (2022) IBEX: an iterative immunolabeling and chemical bleaching method for high-content imaging of diverse tissues. Nat Protoc 17(2):378–401
4. Radtke AJ et al (2020) IBEX: a versatile multiplex optical imaging approach for deep phenotyping and spatial analysis of cells in complex tissues. Proc Natl Acad Sci U S A 117(52):33455–33465
5. Lowekamp BC et al (2013) The design of SimpleITK. Front Neuroinform 7:45
6. Yaniv Z, Lowekamp B (2023) SimpleITK Imaris Extensions. DOI:10.5281/zenodo.7854019
7. Yaniv Z et al (2023) Iterative Bleaching Extends Multiplexity (IBEX) Knowledge-Base (v0.4.0). DOI:10.5281/zenodo.17211279
8. Gola A et al (2021) Commensal-driven immune zonation of the liver promotes host defence. Nature 589(7840):131–136
9. Madissoon E et al (2023) A spatially resolved atlas of the human lung characterizes a gland-associated immune niche. Nat Genet 55(1):66–77
10. Radtke AJ et al (2022) A multi-scale, multiomic atlas of human normal and follicular lymphoma lymph nodes. bioRxiv 2022:494716
11. Richoz N et al (2022) Distinct pathogenic roles for resident and monocyte-derived macrophages in lupus nephritis. JCI Insight 7(21):e159751
12. Speranza E et al (2022) Age-related differences in immune dynamics during SARS-CoV-2 infection in rhesus macaques. Life Sci Alliance 5(4):e202101314
13. Radtke AJ et al (2021) Iterative Bleaching Extends multi-pleXity (IBEX) 2D and 3D Microscopy Data. DOI:10.5281/zenodo.4632320
14. Akoya Biosciences (2022) Opal Polaris 7-Color Manual IHC Kit (NEL861001KT). Online [Protocol]. https://www.akoyabio.com/wp-content/uploads/2021/11/NEL861-Product-Insert.pdf
15. Quardokus EM et al (2023) Organ mapping antibody panels: a community resource for standardized multiplexed tissue imaging. Nat Methods 20(8):1174–1178
16. Schlehlein H et al (2023) HuBMAP CCF 3D Reference Object Library. Accessed December 1, 2025
17. Carson FL, Cappellano CH (2016) Histotechnology: a self-instructional text, 4th edn. American Society for Clinical Pathology, Chicago, p. 352. xvi
18. Rosenberg SA, Spiess P, Lafreniere R (1986) A new approach to the adoptive immunotherapy of cancer with tumor-infiltrating lymphocytes. Science 233(4770):1318–1321
19. Hingorani SR et al (2005) Trp53R172H and KrasG12D cooperate to promote chromosomal instability and widely metastatic pancreatic ductal adenocarcinoma in mice. Cancer Cell 7(5):469–483
20. Howat WJ et al (2014) Antibody validation of immunohistochemistry for biomarker discovery: recommendations of a consortium of academic and pharmaceutical based histopathology researchers. Methods 70(1):34–38
21. MacNeil T et al (2020) Antibody validation for protein expression on tissue slides: a protocol for immunohistochemistry. Biotechniques 69(6):460–468

Chapter 2

Multiplex Immunofluorescence Staining of Paraffin-Embedded Tissue: Coverslip Mounting of Tissue Sections Improves Z-axis Optical Resolution in Widefield Microscopy

Gitte A. Pedersen, Søren H. Elsborg, Rikke Nørregaard and Lene N. Nejsum

Abstract

Immunofluorescence (IF) microscopy is essential for studying protein expression and localization. Multiplex IF enables sequential staining of the same tissue section for comprehensive analysis but often involves harsh treatments or expensive reagents that can damage tissues and reduce signal quality. Here, we present a detailed protocol for multiplex IF using indirect antibody labeling, a mild stripping buffer, and cost-effective reagents. Importantly, mounting paraffin-embedded tissue sections on gelatin-coated coverslips enhances Z-axis optical resolution in widefield imaging.

Keywords Multiplex immunofluorescence, Paraffin-embedded tissue, Widefield microscopy, Tissue staining, Antibody stripping, Enhanced optical resolution

1 Introduction

Immunofluorescence (IF) microscopy is an invaluable tool for investigating the expression levels and subcellular localization of specific proteins in cells and tissue. Typically, tissue IF is performed by labeling tissue sections attached to microscope slides. After labeling, the sample is mounted with a coverslip using mounting medium and imaged with a fluorescence microscope. However, conventional IF methods are limited to the number of proteins that can be detected simultaneously. To overcome this challenge, protocols have been developed that enable multiple rounds of staining on the same tissue section, referred to as multiplex IF [1–4]. Multiplex IF is particularly valuable when samples are limited (e.g., tissue biopsies) and for enabling more comprehensive analyses of protein co-expression.

The authors Gitte A. Pedersen and Søren H. Elsborg contributed equally.

Timothy L. Frankel and Arvind Rao (eds.), *Cellular Spatial Characterization and Analysis*, Methods in Molecular Biology, vol. 2995, https://doi.org/10.1007/978-1-0716-5027-1_2,

Existing multiplex IF methods often rely on harsh chemical treatments to strip bound antibodies [1–3] or on chemical bleaching to inactivate fluorophores [4, 5], both of which can damage the tissue. Additionally, the repeated mounting and remounting of the tissue with mounting medium and coverslips increase the risk of tissue damage. In response to these challenges, we recently developed a multiplex IF protocol (originally published in *APMIS* in 2023 [6]) that employs indirect antibody labeling, a mild stripping buffer and cost-effective, commercially available reagents. Importantly, in this protocol, tissue sections are attached directly to gelatin-coated coverslips instead of microscope slides (Fig. 1). Following staining, the coverslips are mounted in a chamber for live-cell imaging, covered with PBS and imaged. This approach eliminates the need for traditional slide mounting with mounting medium. Importantly, imaging the tissue section directly through the coverslip significantly enhances the Z-axis optical resolution when using standard widefield microscopes (Fig. 2). Additionally, this method is compatible with H&E or PAS staining as the final stain.

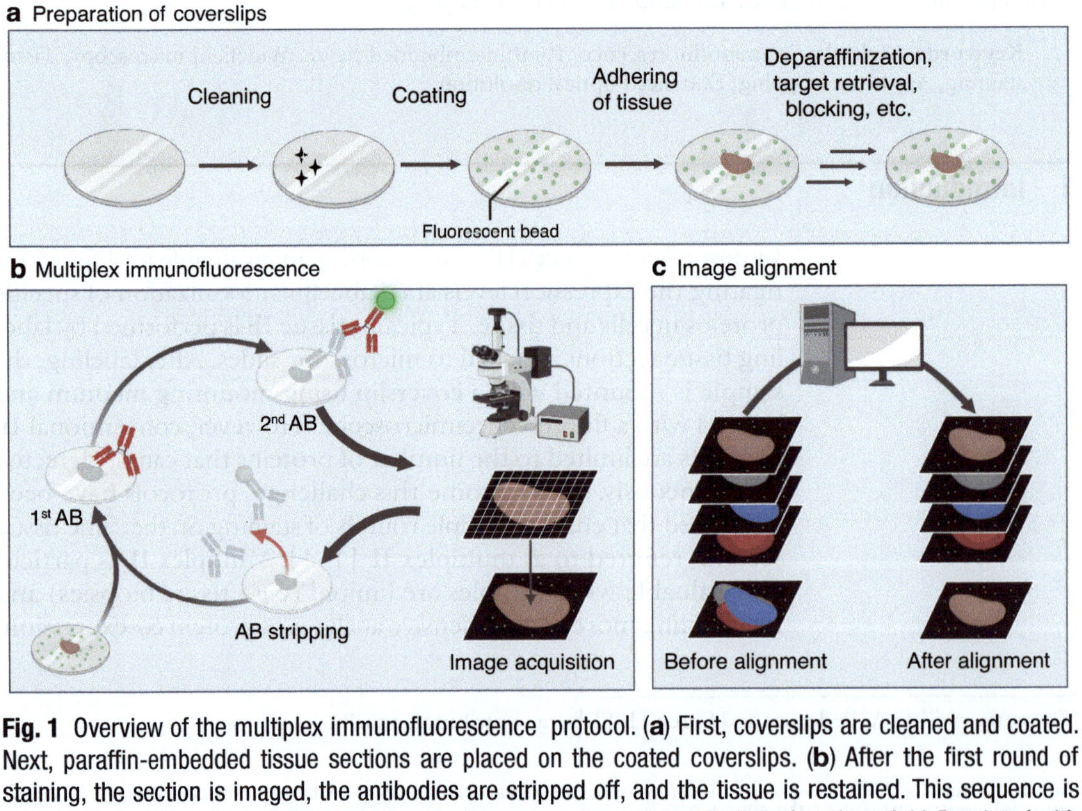

Fig. 1 Overview of the multiplex immunofluorescence protocol. (**a**) First, coverslips are cleaned and coated. Next, paraffin-embedded tissue sections are placed on the coated coverslips. (**b**) After the first round of staining, the section is imaged, the antibodies are stripped off, and the tissue is restained. This sequence is repeated for multiplexing. (**c**) After imaging, the images can be registered, aligned, and overlaid. Reprinted with permission from [6]. Abbreviations: AB, Antibody

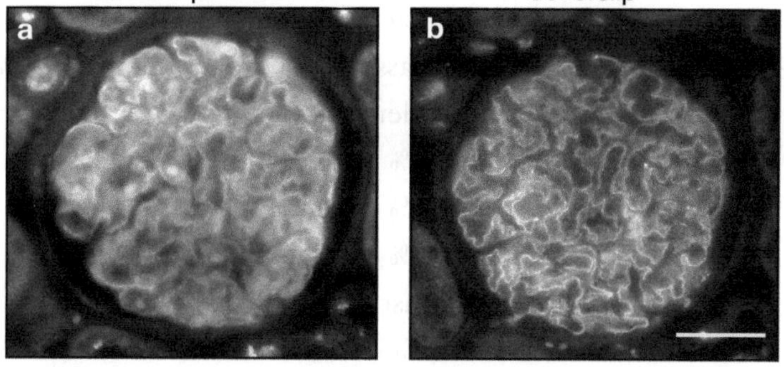

Fig. 2 Improved Z-resolution using coverslips compared to microscope slides. Human kidney tissue embedded in paraffin was serially sectioned and placed onto (**a**) a microscope slide or (**b**) a coverslip and stained for podocin, a marker of podocytes in the glomerulus. The sections were treated and imaged under identical conditions. Microscope: Nikon Ti2 Eclipse inverted widefield microscope. Objective: 60× oil. Scale bar: 50 μm. Reprinted with permission from [6]

2 Materials

Prepare all solutions using analytical-grade reagents and ultrapure water. Store solutions at room temperature (RT) unless otherwise indicated.

2.1 Coating of Coverslips

1. Glass coverslips, thickness should match the objectives (for images in this protocol no. 1.5 coverslips were used).
2. Mini-rack for coverslips (e.g., Wash-N-Dry coverslips rack (Z743685-1EA, Sigma-Aldrich)).
3. 0.45 μm filter units.
4. 20 ml or 50 ml syringes.
5. FluoSpheres 1 μm yellow-green fluorescent (available in various colors and sizes).
6. 70% ethanol.
7. Coating solution: 0.5% gelatin, 1 mM $CrK(SO_4)_2 \times 12H_2O$ (*see* **Note 1**).
   - Dissolve 1 g of gelatin in 200 ml ddH_2O in a 250 ml conical flask by stirring and heating to approximately 80°C.
   - Add 0.1 g of $CrK(SO_4)_2 \times 12H_2O$ and filter through a 0.45 μm filter into a glass beaker (*see* **Note 2**).
   - Add fluorescent beads immediately before coating, using a 1:4000 dilution (may require optimization for optimal results).

2.2 Immunofluorescence Staining of Tissue on Coverslips

1. Paraffin sections (~3 μm thickness) (this protocol was optimized for human kidney tissue).
2. Glass jars for ethanol dehydration.
3. Xylene.
4. 99% ethanol.
5. 96% ethanol.
6. 70% ethanol.
7. Plastic jars for microwave.
8. TEG buffer: 10 mM Tris, 0.5 mM EGTA, pH 9.
   - Weigh 1.21 g of Tris-base and 0.19 g of EGTA, add ddH_2O to 1 l. Adjust pH to 9 if necessary.
9. PBS buffer: 137 mM NaCl, 2.7 mM KCl, 10 mM Na_2HPO_4, pH 7.4, 1.8 mM KH_2PO_4.
   - For a 10× solution: Weigh 2.4 g KH_2PO_4, 14.4 g Na_2HPO_4, 2 g KCl, 80 g NaCl, add ddH_2O to 1 l, and adjust pH to 7.4. Dilute to 1× before use.
10. Shielding buffer: 50 mM NH_4Cl in PBS.
    - Weigh 2.674 g of NH_4Cl, and dissolve in 1 l of PBS.
11. Blocking buffer: 1% BSA, 0.2% gelatin, 0.05% saponin in PBS.
    - Weigh 0.1 g gelatin and 0.025 g saponin and add ~30 ml PBS. Gently heat to ~50°C to dissolve the gelatin. Bring to 50 ml with PBS and add 0.5 g BSA. Store at 4°C. Prepare fresh at least every 14 days.
12. Staining buffer: 0.1% BSA, 0.3% Triton X-100 in PBS.
    - Add 0.05 g of BSA and 150 μl of Triton X-100 to 50 ml of PBS. Store at 4°C.
13. Primary and secondary antibodies of interest and a nuclear stain (e.g., Hoechst 33342 (Thermo Fisher Scientific, Waltham, MA, USA)).
14. Chamlide magnetic chamber for microscopy (Live Cell Instrument Co, Republic of Korea).
15. Inverted fluorescence microscope (a Nikon Eclipse Ti2 microscope equipped with a 60× oil objective was used for this protocol).

2.3 Stripping of Antibodies from Tissue on Coverslips

1. 6-well plates.
2. Oven set to 56°C.
3. TBS-Ts buffer: 20 mM Tris, 150 mM NaCl, 0.01% Tween-20, 100 mM sucrose (*see* **Note 3**).

- Weigh 2.4 g of Tris-HCl, 0.56 g of Tris-base, and 8.8 g of NaCl and add water to a volume of 1000 ml. Add 100 μl of Tween-20. Weigh 34.2 g of sucrose and add to the solution. For frequent use, it might be time saving to prepare a 10× TBS buffer for easy preparation of the 1× TBS-Ts buffer. Store at 4°C.

4. 10% SDS buffer.
   - Weigh 50 g of SDS in the fume hood and add 500 ml of ddH_2O.
5. 0.5 M Tris, pH 6.8.
   - Weigh 30.3 g of Tris-base, add 490 ml ddH_2O and adjust pH to 6.8. Bring volume to 500 ml.
6. PBS buffer: See Sect. 2.2.
7. 1 M DTT.
   - Dissolve DTT in ddH_2O to a 1 M concentration (add 6.48 ml ddH_2O to 1 g of DTT), aliquot and store at −20°C. Work with DTT should be carried out in the fume hood.

3 Methods

3.1 Coating of Coverslips

1. Clean glass coverslips in soapy water, rinse thoroughly with clean water until no foam remains (*see* **Note 4**).
2. Rinse coverslips in 70% ethanol on both sides.
3. Air-dry on a paper tissue or manually using Kleenex.
4. Place the cleaned and dried coverslips in a mini-rack.
5. Add fluorescent beads to the coating solution (*see* **Note 5**).
6. Immerse the coverslip rack into the coating solution for 5 s while very gently moving the rack back and forth. Remove the rack for 5 s and repeat this cycle of 5-s coating and 5-s pause five times. Tap excess liquid off onto a paper towel.
7. Dry at RT for at least 48 h in the dark to protect the fluorescence of the beads. Can be stored at RT for several months before use (Fig. 3a).

3.2 Immunofluorescence Staining of Tissue on Coverslips

1. Section kidney or other tissue to approximately 3 μm thickness and place onto the coated coverslips (place the tissue section as centered on the coverslips as possible), and dry for a minimum of 20 min at 60°C or overnight at 37°C. Can be stored at RT for several months (Fig. 3a). Keep dark.

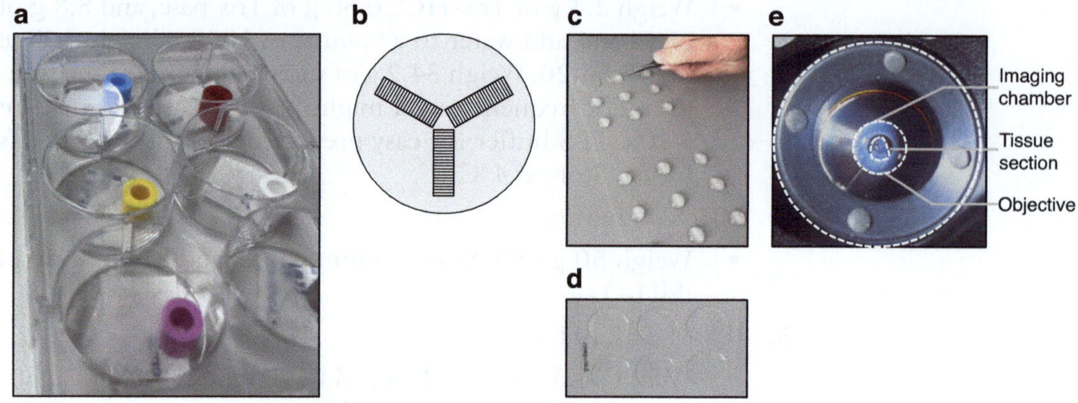

Fig. 3 Key elements and equipment for successful staining. (**a**) After the tissue has been attached and dried, the coverslips can be stored for several months in 6-well plates, tipped with a plastic device on top of parafilm to prevent the coverslips from sticking to the bottom of the wells. (**b**) A schematic representation of the arrangement of the plastic jars within the microwave viewed from above. This formation ensures even and gentler boiling of the coverslips. (**c**) Drop incubation: Drops of solutions or buffers are placed on parafilm. Water between the table and the parafilm prevented movement and kept the parafilm flat. The coverslips are then placed on top of the drops with the tissue facing downward. (**d**) Coverslips incubating with primary antibodies. (**e**) Setup of the imaging chamber. The imaging chamber is assembled with the tissue facing up, using PBS as the imaging medium.

2. Incubate coverslips in xylene for at least 2 h (*see* **Note 6**) in the fume hood to dissolve the paraffin. Note: Place in a coverslip rack approved for xylene treatment.
3. Rehydrate the tissue in a series of decreasing ethanol concentrations:
   - 3 × 5 min in 99% ethanol.
   - 2 × 5 min in 96% ethanol.
   - 1 × 5 min in 70% ethanol.
4. Rinse three to four times in distilled water.
5. Transfer the coverslips to plastic jars for target retrieval in a microwave oven and cover with TEG buffer (*see* **Note 7**).
6. If working with only 1–2 jars, make extra jars with empty racks and water, so there are three full jars in total and place these in the microwave in a "nuclear" pattern, to ensure even heating across the tissue (Fig. 3b).
7. Heat until boiling (~7–8 min at 750 W), then reduce the power (~200 W) and maintain soft boiling for 10 min.
8. Cool on ice for ~30 min until it reaches RT.
9. Incubate the coverslips in shielding buffer for 30 min to shield aldehyde groups.

10. Perform blocking and staining steps by drop incubation (Fig. 3c, d). Place parafilm on the benchtop and dispense drops on top, upon which the coverslips are placed with the tissue-side facing down. Incubate 3 × 10 min in blocking buffer.
11. Incubate with primary antibody diluted in staining buffer placed in a humidity chamber for 30 min at RT and then overnight at 4°C.
12. The following day, allow the humidity chamber to reach RT, which takes approximately 30 min after moving the chamber from 4°C to RT.
13. Wash the coverslips 3 × 5 min in PBS using drop incubation.
14. Incubate the coverslips with fluorescently labeled secondary antibody and a nuclear stain, such as Hoechst 33342 (Thermo Fisher Scientific, Waltham, MA, USA), diluted in staining buffer for 30 min. Keep dark.
15. Wash the coverslips 3 × 5 min in PBS.
16. Transfer the coverslips to a six-well plate with the tissue-side facing up. Store in PBS at 4°C until imaging. Keep dark. Do not store more than 2–3 days.
17. For imaging, place the coverslip in a chamber for live imaging and cover with PBS (Fig. 3e) (*see* **Note 8**).
18. After imaging, the sections can be stripped (Sect. 3.3) or stored in PBS at 4°C for up to a week.

3.3 Stripping of Antibodies from Tissue on Coverslips

1. Transfer coverslips to TBS-Ts buffer in a new six-well plate. Keep dark.
2. Prepare the stripping buffer in the fume hood: For 25 ml of stripping buffer, mix in a 50 ml tube:
   - 15 ml of ddH_2O
   - 5 ml 10% SDS
   - 5 ml 0.5 M Tris, pH 6.8
   - 250 μl 1 M DTT (thaw in the fume hood at RT).

   Prepare fresh stripping buffer each time. DTT will inactivate over time and can then be disposed according to regulations.
3. Incubate coverslips in the stripping buffer for 1 h at 56°C.
4. Cool to RT and wash coverslips 5 × 5 min in TBS-Ts in the fume hood.
5. Transfer coverslips to a new six-well plate containing PBS, while keeping them dark.
6. Perform fluorescent microscopy to check if the stripping procedure has worked efficiently. Use DIC or GFP channel for

autofluorescent tissues such as kidney, to locate the tissue, and use the same acquisition settings, i.e., exposure times and light intensity as in the original experiment (*see* **Note 9**). Importantly, to test if the primary antibody has been stripped off, you must re-incubate with the fluorescently labelled secondary antibody before imaging.

7. If successfully stripped, the tissue can be restained starting from the blocking step of the immunofluorescence staining protocol, Sect. 3.2.10.
8. After the final round of staining, the images can be overlaid in ImageJ/FIJI [7] (*see* **Note 10**).

4 Notes

1. Chromium ions create a positively charged surface on the glass coverslips that mimics the Superfrost Plus Microscope Slides that are normally used to attach tissue to for immunohistochemistry procedures. Because most tissues are negatively charged, they adhere to a positively charged surface through electrostatic forces.
2. The coating solution is very viscous and is difficult to filter, especially if the solution becomes too cold before filtering.
3. Sucrose and other disaccharides have a protective effect on the epitopes of proteins in the tissue. This is mediated by hydrogen bonding between the hydroxyl (OH) groups of the disaccharide and polar groups on the proteins, which preserves the conformation of the proteins.
4. If the coverslips are not thoroughly cleaned before coating, the tissue may detach during the IF procedure, likely during the antigen retrieval step when the coverslips are heated in a microwave oven.
5. The fluorescent beads can be used as reference markers during microscopy to identify and mark identical positions on the coverslip. This enables us to overlay images from different rounds of staining, stripping off antibodies and restaining the tissue.
6. This protocol uses overnight or 2-h xylene incubation as a standard procedure. However, shorter incubation times may also work.
7. Target retrieval reverses the crosslinking of proteins that occurs during paraffin fixation of the tissue. The purpose of this step is to unmask epitopes, allowing antibodies to access their targets during the staining procedure.

8. If a final image is generated with the different images overlaid, ensure that:
   - The same region is captured each time especially if only smaller regions of the tissue section are imaged.
   - The different images are acquired centered on the same region.
   - The tissue on the coverslips is oriented identically.
   - A reference image (e.g., nuclei stain or autofluorescence) is acquired in each round. Without a reference, image alignment may not be possible.

9. All antibodies have different stripping efficiencies; therefore, this step needs to be optimized for each new antibody, including both primary and secondary antibodies. In general, most antibodies could be stripped to an efficiency of 80–100%, and only a few antibodies were difficult to remove. Therefore, hard-to-remove antibodies should be limited and placed in the very end of the staining sequence.
10. To overlay the images into a single composite, the Fiji Plugin *HyperStackReg* (V5.6) [8] was used. First, all images should be opened in Fiji and concatenated (Image › Stacks › Tools › Concatenate). It is important to have a reference channel for each round (e.g., the nuclei or the autofluorescence). Next, select a Transformation method; in most cases use the *Rigid Body* because no scaling is performed on the images. For processing multiple files, a macro has been developed to automate the procedure (*HyperStackReg_processFolder.*)

Acknowledgments

The multiplex method was originally published in *APMIS* in 2023 [6] which was supported by ODIN (the Open Discovery Innovation Network) supported by the Novo Nordisk Foundation (grant number NNF20SA0061466) toward the FRIGG project (FResh Human KIdney Tissue: ExplorinG biomarkers and intervention tarGets in chronic kidney disease).

Conflict of Interest Statement The multiplex method was originally published in APMIS in 2023 which was supported by ODIN (the Open Discovery Innovation Network) supported by the Novo Nordisk Foundation (grant number NNF20SA0061466) towards the FRIGG project (FResh Human KIdney Tissue: ExplorinG biomarkers and intervention tarGets in chronic kidney disease).

References

1. Bolognesi MM, Manzoni M, Scalia CR, Zannella S, Bosisio FM, Faretta M et al (2017) Multiplex staining by sequential immunostaining and antibody removal on routine tissue sections. J Histochem Cytochem 65(8):431–444
2. Cattoretti G, Bosisio FM, Marcelis L, Bolognesi MM (2019) Multiple Iterative Labeling by Antibody Neodeposition (MILAN). Research Square. https://doi.org/10.21203/rs.2.1646/v5
3. Gerdes MJ, Sevinsky CJ, Sood A, Adak S, Bello MO, Bordwell A et al (2013) Highly multiplexed single-cell analysis of formalin-fixed, paraffin-embedded cancer tissue. Proc Natl Acad Sci U S A 110(29):11982–11987
4. Radtke AJ, Chu CJ, Yaniv Z, Yao L, Marr J, Beuschel RT et al (2022) IBEX: an iterative immunolabeling and chemical bleaching method for high-content imaging of diverse tissues. Nat Protoc 17(2):378–401
5. Lin JR, Izar B, Wang S, Yapp C, Mei S, Shah PM et al (2018) Highly multiplexed immunofluorescence imaging of human tissues and tumors using t-CyCIF and conventional optical microscopes. Elife 7:e31657
6. Elsborg SH, Pedersen GA, Madsen MG, Keller AK, Nørregaard R, Nejsum LN (2023) Multiplex immunofluorescence staining of coverslip-mounted paraffin-embedded tissue sections. Apmis 131(8):394–402
7. Schindelin J, Arganda-Carreras I, Frise E, Kaynig V, Longair M, Pietzsch T et al (2012) Fiji: an open-source platform for biological-image analysis. Nat Methods 9(7):676–682
8. Sharma V (2018) ImageJ plugin HyperStackReg V5.6 (v5.6). Zenodo. https://doi.org/10.5281/zenodo.2252521

Chapter 3

Evaluation of Murine Tissue Architecture and Cellular Spatial Relationships in Murine Tumor Microenvironments Utilizing Multiplex Fluorescent Immunohistochemistry

Andrew Spiteri, Alberto Olivei, Jake McGue, Aadith Kumar, Rashmi Kumar, Brian D. Griffith and Timothy L. Frankel

Abstract

The tumor microenvironment (TME) is composed of tumor cells and surrounding stroma, including immune, mesenchymal, and vascular cells, as well as soluble factors. Traditional techniques to interrogate cellular interactions and infiltration are limited by the loss of tissue architecture or by labeling only a small number of antigens. Multiplex fluorescent immunohistochemistry (mfIHC) is a tissue staining technique that involves tyramide-based signal amplification to covalently bind a fluorophore to an antigen of interest, followed by removal of the primary and secondary antibodies, thereby permitting co-staining and localization of multiple antigens on a single sample. mfIHC retains spatial information, allowing for in-depth analysis of cellular phenotypes and their interactions within the TME. Described here is an overview of the mfIHC experimental design, staining, and image analysis in murine tissues utilizing a manual technique and the Akoya OPAL system.

Keywords Immunofluorescence, Tumor immunology, Multiplex fluorescent immunohistochemistry, Tumor microenvironment, Cellular engagement

1 Introduction

The tumor microenvironment (TME) is composed of both cancer cells and the surrounding stroma, containing immune, mesenchymal, and vascular cells, in addition to soluble factors like cytokines and chemokines. The complex interactions among tumor cells and the supporting stroma impact tumor progression, propensity to metastasize, and the overall response to treatment [1–3]. Additionally, the impact of regional differences within the TME in both immune infiltration and the presence of selective pressures, like availability of nutrients, hypoxia, or acidosis, on tumor progression and response to therapy is increasingly apparent [4]. For example, in Merkel cell carcinoma, the colocalization of programmed cell death protein 1 (PD-1) and its ligand

Timothy L. Frankel and Arvind Rao (eds.), *Cellular Spatial Characterization and Analysis*, Methods in Molecular Biology, vol. 2995, https://doi.org/10.1007/978-1-0716-5027-1_3,

programmed death-ligand 1 (PD-L1) was more predictive of response to anti-PD-1 immunotherapy than PD-L1 expression alone [5].

Prior techniques to evaluate the TME, including immunohistochemistry (IHC), immunofluorescence (IF), and flow cytometry, have significant limitations in interrogating these important spatial relationships. Traditional IHC relies upon binding of a primary antibody against a target of interest either directly to an enzyme, like horseradish peroxidase (HRP), or to a species-specific secondary antibody bound to an enzyme. This allows for a reaction to deposit chromogen at the site of antibody binding, with counterstaining of background tissue, for visualization in the visible spectrum [6]. However, IHC is subject to multiple limitations, including colocalization of one or two antigens due to significant overlap in the visible spectrum, low sensitivity for poorly antigenic targets, and high interobserver variability [6–9]. IF allows for similar data to IHC but with better detection and colocalization of a wide variety of antigens due to the detection of signals outside of the visible spectrum, where the final antibody is conjugated to a single fluorophore [10]. Limitations of IF include tissue autofluorescence, photobleaching, cross-species reactivity, and fading of signal intensity with time [11, 12]. Flow cytometry involves processing fresh tissue into a single-cell suspension stained with labeled fluorescent antibodies. Although flow cytometry allows for multiantigen staining of individual cells, limitations include the loss of tissue architecture and spatial information during processing, as well as the need for significant compensation of signals [13, 14].

Multiplex fluorescent immunohistochemistry (mfIHC) is a technique that utilizes tyramide signal amplification (TSA) and multispectral imaging to simultaneously detect multiple antigens in a single tissue sample. TSA involves the covalent binding of tyramide-conjugated fluorophores to antigens of interest, followed by the removal of the antibodies to allow for another round of antibody binding and TSA amplification with a different fluorophore. Multispectral microscopes can detect six to eight antigens and a nuclear counterstain in a single assay with retention of spatial location, allowing for a more comprehensive overview of tissue composition, subpopulation density, and cellular interactions [12, 15]. During mfIHC, formalin-fixed paraffin-embedded tissue is adhered to a charged slide and subjected to antigen retrieval, followed by staining with a primary antibody to an epitope of interest and an HRP-conjugated secondary antibody. TSA amplification is then performed, followed by heating of the slides to remove the previously applied primary and secondary antibodies, leaving the fluorophore bound to the epitope. Subsequently, multiple rounds of staining can be performed with limited cross-reactivity [8, 16]. TSA amplification allows for subtraction of tissue autofluorescence, and panel design with limited spectral overlap among fluorophores limits the need for manual compensation. Codetection of up to eight antigens allows for complex cellular phenotyping, and analysis of the multispectral images can provide key information on cellular location and interactions within the tumor microenvironment [15, 17]. Limitations of mfIHC include the considerable time needed for optimization, as the order of staining can impact antigenicity [18], and decreased specificity from overactive tyramide deposits, which lead to off-target labeling [15]. Moreover, differing protocols and commercial systems can limit the reproducibility of this technique [15, 19]. Described here is an overview of the experimental design, staining, and imaging strategy for mfIHC of murine FFPE tissue utilizing a manual technique and the Akoya OPAL system.

2 Materials

2.1 Staining Reagents

1. Primary antibody
2. HRP secondary antibody
3. Opal fluorophore stocks (480, 520, 570, 620, 690, 780)
4. TSA-DIG (Tyramide signal amplification plus digoxigenin)
5. 1× Amplification diluent (Amp diluent)

2.2 Antigen Retrieval Buffers

1. 1× Citrate buffer (pH 6)
2. 1× Tris-EDTA buffer (pH 9)

2.3 Wash Buffers

1. Tris-buffered saline (TBS)
2. Tris-buffered saline, 0.1% Tween 20 (TBST)

2.4 Equipment

1. Heat-resistant slide containers (12 recommended) (*see* **Note 1**)
2. Hybridization oven
3. Plastic slide rack (heat and chemical resistant)
4. Immunohistochemistry staining tray
5. Vacuum with pipette attachment
6. Microwave with Inverter Technology

3 Methods

3.1 Slide Preparation

3.1.1 Cut Formalin-Fixed, Paraffin-Embedded (FFPE) Tissue onto Charged Slides

1. Cut 5 μm sections of FFPE tissue and adhere to positively charged slides (*see* **Note 2**).
2. Allow the slides to dry on a flat surface with the tissue side up for 24 h at room temperature or 1 h at 50–60°C (*see* **Note 3**).
3. Store the dried slides at 4°C until ready for use (*see* **Note 4**).

3.2 Staining Preparation

3.2.1 Deparaffinization and Tissue Rehydration

1. Place the slides in a heat-resistant slide rack and bake for 1 h at 60°C in a hybridization oven. Allow the slides to cool at room temperature for at least 10 min after baking.
2. Rehydrate the tissue by placing the slides through the following series: xylene in triplicate, 100% ethanol, 95% ethanol, and 70% ethanol. Submerge the slides for 10 min at each step.
3. Wash the slides in deionized water for 2 min, followed by 10% neutral buffered formalin for 30 min. Wash with deionized water for 2 min to remove excess neutral buffered formalin (*see* **Note 5**).

3.2.2 Heat-Induced Epitope Retrieval (HIER)

1. Place the slide rack in a heat-resistant slide container and submerge with citrate (pH 6) or tris-EDTA (pH 9) antigen retrieval buffer (*see* **Note 6**).
2. Cover the heat-resistant slide container with plastic wrap and secure with a rubber band.
3. Place the heat-resistant box against the microwave plate's edge. The slides should be microwaved for 45 s at 100% power and then for 15 min at 20% power (*see* **Note 7**).
4. Remove the heat-resistant box from the microwave and use the box cover to vent about 1/3 of the opening. Allow the slides to cool for at least 20 min (*see* **Note 8**).

3.2.3 Primary Antibody, Opal Fluorophore, and Wash Buffer Preparations

1. Dilute the primary antibody in antibody dilutant. Prepare 100–200 μl per slide depending on the size of the tissue.
2. Allow the stock Opal fluorophores to reach room temperature and prepare in the following manner (*see* **Note 9**):
   a. Opal 480–690: Reconstitute with 75 μl of DMSO. Vortex and allow the lyophilizate to rest for 15 min. Prepare the working fluorophore solution by diluting 1:50 with AMP dilutant. Store in the dark at 4°C until ready for use.
   b. TSA-Dig: Reconstitute with 75 μl of DMSO. Vortex and allow the lyophilizate to rest for 15 min. Prepare the working solution by diluting 1:100 with AMP dilutant. Store in the dark at 4°C until ready for use.
   c. Opal 780: Reconstitute with 300 μl of deionized water. Vortex and allow the lyophilizate to rest for 15 min. Prepare the working fluorophore solution by diluting 1:100 with antibody dilutant. Store in the dark at 4°C until ready for use.
3. Dilute 10× TBS stock (1.5 M NaCl, 0.1 M Tris-HCl, pH 7.4) to a 1× working solution with deionized water. Add Tween-20 such that the final formulation of the TBST wash buffer contains 0.1% Tween-20.

3.3 Slide Staining Protocol (see Note 10)

3.3.1 Peroxidase Blocking

1. Wash slides with deionized water then TBST for 2 min each. Use a separate slide box for each wash.
2. Remove a slide and dry with a delicate task wipe. Avoid touching the tissue directly. Using a hydrophobic barrier pen, trace a barrier around the tissue. Place TBST onto the tissue to avoid drying. Repeat for the remaining slides.
3. Aspirate off the TBST without directly touching or disrupting the tissue. Apply three to four drops of peroxidase blocking solution and incubate at room temperature for 10 min.

3.3.2 Primary Antibody Application

1. Aspirate the blocking solution and incubate the tissue with approximately 150 μl of working primary antibody solution per slide in a humidified chamber for 1 h at room temperature.
2. After incubation, remove the primary antibody solution and wash the slides three times in a slide box with fresh TBST for 2 min each (*see* **Note 11**).

3.3.3 Secondary Antibody Application

1. Load the humidified chamber as detailed in step 3.3.1.2, excluding the reapplication of the hydrophobic barrier.
2. Gently aspirate TBST and incubate the tissue in three to four drops of secondary antibody. Incubate for 45 min in the humidified chamber.
3. After incubation, remove the secondary antibody solution and wash the slides three times in a slide box with fresh TBST for 2 min each.

3.3.4 Fluorophore Application

1. Load the slides into the humidified chamber as before.
2. Aspirate TBST and add 100 μl per slide of the appropriate fluorophore working solution. Incubate for 10 min at room temperature in the humidified chamber.
3. Remove the excess fluorophore solution and wash slides three times with fresh TBST.

3.3.5 Binding of the Fluorophore and Removal of the Primary and Secondary Antibodies

1. As detailed in Sect. 3.2.3, microwave the slides to remove the primary and secondary antibodies, and covalently bind the fluorophore to the epitope of interest.
2. The protocol can be paused here if desired, with slides submerged in antigen retrieval buffer overnight at room temperature. If pausing, ensure the slide box is covered with plastic wrap to limit evaporation.
3. Once the multiplex positions are determined as detailed in Sect. 3.4, repeat the above steps (Sects. 3.3.1–3.3.5) for the remaining antibody-fluorophore pairs, excluding the final position.

3.3.6 Final Antibody Position and TSA-Dig Amplification

1. Repeat steps in Sects. 3.3.1–3.3.3 to perform peroxidase blocking, primary antibody application, and secondary antibody application for the final antibody position.
2. Load the slides into the humidified chamber as before. Incubate in 150 μl of Opal TSA-Dig solution for 10 min at room temperature.
3. Remove the excess TSA-Dig solution and wash three times in fresh TBST as before.
4. Microwave as in Sect. 3.2.2 to allow for the removal of primary and secondary antibodies. After cooling, wash in a slide box with deionized water, then TBST.
5. Load the slides into the humidified chamber as before. After aspirating the TBST, incubate the slides in 100 μl of the final working fluorophore solution for 1 h.
6. Remove the excess fluorophore solution. Wash in a slide box with fresh TBS solution three times for 2 min each.

3.3.7 DAPI Application and Mounting

1. Add three drops of 4′,6-diamidino-2-phenylindole (DAPI) to 1 ml of TBS to prepare the DAPI working solution. Vortex. Store at 4°C in the dark until ready for use.
2. Load the slides into the humidified chamber, utilizing TBS to ensure slides do not dry out. After aspirating TBS, add approximately 150 μl of DAPI solution to each slide. Incubate for 10 min.
3. Remove the excess DAPI. Wash slides in a slide box with fresh TBS for 2 min then deionized water for 2 min.
4. Remove the hydrophobic barrier by placing slides in fresh xylene for approximately 1 min. Ensure slides are not submerged longer than 2 min.
5. Use an antifade mountant to mount coverslips, avoiding air bubbles. Allow the slides to dry overnight.

3.4 Multiplex Optimization via Monoplex Testing

3.4.1 Use Traditional IHC to Determine the Optimal Antibody Concentration for Multiplex

1. Complete the IHC on your tissue of interest for the best results. However, any tissue with an abundance of epitopes specific for the tested antibody is also acceptable.
2. Prepare and use a working primary antibody concentration below, equal to, and above the company-recommended antibody concentration.
3. Visualize the slides side by side and record the best performing antibody concentration for use in the multiplex (*see* **Note 12**).

3.4.2 Complete Monoplexes to Determine the Optimal Primary Antibody Sequence for Multiplex (Fig. 1)

1. For each antibody in the anticipated multiplex staining panel, prepare an equal number of slides as antibodies in the multiplex. For example, if staining for three antibodies, prepare three slides for each of the three antibodies. Each slide should contain tissue with an ample amount of epitope for each optimized primary antibody.

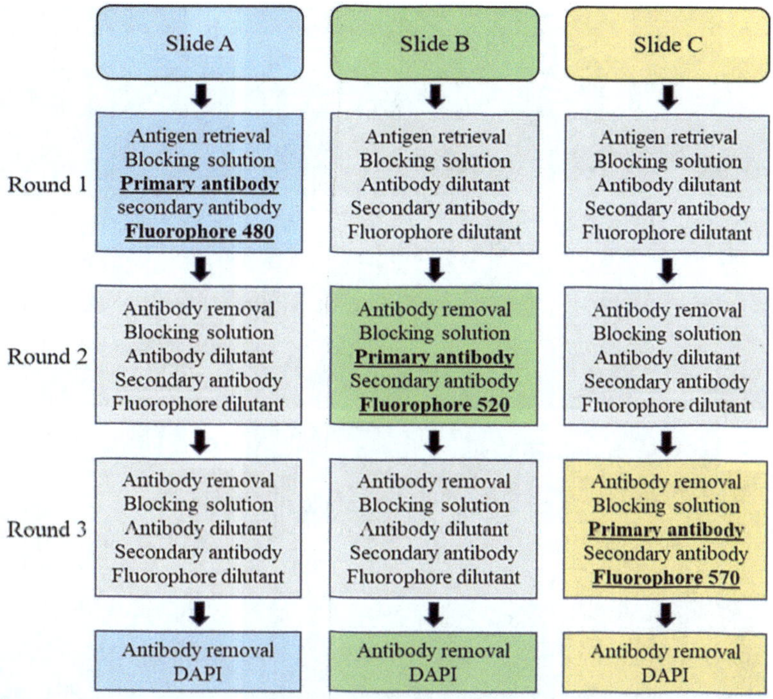

Fig. 1 Workflow of a monoplex position test. Example workflow for a position test of a single primary antibody, for anticipated use in a multiplex examining three antibodies total. The primary antibody of interest is at position 1 in Slide A, position 2 in Slide B, and position 3 in slide C

2. Perform a monoplex stain with the antibody in a unique position for each individual antibody, following the staining procedures outlined in Sects. 3.3.1–3.3.7. For example, if using three antibodies, each slide would have one primary antibody applied in one of three unique positions. If the slides do not require a primary antibody for the particular round of staining, replace with antibody and fluorophore diluent solutions.

3.4.3 Utilize a Fluorescent Microscope to Image and Evaluate Each Monoplex

1. Focus the fluorescent microscope on a region of positive cells.
2. Evaluate the fluorescent intensity of the stained marker. A strong positive signal will typically have an exposure time between 1 and 250 ms^{-1}.
3. Compare this intensity to the adjacent background. If the intensity of the positive signal is five to ten times greater than the background, it is in a viable position.
4. If the signal intensity is sufficient for multiple positions, qualitatively evaluate which position stained the most specifically with the least amount of background interference.
5. Refer to Fig. 2 for an example of a completed monoplex test.

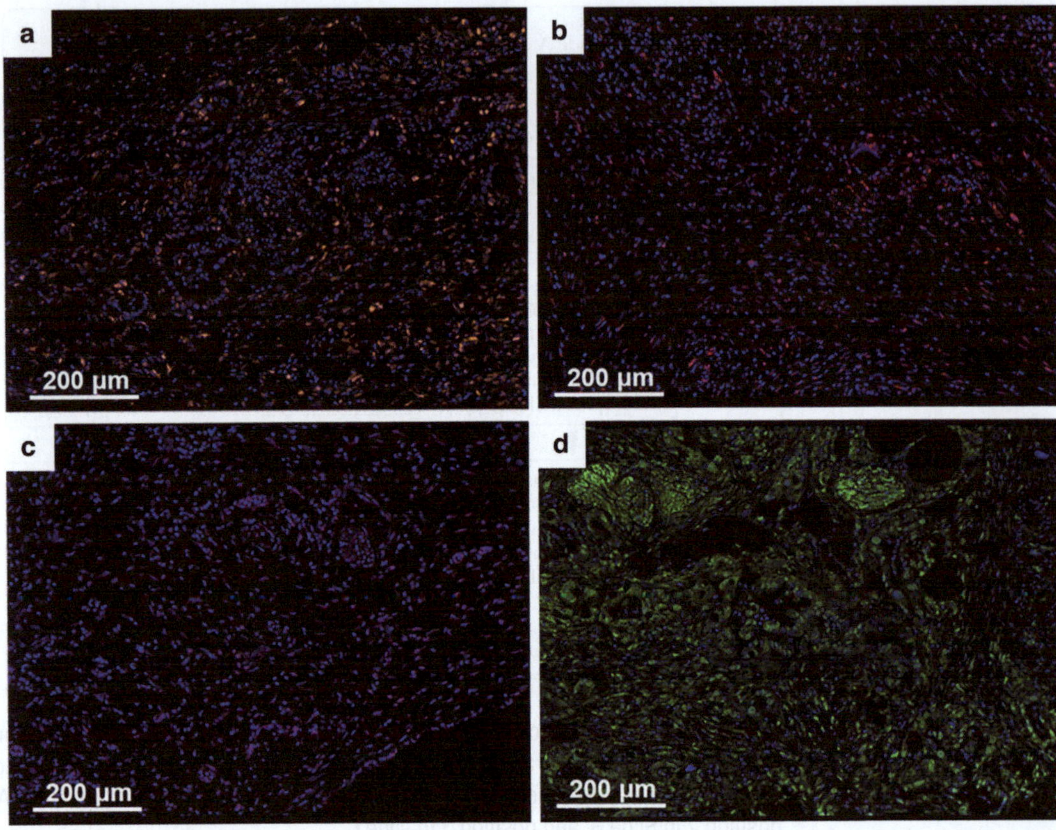

Fig. 2 Example of a monoplex position test. An example monoplex position test for phosphorylated extracellular signal-regulated kinases (pERK) in murine tonsillar tissue. (**a**) Staining of pERK (orange) in position 4 (orange) with the Opal 620 fluorophore showing the strongest signal with specific staining. This is an ideal position for pERK. (**b**) Staining of pERK (red) at position 1 with Opal 480 fluorophore showing intermediate signal strength and good specificity. It is a viable position. (**c**) Staining of pERK (magenta) at position 6 with the Opal 780 fluorophore revealing weak signal intesnsity and poor staining quality. (**d**) Staining of pERK (green) at position 2 with the Opal 520 fluorophore. Poor staining quality evidenced by strong background autofluorescence and poor signal intensity.

3.5 Multiplex Staining

3.5.1 Perform the Multiplex Stain After Optimization (Fig. 3)

1. Obtain your relevant slides as well as a blank slide for autofluorescence subtraction following imaging. The blank slide does not receive any working solution. Instead of treating with the primary antibody and fluorophore, use antibody dilutant and the fluorophore diluent (Amp diluent), respectively (*see* **Note 13**).
2. Note the appropriate primary antibody sequence as described in Sect. 3.4.3. Assign a fluorophore to each primary antibody (*see* **Note 14**).
3. Stain the multiplex as described in Sects. 3.3.1–3.3.7.
4. Refer to Fig. 4 for an example of a completed multiplex stain.

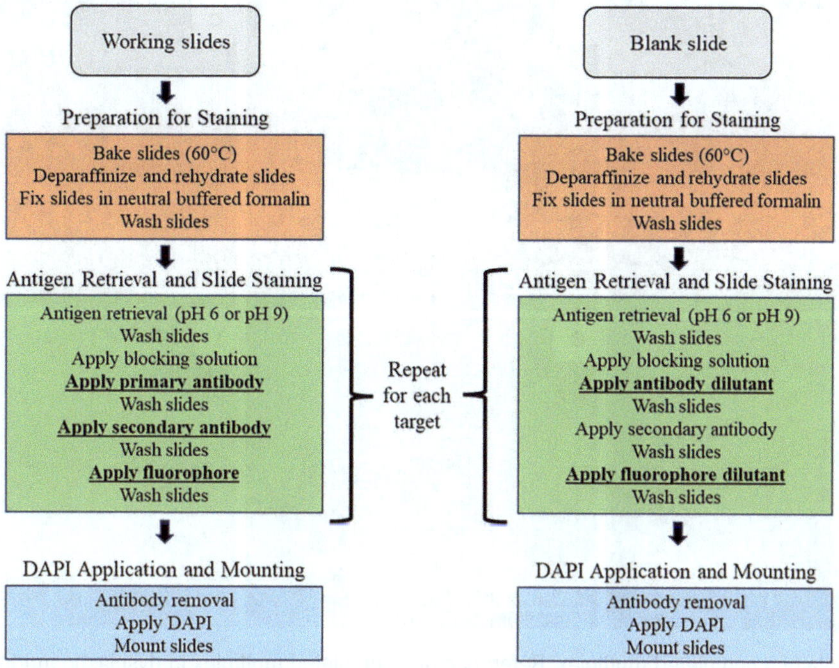

Fig. 3 Multiplex fluorescent immunohistochemistry (mflHC) workflow. Overview of the staining process for a complete multiplex experiment after optimizing primary antibody positions. Adapted from Lazarus et al. [20]

4 Notes

1. Allocate slide containers for each washing solution to avoid cross-contamination (3× TBS/TBST, 3× xylene, 3× ethanol, 1× deionized water, 1× citrate buffer, 1× Tris-EDTA buffer).
2. The extra adherence granted by using charged slides helps the tissue survive multiple washes and antigen retrieval steps.
3. We recommend 24 h at room temperature to avoid the risk of extended drying and high temperatures causing decreased immunogenicity, but the accelerated option exists if necessary.
4. Cooling the slides helps preserve the immunogenicity of epitopes of interest. We recommend using these slides as soon as possible for the best results, or within 2–3 weeks. Each epitope has a different survivability.
5. It is important to use distilled water for proper adherence and mounting of tissue.
6. Use the company-recommended antigen retrieval buffer for the associated primary antibody. If not provided, we recommend first using citrate buffer for membrane and cytoplasmic epitopes and Tris-EDTA buffer for nuclear epitopes.

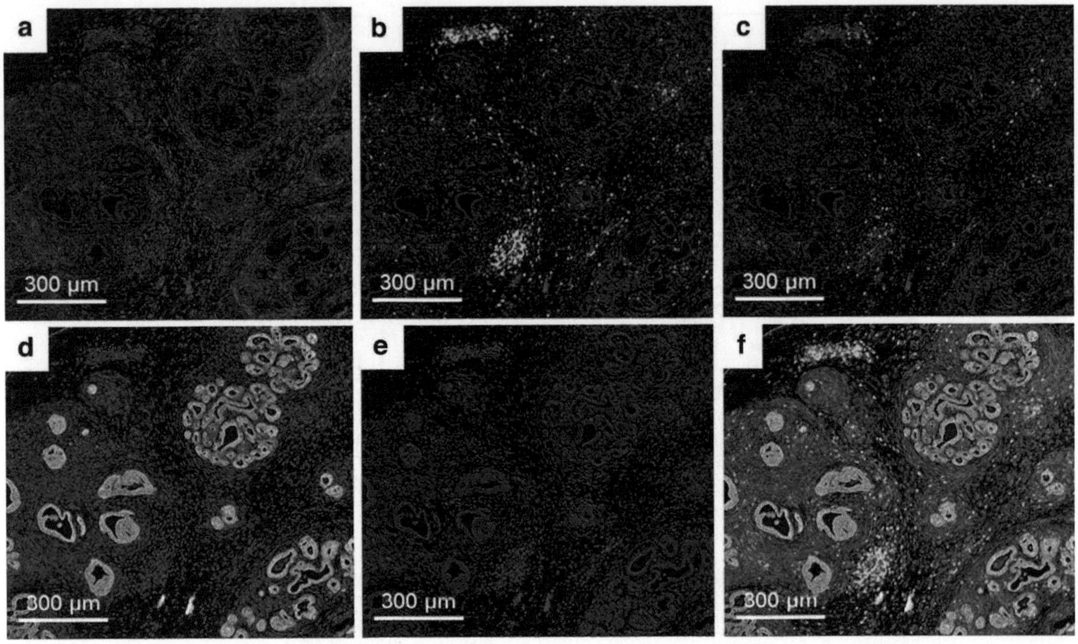

Fig. 4 Example of a completed multiplex. Reference of a completed multiplex in dysplastic murine pancreatic tissue after panel optimization. (**a**) F4/80 (orange) stain in position 1 with the Opal 480 fluorophore. (**b**) CD3 (green) stain in position 2 with the Opal 520 fluorophore. (**c**) CD8 (yellow) stain in position 3 with the Opal 570 fluorophore. (**d**) Cytokeratin-19 (CK19, white) in position 5 with the Opal 690 fluorophore. (**e**) FoxP3 (magenta) stain in position 6 with the Opal 780 fluorophore, demonstrating mild tissue autofluorescence but moderate intensity signal. (**f**) Full multiplex composite image (DAPI—blue, F4/80—orange, CD3—green, CD8—yellow, CK19—white, FoxP3—magenta)

7. Use a microwave with inverter technology for even heating.
8. Following application of the first fluorophore, it is best to limit ambient light exposure to avoid excessive tissue autofluorescence. Venting in this way is a compromise that allows the slides to cool down while maintaining some light protection.
9. Fluorophore solutions are stable for 24–48 h when stored at 4°C. Additionally, fluorophore concentrations may need further optimization depending on the primary antibody being used and previous results.
10. It is recommended to perform monoplex testing, as detailed in Sect. 3.4, to determine the ideal antibody position prior to initiating multiplex staining, as detailed in Sect. 3.5. Sect. 3.3 details the generic slide staining workflow to be utilized in both monoplex testing and multiplex staining.
11. Gently agitate the slides once submerged in the TBST to ensure thorough washing. Moreover, we recommend making fresh TBST with each experiment to ensure a clean image.

12. The best-performing antibody will stain specifically and strongly to the epitope of interest with minimal background interference.
13. The blank slide should be the same tissue type as your slides of interest for the best results when subtracting autofluorescence.
14. Fluorophore assignments may also require further optimization. It is recommended to use brighter fluorophores for less abundant epitopes. Additionally, to minimize spectral overlap, epitopes that colocalize should be matched with fluorophores as far away as possible on the spectrum.

Conflict of Interest Statement

The authors have no conflicts of interest to declare that are relevant to the content of this chapter.

References

1. Chen F, Zhuang X, Lin L, Yu P, Wang Y, Shi Y et al (2015) New horizons in tumor microenvironment biology: challenges and opportunities. BMC Med 13:45
2. Paluskievicz CM, Cao X, Abdi R, Zheng P, Liu Y, Bromberg JS (2019) T regulatory cells and priming the suppressive tumor microenvironment. Front Immunol 10:2453
3. Schulz M, Salamero-Boix A, Niesel K, Alekseeva T, Sevenich L (2019) Microenvironmental regulation of tumor progression and therapeutic response in brain metastasis. Front Immunol 10:1713
4. Junttila MR, de Sauvage FJ (2013) Influence of tumour micro-environment heterogeneity on therapeutic response. Nature 501(7467):346–354
5. Giraldo NA, Nguyen P, Engle EL, Kaunitz GJ, Cottrell TR, Berry S et al (2018) Multidimensional, quantitative assessment of PD-1/PD-L1 expression in patients with Merkel cell carcinoma and association with response to pembrolizumab. J Immunother Cancer 6(1):99
6. Katikireddy KR, O'Sullivan F (2011) Immunohistochemical and immunofluorescence procedures for protein analysis. Methods Mol Biol 784:155–167
7. Tan WCC, Nerurkar SN, Cai HY, Ng HHM, Wu D, Wee YTF et al (2020) Overview of multiplex immunohistochemistry/immunofluorescence techniques in the era of cancer immunotherapy. Cancer Commun (Lond) 40(4):135–153
8. Stack EC, Wang C, Roman KA, Hoyt CC (2014) Multiplexed immunohistochemistry, imaging, and quantitation: a review, with an assessment of Tyramide signal amplification, multispectral imaging and multiplex analysis. Methods 70(1):46–58
9. Taylor CR, Levenson RM (2006) Quantification of immunohistochemistry–issues concerning methods, utility and semiquantitative assessment II. Histopathology 49(4):411–424
10. Wharton Jr.KA, Wood D, Manesse M, Maclean KH, Leiss F, Zuraw A (2021) Tissue multiplex analyte detection in anatomic pathology – pathways to clinical implementation. Front Mol Biosci 8:672531
11. Lichtman JW, Conchello JA (2005) Fluorescence microscopy. Nat Methods 2(12):910–919
12. Harms PW, Frankel TL, Moutafi M, Rao A, Rimm DL, Taube JM et al (2023) Multiplex immunohistochemistry and immunofluorescence: a practical update for pathologists. Mod Pathol 36(7):100197
13. Adan A, Alizada G, Kiraz Y, Baran Y, Nalbant A (2017) Flow cytometry: basic principles and applications. Crit Rev Biotechnol 37(2):163–176
14. Zaritskaya L, Shurin MR, Sayers TJ, Malyguine AM (2010) New flow cytometric assays for monitoring cell-mediated cytotoxicity. Expert Rev Vaccines 9(6):601–616
15. Boisson A, Noel G, Saiselet M, Rodrigues-Vitoria J, Thomas N, Fontsa ML et al (2021) Fluorescent multiplex immunohistochemistry coupled with other state-of-the-art techniques to systematically characterize the tumor immune microenvironment. Front Mol Biosci 8:673042

16. Zhang W, Hubbard A, Jones T, Racolta A, Bhaumik S, Cummins N et al (2017) Fully automated 5-plex fluorescent immunohistochemistry with tyramide signal amplification and same species antibodies. Lab Invest 97(7):873–885
17. Lazarus J, Maj T, Smith JJ, Perusina Lanfranca M, Rao A, D'Angelica MIet al (2018) Spatial and phenotypic immune profiling of metastatic colon cancer. JCI Insight 3(22):e121932
18. Ehrenberg AJ, Morales DO, Piergies AMH, Li SH, Tejedor JS, Mladinov M et al (2020) A manual multiplex immunofluorescence method for investigating neurodegenerative diseases. J Neurosci Methods 339:108708
19. Laberiano-Fernandez C, Hernandez-Ruiz S, Rojas F, Parra ER (2021) Best practices for technical reproducibility assessment of multiplex immunofluorescence. Front Mol Biosci 8:660202
20. Lazarus J, Akiska Y, Perusina Lanfranca M, Delrosario L, Sun L, Long D et al (2019) Optimization, design and avoiding pitfalls in manual multiplex fluorescent immunohistochemistry. J Vis Exp (149)

Chapter 4

Autostaining Immune Multiplex Immunohistochemistry Panels and Imaging Analysis

Hidetoshi Mori and Alexander D. Borowsky

Abstract

Immune cells often require several markers for positive identification. While flow-cytometry can provide detailed multi-parameter cell identification it does not retain the cell localization. Multiplex immunohistochemistry provides a valuable technique for cell profiling with localization in the tissue microenvironment. In this study, we present the staining procedures for human immune-cell multiplex panels, employing tyramide signal amplification-based immunohistochemistry on an autostainer. Additionally, we explore the imaging analysis techniques applied to the stained tissues. These panels enable the visualization of immune cell markers on formalin-fixed paraffin-embedded tissues.

Keywords Autostaining, Imaging analysis, Immune cells, Multiplex immunohistochemistry

1 Introduction

Increasing numbers of studies prove the value of spatially defined multi-omics analyses, particularly in the characterization of the tissue/tumor microenvironment. In pathological analysis, it is crucial to define cell types, the levels of biomarkers, and their distributions in order to characterize the immune interaction patterns. Recent studies show predictive power for choosing optimal therapies. In routine pathological analysis, cell characterization with marker proteins has been performed through single marker chromogenic IHC. Chromogenic IHC which is based on enzymatic color development is best used as a qualitative (yes/no per cell) assay and harder to optimize for quantitative marker analysis. Additionally, it is challenging to co-register multiple markers on stained serial sections and impossible to co-register individual cells on serial sections. Particularly, when studying immune cells' activities in the target tissue for immunotherapy strategies, it becomes necessary to detect multiple markers to identify immune cells and assess immune checkpoint status.

Timothy L. Frankel and Arvind Rao (eds.), *Cellular Spatial Characterization and Analysis*, Methods in Molecular Biology, vol. 2995, https://doi.org/10.1007/978-1-0716-5027-1_4,

To address these challenges, the use of TSA-based multiplex immunohistochemistry [1, 2] offers a seamless transition from routine chromogenic IHC experiments without significant changes to the staining protocol. In this context, we have developed two immune multiplex panels to visualize the immune microenvironment in human cancerous tissues [1]. The first multiplex immune panel (IP1) enables the detection of CD3, CD20, FOXP3, CD117, cytokeratins, and Ki67. The second panel (IP2) is designed to detect CD3, CD8, PD1, PDL1, CD68, and cytokeratins. Responding to the high demand for detecting HLA-DR on tumor cells, which has implications for patient prognosis [3–6], we have re-optimized the IP1 panel as IP1.2 panel to include CD3, CD20, FOXP3, HLA-DR, cytokeratins, and Ki67. Overall, these developments in multiplex IHC techniques allow for a comprehensive analysis of the immune microenvironment in human cancerous tissues. Here, we introduce the detailed procedure for autostaining these immune panels and provide insights into their optimization. By utilizing these innovative techniques, researchers and pathologists can gain a deeper understanding of the tissue microenvironment and make more informed decisions regarding therapeutic approaches.

2 Materials

2.1 Equipment

1. BOND RX fully automated research stainer (Leica Biosystems)
2. Vectra/Polaris automated Quantitative Pathology Imaging System (Akoya Biosciences)

2.2 Reagents

1. Milli-Q water (indicated as Kit wash in the procedure)
2. APEX BOND slide (Leica Biosystems)
3. BOND Universal Covertile (Leica Biosystems)
4. BOND dewax solution (Leica Biosystems)
5. Alcohol: 100% Ethanol
6. BOND wash solution (Leica Biosystems)
7. BOND ER Solution 1 (Leica Biosystems)
8. BOND ER Solution 2 (Leica Biosystems)
9. PKI Blocking buffer (Opal Antibody diluent/block; Akoya Biosciences)
10. Opal Polymer HRP (1× Opal Anti-Ms+Rb HRP in Opal 6-Plex detection kit; Akoya Biosciences)
11. PV mS 50%: 50% (v/v) PowerVision poly-HRP anti-Mouse IgG (Leica Biosystems) diluted with antibody diluent in Opal 6-Plex detection kit or Opal Antibody diluent/block.

12. PV Rb 50%: 50% (v/v) PowerVision poly-HRP anti-rabbit IgG (Leica Biosystems) diluted with antibody diluent in Opal 6-Plex detection kit or Opal Antibody diluent/block.
13. TSA Biotin Reagent Pack (This kit contains 1× Amplification buffer, TSA Biotin, and DMSO; Akoya Biosciences).
14. DAPI solution: 25 μg/ml DAPI
15. Fluoromount-G (Thermo Fisher Scientific)

2.3 Primary Antibodies

Antibodies are indicated with Company, clone name, catalog #, and the dilution for the final concentration. The antibody must be diluted in Antibody Diluent using the indicated concentration provided below. If "ready to use" (RTU) is indicated, there is no need to dilute the antibody. It can be used directly without any further dilution.

1. Anti-FOXP3 (Abcam clone 236A/E7, 1:150)
2. Anti-CD20 (Ventana, clone L26, 1:2 from RTU)
3. Anti-Pan-cytokeratin (Dako, clone AE1/AE3, 1:300 for IP1.2 and 1:150 for IP2.2)
4. Anti-Ki67 (Ventana, clone 30-9, 1:2 from RTU)
5. Anti-CD3 (Ventana, clone 2GV6, 1:2 from RTU)
6. Anti-HLADR (Abcam, clone: EPR3962, 1:100)
7. Anti-CD8 (Leica Biosystems, clone: 4B11, 1:100)
8. Anti-PDL1 (Cell Signaling Technology, clone: E1L3N, 1:250)
9. Anti-CD68 (Dako, clone: PG-M1, 1:100)
10. Anti-PD1 (Abcam, clone: EPR4877, 1:100)

3 Methods

3.1 Autostaining

The following procedures are specifically designed and optimized for BOND RX autostainer. If a different autostaining platform is used, it may be necessary to adjust the protocol to suit the specific requirements.

3.2 Preparing Tissue Sections

Prepare formalin-fixed paraffin-embedded tissue sections at a thickness of 4 μm on APEX BOND glass slides. It is crucial that the tissue section is placed in the center of the slide to accommodate the mounting of the BOND Universal Covertile. Placing the tissue section in the center ensures effective reagent flow on the tissue area, thereby guaranteeing optimal staining results (*see* **Note 1**). Tissue slides are usually baked at 55–60 °C for at least 1 h in thermal benchtop oven (*see* **Note 2**).

3.3 Dewaxing Procedure

Dewaxing the slide will be performed in BOND RX with nine steps of the procedure. Following procedure is a setting for BOND RX. Each step will be indicated with Step type, treatment time (min), temperature. The reagent size, which will be indicated as "Dispense type," is always at 150 μl.

1. Bond dewax solution (Reagent, 0.5 min, 72°C). Repeat two more times.
2. Alcohol (Wash, 0 min, Ambient). Repeat two more times.
3. Bond dewax solution (Wash, 0 min, 72°C). Repeat two more times.

3.4 Antigen Retrieval Pretreatment

This antigen retrieval step is used as a pretreatment prior to run staining procedure.

1. Bond ER Solution 2 (Reagent, 0 min, Ambient, Dispense type: 150 μl). Repeat one more time.
2. Bond ER Solution 2 (Reagent, 40 min, 100°C, Dispense type: Intermediate).
3. Bond ER Solution 2 (Reagent, 0 min, Ambient, Dispense type: 150 μl).
4. Bond dewax solution (Reagent, 0 min, Ambient, Dispense type: 150 μl). Repeat two more times.
5. Bond dewax solution (Reagent, 3 min, Ambient, Dispense type: 150 μl).

3.5 Preparing Reagents

Each reagent should be prepared in a sufficient quantity for each individual reaction. When using the BOND RX system, it is important to note that an additional dead volume (approximately 500 μl) is required for reagents such as primary and secondary antibodies, Opal-TSA, and DAPI solution. It is recommended to prepare these reagents immediately before setting the slides in the BOND RX system and to avoid recycling them for subsequent runs.

3.6 Setting up BOND RX

3.6.1 Setting for IP1.2

This procedure is for staining IP1.2 panel to stain CD3, CD20, FOXP3, HLA-DR, cytokeratins, and Ki67. The following procedure is indicated same as "Dewaxing procedure." Primary antibody reagents are allocated as Open1 (FOXP3), Open2 (CD20), Open3 (Pan Cytokeratin), Open4 (Ki67), Open5 (CD3), Open6 (HLA-DR), and Open11 (DAPI solution).

1. Kit wash (Reagent, 10 min, Ambient, Dispense type: 150 μl).
2. Bond wash solution (Wash, 1 min, Ambient, Dispense type: Open).
3. Bond wash solution (Wash, 1 min, Ambient, Dispense type: 150 μl).

4. Bond wash solution (Wash, 0 min, Ambient, Dispense type: 150 μl).
5. Bond wash solution (Wash, 0 min, Ambient, Dispense type: 150 μl).
6. PKI blocking buffer (Reagent, 30 min, Ambient, Dispense type: 150 μl).
7. Open 1 (Reagent, 32 min, 36°C, Dispense type: 150 μl).
8. Bond wash solution (Wash, 0 min, Ambient, Dispense type: 150 μl).
9. Bond wash solution (Wash, 2 min, Ambient, Dispense type: 150 μl).
10. Bond wash solution (Wash, 2 min, Ambient, Dispense type: 150 μl).
11. Bond wash solution (Wash, 0 min, Ambient, Dispense type: 150 μl).
12. Bond wash solution (Wash, 0 min, Ambient, Dispense type: 150 μl).
13. PV mS 50% (Reagent, 10 min, Ambient, Dispense type: 150 μl).
14. Repeat steps #8–12.
15. Opal 570 reagent (Reagent, 10 min, Ambient, Dispense type: 150 μl).
16. Repeat steps #8–12.
17. Bond ER Solution 1 (Reagent, 0 min, Ambient, Dispense type: 150 μl).
18. Bond ER Solution 1 (Reagent, 0 min, 98°C, Dispense type: 150 μl).
19. Bond ER Solution 1 (Reagent, 20 min, 98°C, Dispense type: Intermediate).
20. Bond ER Solution 1 (Reagent, 0 min, Ambient, Dispense type: 150 μl).
21. Repeat steps #8–12.
22. PKI blocking buffer (Reagent, 10 min, Ambient, Dispense type: 150 μl).
23. Open 2 (Reagent, 32 min, 36°C, Dispense type: 150 μl).
24. Bond wash solution (Wash, 0 min, Ambient, Dispense type: 150 μl).
25. Bond wash solution (Wash, 1 min, Ambient, Dispense type: 150 μl).
26. Bond wash solution (Wash, 0 min, Ambient, Dispense type: 150 μl).

27. Opal Polymer HRP (Reagent, 10 min, Ambient, Dispense type: 150 μl).
28. Bond wash solution (Wash, 0 min, Ambient, Dispense type: 150 μl).
29. Bond wash solution (Wash, 1 min, Ambient, Dispense type: 150 μl).
30. Bond wash solution (Wash, 0 min, Ambient, Dispense type: 150 μl).
31. Bond wash solution (Wash, 0 min, Ambient, Dispense type: 150 μl).
32. Opal 520 reagent (Reagent, 16 min, Ambient, Dispense type: 150 μl).
33. Repeat steps #28–31.
34. Repeat steps #17–20.
35. Repeat steps #28–31.
36. PKI blocking buffer (Reagent, 10 min, Ambient, Dispense type: 150 μl).
37. Open 3 (Reagent, 32 min, 36°C, Dispense type: 150 μl).
38. Repeat steps #8–12.
39. Opal Polymer HRP (Reagent, 10 min, Ambient, Dispense type: 150 μl).
40. Repeat steps #8–12.
41. Opal 690 reagent (Reagent, 16 min, Ambient, Dispense type: 150 μl).
42. Repeat steps #8–12.
43. Repeat steps #17–20.
44. Repeat steps #28–31.
45. Repeat steps #17–20.
46. Repeat steps #28–31.
47. PKI blocking buffer (Reagent, 10 min, Ambient, Dispense type: 150 μl).
48. Open 4 (Reagent, 32 min, 36°C, Dispense type: 150 μl).
49. Repeat steps #24–26.
50. Opal Polymer HRP (Reagent, 10 min, Ambient, Dispense type: 150 μl).
51. Repeat steps #28–31.
52. Opal 620 reagent (Reagent, 16 min, Ambient, Dispense type: 150 μl).
53. Repeat steps #28–31.
54. Bond wash solution (Wash, 0 min, Ambient, Dispense type: 150 μl).

55. Repeat steps #17–20.
56. Repeat steps #28–31.
57. PKI blocking buffer (Reagent, 10 min, Ambient, Dispense type: 150 μl).
58. Open 5 (Reagent, 32 min, 36°C, Dispense type: 150 μl).
59. Repeat steps #24–26.
60. Opal Polymer HRP (Reagent, 10 min, Ambient, Dispense type: 150 μl).
61. Repeat steps #28–31.
62. Bond wash solution (Wash, 0 min, Ambient, Dispense type: 150 μl).
63. Opal 480 reagent (Reagent, 16 min, Ambient, Dispense type: 150 μl).
64. Repeat steps #28–31.
65. Bond wash solution (Wash, 0 min, Ambient, Dispense type: 150 μl).
66. Repeat steps #17–20.
67. Repeat steps #28–31.
68. PKI blocking buffer (Reagent, 10 min, Ambient, Dispense type: 150 μl).
69. Open 6 (Reagent, 32 min, 36°C, Dispense type: 150 μl).
70. Repeat steps #8–12.
71. Opal Polymer HRP (Reagent, 10 min, Ambient, Dispense type: 150 μl).
72. Repeat steps #8–12.
73. TSA-Biotin (Reagent, 0 min, Ambient, Dispense type: 150 μl).
74. TSA-Biotin (Reagent, 10 min, Ambient, Dispense type: 150 μl).
75. Repeat steps #8–12.
76. Alexa 750 Streptavidin (Reagent, 60 min, Ambient, Dispense type: 150 μl).
77. Repeat steps #8–12.
78. Open 11 (Reagent, 0 min, Ambient, Dispense type: 150 μl).
79. Open 11 (Reagent, 10 min, Ambient, Dispense type: 150 μl).
80. Repeat steps #24–26.

3.6.2 Setting for IP2.2

The following settings are for staining IP2.2 panel to stain CD3, CD8, CD68, PDL1, PD1, and cytokeratins. Primary antibody reagents are allocated as Open1 (CD8), Open2 (PDL1), Open3 (Pan-Cytokeratin), Open4 (PD1), Open5 (CD3), Open6 (CD68), and Open11 (DAPI solution). Before running the following procedure,

"Dewaxing procedure" and "Antigen-retrieval pretreatment" indicated for IP1.2 should be applied.

1. Kit wash (Reagent, 10 min, Ambient, Dispense type: 150 μl).
2. Bond wash solution (Wash, 1 min, Ambient, Dispense type: Open).
3. Bond wash solution (Wash, 1 min, Ambient, Dispense type: 150 μl).
4. Bond wash solution (Wash, 0 min, Ambient, Dispense type: 150 μl).
5. Bond wash solution (Wash, 0 min, Ambient, Dispense type: 150 μl).
6. PKI blocking buffer (Reagent, 10 min, Ambient, Dispense type: 150 μl).
7. Open 1 (Reagent, 32 min, 36°C, Dispense type: 150 μl).
8. Bond wash solution (Wash, 0 min, Ambient, Dispense type: 150 μl).
9. Bond wash solution (Wash, 2 min, Ambient, Dispense type: 150 μl).
10. Bond wash solution (Wash, 2 min, Ambient, Dispense type: 150 μl).
11. Bond wash solution (Wash, 0 min, Ambient, Dispense type: 150 μl).
12. Bond wash solution (Wash, 0 min, Ambient, Dispense type: 150 μl).
13. Opal Polymer HRP (Reagent, 10 min, Ambient, Dispense type: 150 μl).
14. Repeat steps #8–12.
15. Opal 570 reagent (Reagent, 0 min, Ambient, Dispense type: 150 μl).
16. Opal 570 reagent (Reagent, 16 min, Ambient, Dispense type: 150 μl).
17. Repeat steps #8–12.
18. Bond ER Solution 1 (Reagent, 0 min, Ambient, Dispense type: 150 μl).
19. Bond ER Solution 1 (Reagent, 0 min, 95°C, Dispense type: 150 μl).
20. Bond ER Solution 1 (Reagent, 20 min, 95°C, Dispense type: Intermediate).
21. Bond ER Solution 1 (Reagent, 0 min, Ambient, Dispense type: 150 μl).
22. Repeat steps #8–12.

23. Open 2 (Reagent, 32 min, 36°C, Dispense type: 150 μl).
24. Bond wash solution (Wash, 0 min, Ambient, Dispense type: 150 μl).
25. Bond wash solution (Wash, 1 min, Ambient, Dispense type: 150 μl).
26. Bond wash solution (Wash, 0 min, Ambient, Dispense type: 150 μl).
27. PV Rb 50% (Reagent, 10 min, Ambient, Dispense type: 150 μl).
28. Bond wash solution (Wash, 0 min, Ambient, Dispense type: 150 μl).
29. Bond wash solution (Wash, 1 min, Ambient, Dispense type: 150 μl).
30. Bond wash solution (Wash, 0 min, Ambient, Dispense type: 150 μl).
31. Bond wash solution (Wash, 0 min, Ambient, Dispense type: 150 μl).
32. Bond wash solution (Wash, 0 min, Ambient, Dispense type: 150 μl).
33. Opal 520 reagent (Reagent, 16 min, Ambient, Dispense type: 150 μl).
34. Repeat steps #28–31.
35. Repeat steps #18–21.
36. Repeat steps #28–31.
37. PKI blocking buffer (Reagent, 10 min, Ambient, Dispense type: 150 μl).
38. Open 3 (Reagent, 32 min, 36°C, Dispense type: 150 μl).
39. Repeat steps #8–12.
40. Opal Polymer HRP (Reagent, 10 min, Ambient, Dispense type: 150 μl).
41. Repeat steps #8–12.
42. Opal 690 reagent (Reagent, 16 min, Ambient, Dispense type: 150 μl).
43. Repeat steps #8–12.
44. Repeat steps #18–21.
45. Repeat steps #8–12.
46. Repeat steps #18–21.
47. PKI blocking buffer (Reagent, 10 min, Ambient, Dispense type: 150 μl).
48. Open 4 (Reagent, 32 min, 36°C, Dispense type: 150 μl).

49. Repeat steps #24–26.
50. PV Rb 50% (Reagent, 10 min, Ambient, Dispense type: 150 μl).
51. Repeat steps #28–32.
52. Opal 620 reagent (Reagent, 0 min, Ambient, Dispense type: 150 μl).
53. Opal 620 reagent (Reagent, 16 min, Ambient, Dispense type: 150 μl).
54. Repeat steps #28–32.
55. Repeat steps #18–21.
56. Repeat steps #28–31.
57. Open 5 (Reagent, 32 min, 36°C, Dispense type: 150 μl).
58. Repeat steps #24–26.
59. Opal Polymer HRP (Reagent, 10 min, Ambient, Dispense type: 150 μl).
60. Repeat step #28–32.
61. Opal 480 reagent (Reagent, 16 min, Ambient, Dispense type: 150 μl).
62. Repeat steps #28–32.
63. Repeat steps #18–21.
64. Repeat steps #28–31.
65. PKI blocking buffer (Reagent, 10 min, Ambient, Dispense type: 150 μl).
66. Open 6 (Reagent, 32 min, 36°C, Dispense type: 150 μl).
67. Repeat steps #8–12.
68. Opal Polymer HRP (Reagent, 10 min, Ambient, Dispense type: 150 μl).
69. Repeat steps #8–12.
70. TSA-Biotin (Reagent, 0 min, Ambient, Dispense type: 150 μl).
71. TSA-Biotin (Reagent, 10 min, Ambient, Dispense type: 150 μl).
72. Repeat steps #8–12.
73. Alexa 750 Streptavidin (Reagent, 0 min, Ambient, Dispense type: 150 μl).
74. Alexa 750 Streptavidin (Reagent, 60 min, Ambient, Dispense type: 150 μl).
75. Repeat steps #8–12.
76. Open 11 (Reagent, 0 min, Ambient, Dispense type: 150 μl).
77. Open 11 (Reagent, 10 min, Ambient, Dispense type: 150 μl).
78. Repeat steps #24–26.

3.7 Mounting Slides

Fluoromount-G is utilized for mounting coverglass. Avoid air bubble formation remove/press and blot out any excess mounting solution. To ensure the complete solidification of mounting solution and secure the position of the coverglass, stained slides should be dried overnight on a flat, even surface (we use a chemical fume hood).

3.8 Scanning Images

Stained slides can be scanned using a multispectral imaging scope (Vectra/Polaris automated Quantitative Pathology Imaging System or Phenoimager, Akoya Biosciences). The procedure for scanning images on these platforms should follow manufacturer's instructions. The scanned images are saved as qptiff files which can be reviewed using Phenochart software provided by Akoya Biosciences (Fig. 1a). As multispectral imaging captures multiple fluorescence signals simultaneously, it is necessary to analyze unmixed images to obtain accurate signal representation for each marker. The image can be annotated on Phenochart and opened on inForm software. Once the image is opened on the inForm, the image can be analyzed for tissue segmentation, cell segmentation, cell classification, and scoring markers [1, 2]. The inForm software can also convert the image into multi-layered TIFF files which can be opened on other imaging platform such as QuPath [7].

3.9 Stitching Tile Images

In inForm, the imaging analysis is primarily based on rectangular annotations of a particular size. Consequently, the converted TIFF images will also maintain the same rectangular format as the original image. While the analysis within inForm primarily focuses on designated regions of interest (ROIs), it is often preferred to perform imaging analysis on wide areas of the original tissue image.

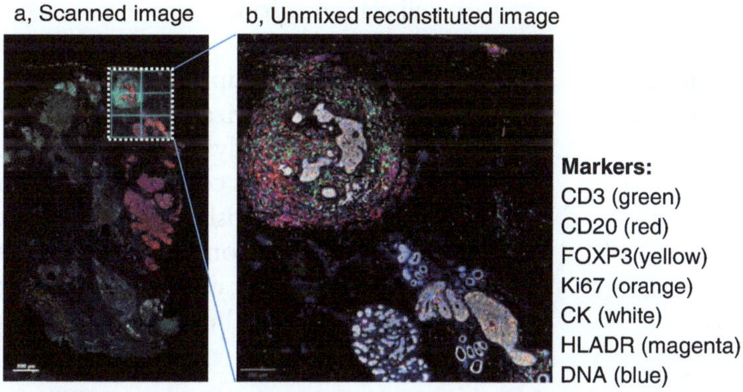

Fig. 1 Multiplex immunohistochemical staining of breast cancer tissue. (**a**) Phenochart image (qptiff file) showing multiplex IHC IP1.2 stained breast cancer tissue before signal unmixing. The white-dot box area is scanned at higher resolution, with each rectangle representing a specific region of interest. (**b**) Reconstituted Tile image from white-box area of (**a**) showing CD3, CD20, FOXP3, Ki67, CK, HLADR, and DNA in indicated colors

To facilitate this, the converted TIFF images can be stitched back together to reconstruct the target tissue lesion. This reconstructed image (tile image: OME.TIFF file) can be prepared using QuPath (Fig. 1b) (*see* **Note 3**). Once the reconstructed image is created, it can be analyzed using software such as QuPath or other imaging platform that offer comprehensive image analysis and evaluation capabilities. The extension script for stitching on QuPath platform (v0.4.4 or earlier version) can be acquired at QuPath github website (https://qupath.github.io/) (*see* **Note 4**).

3.10 Imaging Analysis

Imaging analysis can be conducted using various imaging platforms. Here, a simplified analysis using QuPath on tile image is introduced. Imaging analysis on QuPath performs best with ample RAM memory (i.e., 24 GB or more) especially when analyzing larger image or a project with multiple images. Therefore, using the PC with ample RAM memory is recommended especially for analyzing tiled image(s).

3.11 Generating a Project

To expedite the preparation of classifiers for tissue and cell and optimize RAM memory usage, it is advisable to generate a master project folder. Multiple images can be loaded into the project, but it is recommended to create a training image from "region annotations" (*see* **Note 5**). This can be achieved by selecting the "Create region annotations" function within the "Classify" menu, specifically under "Training images." Right after preparing all annotations, the project needs to be saved before executing next step. Once annotations are generated on one or more images, "training image" can be generated with "Create training image" in the same "Classify" menu. This "training image" can be used to train tissue segmentation and cell classification. By creating at least two replicated training images, one can be dedicated to tissue segmentation, while the other can focus on cell classification.

3.12 Tissue Segmentation

These immune multiplex panels described here are designed to provide a basic characterization of the tumor immune microenvironment and facilitate the analysis of immune cell activities within and outside of the tumor. In this context, cytokeratin (CK) is utilized as a tissue classifier to distinguish and define the epithelial area, which corresponds to the carcinoma area, with the stroma area negative for CK. After creating the training images in the previous step, one of the training images will be utilized to generate the tissue segmentation classifier.

1. Select "train pixel classifier" selected from "classifier" tab to open a new window for pixel classifier.
2. Tune Classifier, Resolution, Features, Output and Region for generating a classifier.

3. Classify CK positive area by editing "Channels" in "Feature" by checking DNA and CK (and unchecking other markers).
4. Use the image selection tool to annotate the tile image by designating CK positive tissue areas as "Tumor," CK negative tissue areas as "Stroma," and marking non-tissue areas (e.g., glass) as "Ignore*" (Fig. 2a). These annotations can be generated on individual cells or multiple cells.
5. Turn on "Live prediction" to facilitate the annotation process and assess the performance of the classifier. This feature enables real-time interactive comparison between the actual CK positive and negative areas and the classifier's predictions, facilitating the refinement and assessment of the classifier's performance.

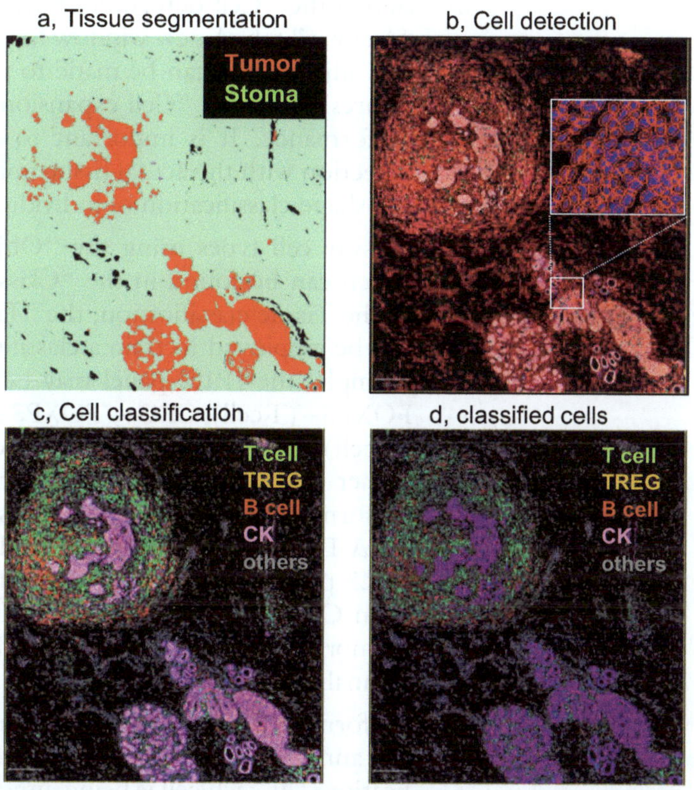

Fig. 2 QuPath imaging analysis for tissue segmentation and cell classification. (**a**) Tissue segmentation identifies tumor region as cytokeratin (CK) positive (red) and CK negative (stroma: green). Non tissue area is also classified as "ignored" (black). The tile image from Fig. 1 was used. (**b**) Cell detection visualizing each DAPI stained nucleus and predicted cytoplasm. (**c**) Cell classification applied on mIHC image. In this case, cells on the image were classified into T cell, TREG, B cell, epithelial cells (CK) and others. (**d**) Classified cell locations are indicated based on individual cell types

3.13 Cell Classification

Cell classification aims to categorize different cell types based on the status of stained markers. The procedure generally involves two main steps: cell detection and object classification. The first step, "Cell detection," involves identifying and delineating individual cells within the image. The second step, "Object classification," involves assigning cell types based on the status of stained markers. By combining cell detection and object classification, the cells in the image can be categorized into different cell types based on the status of stained markers, providing valuable insights into cellular heterogeneity and marker expression patterns within the tissue microenvironment.

1. Prepare a training image by copying a training image which was not used for tissue segmentation.
2. Open the copied training image from the project file and select the entire image as one annotation using the "Create full image annotation" command (Control+Shift+A).
3. Access the "Cell detection" function by selecting it from the "Analyze" tab. A new window for "Cell detection" will appear, and adjustments can be made to parameters such as "Sigma," "Threshold," and "Cell expansion" to optimize cell detection performance. It is important to compare the results of cell detection with the actual tissue image, focusing on nuclear and cell shape classification of individual cells (Fig. 2b).
4. Classify cell types using the "Object classification" function, which can be found in the "Classify" tab of QuPath. Similar to the Tissue classification, the "Train object classifier" feature can be employed to train a classifier for various cell types. For example, the IP1.2 panel may be utilized to classify CD3+/FOXP3− (T cell), CD3+/FOXP3+ (regulatory T cell), CD20+ (B cell), CK+ (tumor/epithelial cell), or marker-negative cells (other cell types). Additionally, further categorization can be performed based on proliferation status (Ki67+ or Ki67−) and HLA-DR expression status (HLADR+ or HLADR−). For the IP2.2 panel, CD3+/CD8+ (cytotoxic T cell), CD3+/CD8− (non-CD8+ T cell), CD68 (macrophage/dendritic cell), CK+ (tumor/epithelial cell), and their PD1 and PDL1 statuses can be analyzed (*see* **Note 6**).
5. Perform "train object classifier" process in real time by manually annotating the target cells with their corresponding classifications. As each cell is being annotated, the classifier is trained and incorporates the labeled examples into its learning algorithm. This interactive approach allows for immediate feedback and refinement of the classifier, ensuring that it becomes more accurate for the cell classification (Fig. 2c).
6. Save the Object classifier once the trained classifier prediction matches each cell definition.

3.14 Preparation to Apply Tissue Segmentation and Cell Classification

1. Annotate ROIs on each image in the project.
2. Open one image and select all annotations on the image.
3. Apply the saved tissue segmentation classifier. If there are annotations used for generating a training image, these annotations should be cleared before applying these classifiers.
4. Select all newly annotated ROIs and click "Classify," "Pixel classification," then select "Load pixel classifier" which will pop up window to choose model for saved tissue classifier file. "Region" on this window can be "everywhere" or "Any annotation ROI" and then select "Create annotation or detection objects from the classification output" with another pop-up window. In this new window, "OK" can be clicked without selecting "Choose parent objects" to generate Tumor area and Stromal area (Fig. 2a).
5. Click "OK" on pop-up window. This procedure will generate two new annotations named "Annotation (Tumor)" and "Annotation (Stroma)" in "Annotations" window on the left analysis pane.
6. Select these two new annotations on the list and apply cell detection with same parameters used in former cell classification procedure (Fig. 2b), then apply cell classifier by selecting "Load object classifier" from "Classify" tab.
7. Select cell classifier on pop-up "Object Classifiers" window. This command will show various type of cells with different colors on the tissue image (Fig. 2c, d).
8. Save tissue segmentation and cell classification.
9. Export measurements from "Measure" tab and click "export measurements" which will pop-up a window to select what will be saved. Selecting "Annotations" on "export type" will summarize each annotation's cell counts for each cell type and area which can be converted to each cell density at each annotation. Selecting "Cell" on "export type" will generate individual cell type, parent (tumor or stroma), XY coordination and each individual marker's intensities in nucleus, cytoplasm, and entire cell. These parameters can be used to compare each marker's intensity or further classification like virtual FACS analysis and spatial associations.

4 Notes

1. Due to the necessity of using BOND Universal Covertile, it is essential to position the tissues relatively at the center area of the APEX BOND slide. Care should be taken to avoid sandwiching the tissue section between the slide and the Covertile, as well as preventing the tissue from touching the inner edge

of the Covertile. Positioning the tissues correctly on the slide ensures sealing and prevents reagent leakage during the staining process.

2. This baking process helps to improve tissue adhesion to the slide, ensuring that the tissue section remains intact during subsequent staining in the autostainer. However, certain tissue types, such as adipose tissue or collagen-rich tissues, may have a higher tendency to detach from the slide. In such cases, it is advisable to extend the baking time overnight to enhance tissue adhesion and minimize detachment issues.
3. The installer for QuPath can be downloaded from the QuPath website (https://qupath.github.io).
4. Using a computer with a large RAM memory is recommended when running a stitching script to handle the potentially large data size generated during the process effectively and ensure optimal performance.
5. There are differences in staining intensities between staining batches, which can pose difficulties in building the classifier. To ensure accurate imaging analysis, it is recommended to use images from one staining batch for building the classifier and applying it exclusively to images from the same staining batch.
6. While more complex marker combinations can be defined, training the classifier with numerous cells can slow down QuPath by straining the CPU and RAM memory usage. For efficient imaging analysis, it is advisable to initially classify simple cell types (e.g., Fig. 2c). Additional markers can then be utilized to further classify cells based on the data obtained from cell segmentation, allowing for a quicker and manageable analysis process.

Acknowledgments

We thank Dr. Michael Campbell at the University of California San Francisco for scanning image and Akoya Biosciences for technical support for optimizing autostaining conditions and imaging analysis.

Conflict of Interest The authors have no conflicts of interest to declare that are relevant to the content of this chapter.

References

1. Mori H, Bolen J, Schuetter L, Massion P, Hoyt CC, VandenBerg S, Esserman L, Borowsky AD, Campbell MJ (2020) Characterizing the tumor immune microenvironment with tyramide-based multiplex immunofluorescence. J Mammary Gland Biol Neoplasia 25(4):417–432. https://doi.org/10.1007/s10911-021-09479-2
2. Stack EC, Wang C, Roman KA, Hoyt CC (2014) Multiplexed immunohistochemistry, imaging, and quantitation: a review, with an assessment

of tyramide signal amplification, multispectral imaging and multiplex analysis. Methods 70(1): 46–58. https://doi.org/10.1016/j.ymeth.2014.08.016

3. Dunne MR, Michielsen AJ, O'Sullivan KE, Cathcart MC, Feighery R, Doyle B, Watson JA, O'Farrell NJ, Ravi N, Kay E, Reynolds JV, Ryan EJ, O'Sullivan J (2017) HLA-DR expression in tumor epithelium is an independent prognostic indicator in esophageal adenocarcinoma patients. Cancer Immunol Immunother 66(7): 841–850. https://doi.org/10.1007/s00262-017-1983-1
4. Matoba K, Iizuka N, Gondo T, Ishihara T, Yamada-Okabe H, Tamesa T, Takemoto N, Hashimoto K, Sakamoto K, Miyamoto T, Uchimura S, Hamamoto Y, Oka M (2005) Tumor HLA-DR expression linked to early intrahepatic recurrence of hepatocellular carcinoma. Int J Cancer 115(2):231–240. https://doi.org/10.1002/ijc.20860
5. Matsushita K, Takenouchi T, Shimada H, Tomonaga T, Hayashi H, Shioya A, Komatsu A, Matsubara H, Ochiai T (2006) Strong HLA-DR antigen expression on cancer cells relates to better prognosis of colorectal cancer patients: possible involvement of c-myc suppression by interferon-gamma in situ. Cancer Sci 97(1):57–63. https://doi.org/10.1111/j.1349-7006.2006.00137.x
6. Senosain MF, Zou Y, Novitskaya T, Vasiukov G, Balar AB, Rowe DJ, Doxie DB, Lehman JM, Eisenberg R, Maldonado F, Zijlstra A, Novitskiy SV, Irish JM, Massion PP (2021) HLA-DR cancer cells expression correlates with T cell infiltration and is enriched in lung adenocarcinoma with indolent behavior. Sci Rep 11(1), 14424. https://doi.org/10.1038/s41598-021-93807-3
7. Bankhead P, Loughrey MB, Fernandez JA, Dombrowski Y, McArt DG, Dunne PD, McQuaid S, Gray RT, Murray LJ, Coleman HG, James JA, Salto-Tellez M, Hamilton PW (2017) QuPath: open source software for digital pathology image analysis. Sci Rep 7(1), 16878. https://doi.org/10.1038/s41598-017-17204-5

Part II

Spatial Proteomics

Check for updates

Chapter 5

Fully Integrated Sample Preparation-Based Spatial Proteomic Analysis

Qian Kong, Xi Wang and Ruijun Tian

Abstract

To decipher the complex tissue microenvironment for comprehensively elucidating the biological machinery, spatial proteomics is becoming popular. Laser microdissection (LMD) technology combined with integrated sample preparation and high-sensitive liquid chromatography-mass spectrometry (LC-MS) is the most powerful strategy. In this chapter, we describe the protocols for tissue slice preparation and staining, LMD-based histological regions collection, simple and integrated spintip-based proteomics technology (SISPROT) based sample preparation, and highly sensitive LC-MS analysis.

Keywords LMD, SISPROT, LC-MS, Spatial proteomics

1 Introduction

A rich variety of cells make up the tissues and organs of the human body and interact with each other to form an organizational microenvironment [1]. Interrogating the tissue microenvironment is essential for comprehensive analysis of intracellular interaction mechanisms and biological processes [2, 3].

Mass spectrometry (MS) served as a sensitive and accurate tool for proteome profiling, has been systematically applied to reveal the complicated multicellular biological systems [4, 5]. Jiang and co-workers conducted a proteomic analysis of 32 normal tissues in the human body and found some tissue-specific proteins that demonstrate how understanding protein levels can provide insights into regulation and human diseases [6]. However, proteomic studies at the bulk tissue level lose information about cell type heterogeneity and protein spatial localization, and the resulting mass spectrum signal is the average of multiple cells. For this purpose, the past decade has witnessed significant advancements in the field of spatial proteomics, aimed at characterizing the abundance and spatial

Timothy L. Frankel and Arvind Rao (eds.), *Cellular Spatial Characterization and Analysis*, Methods in Molecular Biology, vol. 2995, https://doi.org/10.1007/978-1-0716-5027-1_5,

distribution of proteins in tissue to comprehensively profile the tissue microenvironment.

In order to deciphering the protein abundance and spatial information at high resolution, the spatial proteomic technology currently faces three technical difficulties: (1) The selected regions need to be precisely cut and accurately collected; (2) Integrated and lossless sample preparation process is needed; and (3) High-sensitive MS analysis for limited amount of samples. Laser microdissection (LMD) technology is a powerful technology for separating selected cell populations or histological regions from heterogeneous tissues with spatial information. Many researchers have applied LMD as first choice for target region collection in spatial proteomic studies. Mund et al. introduced a spatial proteomic approach that combines AI-driven cell phenotypic imaging with LMD and ultra-sensitive MS analysis termed deep visual proteomics (DVP) [7]. Data generated by DVP can be well applied to discover protein signatures providing molecular insights into proteome variation at the phenotypic level while retaining complete spatial information. To achieve integrated sample preparation, a simple and integrated spintip-based proteomics technology (termed SISPROT) [8, 9] previously developed by our group has been used in spatial proteomic analysis. Our group first introduced this LMD-SISPROT-based protocol for spatial proteomic analysis in 2018 and subsequently conducted this strategy in immunohistochemical (IHC) staining samples and spatial glycoproteome studies [10–12]. We separated four cell types in one hematoxylin-eosin (H&E) staining slice and identified more than 5000 proteins in 5 $mm^2 \times 10$ μm slice [10]. Combing with the Q-Exactive HF-X mass spectrometer with optimized parameters, quantitative analysis of sample with micrometer scale can be accomplished. Recently, we applied this LMD-SISPROT strategy to spatial protein assessment and identified more than 3000 proteins in 0.01 $mm^2 \times 10$ μm slice. Herein, we present detailed protocols of this LMD-SISPROT-based spatial proteomic analysis strategy.

2 Materials and Reagents

2.1 Preparation of Tissue Section

1. Tissue samples. All tissue samples are obtained from the hospital with approval from the Medical Ethics Committee.
2. Optimal cutting temperature (OCT) medium stored at RT.
3. Phosphate buffer saline (PBS) buffer: PBS powder is dissolved in 18.2 MΩ ultrapure water at the recommended concentration.
4. Leica CM 1900 cryostat, Leica RM 2255 Fully Automated Rotary Microtome, and Leica LMD 7000 system are used in tissue section preparation. And tissue sections are prepared as required thickness and then mounted onto PEN membrane-coated glass slides.

5. Fixing regent for fresh frozen sections: methanol (MeOH) is precooled at −20°C for >1 h for use.
6. Fixing regent for formalin fixation and paraffin embedding (FFPE) sections: 4% formalin (w/v) is diluted by 10% Formalin. Three percent hydrogen peroxide (H_2O_2) is diluted by 30% hydrogen peroxide.
7. For hematoxylin and eosin (H&E) staining: hematoxylin, eosin, and xylene are stored at RT in biosafety cabinet.
8. For IHC staining: 10% goat serum, Primary antibody with indicated concentrations or dilution ratio, HRP-conjugated secondary antibody, and 3,30-diaminobenzidine (DAB) detection kit stored at −20°C.
9. Ethanol (EtOH) series: 100% EtOH, 90% EtOH, 80% EtOH, and 70% EtOH are diluted by ethanol and stored at RT for 6 months.

2.2 Integrated Proteomics Sample Preparation with SISPROT Kit

1. SISPROT Kit (BayOmics). All stock solutions from SISPROT kit are stored at proper conditions according to manufacturer's instructions.
2. Tissue samples are dissolved in lysis buffer from SISPROT Kit and lysed in Bioruptor Pico (Diagenode).
3. Bicinchoninic acid Protein Assay Kit is used for protein concentration determination.
4. CentriVap Vacuum Concentrators.

2.3 LC-MS Analysis

1. In-house 100 μm i.d. capillary column packed with 2–5 mm C4 beads (3 μm/120 Å, 0.5–0.8 cm) as frit and 20 cm C18 beads (1.9 μm/120 Å, 19–20 cm).
2. Q-Exactive HF-X mass spectrometer (Thermo Fisher Scientific) equipped with Easy-nLC 1200 chromatography system (Thermo Fisher Scientific).
3. Mobile phase A: 0.1% formic acid (FA) in water.
4. Mobile phase B: 0.1% FA in acetonitrile (ACN).

3 Methods

3.1 Frozen Tissue Section Preparation

1. Clinical specimens obtained from surgery are immediately frozen in liquid nitrogen and kept frozen in liquid nitrogen or stored at −80°C for further use (*see* **Note 1**).
2. Embed the fresh-frozen tissues by Tissue OCT-Freeze Medium in −20°C and slice into sections with suitable thickness using Leica CM 1900 cryostat at −20°C.

3. The obtained sections are then flat mounted onto a membrane-coated glass slide and maintained at −20°C.
4. Add pre-cooled MeOH to immerse the tissue sections and fix them at −20°C for at least 10 min (*see* **Note 2**).
5. For hematoxylin-eosin (H&E) staining, the sections are stained with hematoxylin and eosin followed by dehydration via an EtOH series and air dryness.
6. For immunohistochemistry (IHC) staining, the detailed steps are as follows:

   (1) Frozen sections are treated with 3% (w/v) H_2O_2 for 10 min to inactivate endogenous peroxidase.

   (2) Then, the sections are washed three times with PBS before blocking with 10% goat serum at 37°C for 30 min, followed by incubating with the corresponding primary antibody with the indicated concentrations for 1 h at 37°C.

   (3) Next, the sections are washed with PBS, then incubated with HRP-conjugated secondary antibody at RT for 30 min.

   (4) Detect the signal with DAB detection kit according to manufacturer's instructions.

   (5) Finally, hematoxylin is used to stain the nucleus, and then sections are dehydrated via EtOH series and air dryness.

3.2 Formalin-Fixed Paraffin-Embedding (FFPE) Tissue Section Preparation

1. Clinical specimens obtained from surgery are immersed in 10% formalin and fixed at RT for 24–48 h.
2. The sections are dehydrated via EtOH series and xylene at RT (*see* **Note 3**).
3. The sections are embedded into heated paraffin sliced into sections with suitable thickness.
4. The obtained sections are placed in a water bath, and flat-mounted onto a membrane-coated glass slide and air-dried overnight.
5. Deparaffinize the sections by xylene and hydrate the sections by EtOH series.
6. The H&E staining and IHC staining processes are performed as steps 5 and 6 in Sect. 3.1.

3.3 Laser Capture Microdissection (LMD)

1. Tissue sections are scanned to evaluate the dissection contour according to pathological and cell type examination. Figure 1 shows the workflow of proteomic analysis.
2. LMD is performed using an LMD7000 system and the periphery of the selected section is dissected.

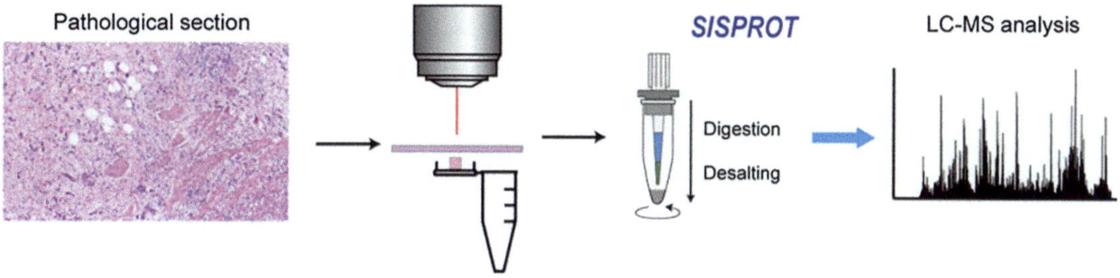

Fig. 1 Workflow of proteomic analysis of tissue sections

3. The entire selected sections fall onto the cap of a 0.2 ml EP tube (*see* **Note 4**). This non-contacting laser catapulting helps to avoid potential contamination.
4. Adjust the parameters of laser, select the target regions, and collect the sections in the cap of the 0.2 ml PCR tube.
5. Mount the cap with PCR tube body in an upside-down position carefully, then transfer the collected sections to the bottom of the tube by centrifuging at 10 000 × *g* for 5 min.

3.4 Proteomic Sample Preparation (SISPROT Process)

The dissected tissue regions by LMD are processed by SISPROT kit according to manufacturer's instructions (*see* **Notes 5, 6, and 7**). All the reagents used in SISPROT kit are shown in italics.

3.4.1 Protein Extraction

Dissected tissue sections in the cap of 0.2 ml PCR tube are directly transferred into the same tube and lysed in 20 μl *Extract buffer* (from SISPROT kit) assisted with non-contacting bath sonication (15 cycles of 5 s on and 5 s off at maximum output power) followed by heating at 90°C for 90 min, then repeat sonication. The samples need to be centrifuged to avoid liquid splashing. Add 3 μl *Acidize* and pipette the sample into PCR tubes for at least five times, centrifuge for 3–5 s, then place the sample on ice.

3.4.2 Enzymatic Digestion on SISPROT Tip

1. Assemble sample processor: Assemble the sample processor as Fig. 2, and place it in the centrifuge.
2. Activate SISPROT Tip: Add 60 μl *Activate*, centrifuge at 400 g for 1 min.
3. Equilibrium SISPROT Tip: Add 60 μl *Wash*, centrifuge at 400 g for 2 min.
4. Load sample: Load all protein sample (~33 μl) to the SISPROT tip and centrifuge at 100 g for 5 min.
5. Wash sample: Add 30 μl *Wash*, centrifuge at 400 g for 2 min; add 30 μl *Activate*, centrifuge at 300 g for 1 min.
6. Reduce sample: Add 30 μl *Reduce*, centrifuge at 100 g for 30 s, incubate for 15 min at room temperature in dark; afterward, centrifuge at 400 g for 1 min.

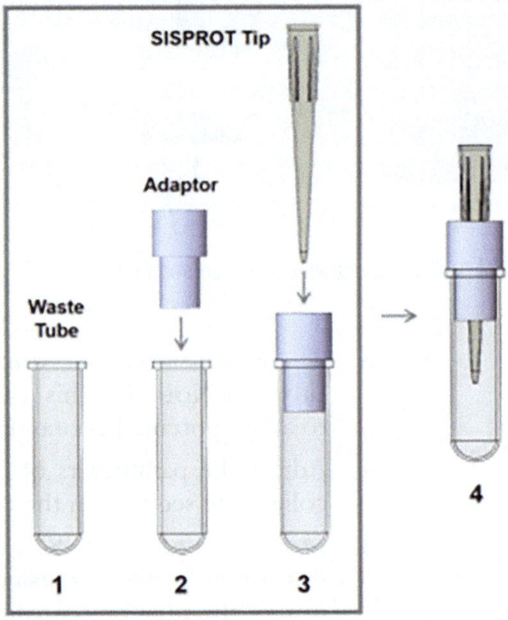

Fig. 2 SISPROT tip assembly diagram

Table 1
Liquid chromatography setup

Time	Duration	Gradient (% B)
0	0	4
1	1	6
49	48	25
54	5	40
55	1	97
60	5	97

7. Wash SISPROT Tip: Add 30 μl *Dissolve A*. centrifuge at 400 g for 1 min.
8. Prepare Digest Solution: Add 55 μl *Dissolve A* into Digest (one tube for six tests) and pipette five times.
9. Enzymatic digestion: Add 4 μl *Digest Solution* into the SISPROT Tip, centrifuge at 100 g for 20 s; add another 4 μl *Digest Solution*, centrifuge at 100 g for 5 s. Subsequently, wrap the entire sample processor with tin foil to protect it from light and incubate for 1 h at 37°C in the oven.

3.4.3 Transfer and Clean-up Peptides

1. Transfer peptides: Take out the sample processor from the oven after enzymatic digestion. Place the processor in the centrifuge, add 60 μl *Transfer* to the SISPROT Tip, centrifuge at 150 g for 5 min.
2. Clean peptides: Add 60 μl *Desalt*, centrifuge at 400 g for 2 min, repeat this step one more time.

Table 2
Mass spectrometry setup

Setting	Value
General	
Polarity	Positive
Default charge	2
Full MS	
Resolution	60 000
AGC target	3e6
Maximum IT	50 ms
Scan range	350 to 1400 *m/z*
dd-MS²/dd-SIM	
Resolution	15 000
AGC target	1e5
Maximum IT	60 ms
Loop count	30
TopN	30
Isolation window	1.6 *m/z*
Fixed first mass	110.0 *m/z*
(N)CE/ stepped nce	27
Spectrum data type	Centroid
dd Settings	
Minimum AGC target	1.80e3
Intensity threshold	3.0e4
Charge exclusion	Unassigned, 1, 6–8, >8
Multiple charge states	One charge state only
Peptides match	Preferred
Exclude isotope	on
Dynamic exclusion	30.0 s

3.4.4 Collect Peptides for LC-MS Analysis

1. Collect peptides: Replace the tube of the sample processor with the *Collection Tube*. Add 60 μl *Elute* into the SISPROT Tip, centrifuge at 150 g for 5 min.
2. Dry and resuspend peptides: Dry the peptides in the *Collection Tube* using vacuum centrifugal concentrator (approx. 2 h). Afterward, add 5–10 μl *Dissolve B* to resuspend peptides. The dried peptides should be stored at −20°C.

3.5 Nano-LC-MS/MS Analysis

The obtained samples are dissolved in 0.1% (v/v) FA and separated by an Easy-nLC 1200 chromatography. The separation column is a 20 cm × 100 μm i.d. analytical column in-house packed with C4 beads and C18 beads. Peptides are separated with a binary buffer system include 0.1% FA (buffer A) and 90% ACN/0.1% FA (buffer B). Total gradient is 60 min with the flow rate of 250 nl/min. Then the peptides are detected by the Q-Exactive HF-X mass spectrometer as parameters in Tables 1 and 2.

3.6 Data Analysis

Raw data are searched against the human Uniprot fasta database (80581 entries, downloaded on Dec 1, 2022) using MaxQuant (v 2.1.1.0). The Default settings are used except for the following values. Deamidation (NQ) is added as dynamic modification. The "Label-free quantification" and "Match between runs" are selected. Statistical and bioinformatics analyses are performed with the Perseus software (v 1.5.5.3) and R language (v 4.2).

4 Notes

1. Clinical specimens obtained from surgery must immediately be frozen in liquid nitrogen and kept frozen in liquid nitrogen or stored at −80°C to maintain the protein activity.
2. Before fixing, it is necessary to pre-cool the MeOH at −20°C for > 1 h.
3. All the organic reagent preparation and staining steps are conducted in a fume hood to ensure safety during sample preparation.
4. In LMD process, ensure that all cut sections are collected in the tube to avoid sample loss.
5. SISPROT Tip must be stored in a dry environment to prevent water vapor from entering the tip. Additionally, it is recommended to check whether the liquid can pass completely after centrifugation during the activation step, as particulate matter in the environment may cause the SISPROT Tip to clog. If there is a significant amount of liquid residue, it is advisable to replace the tip.

6. Before the experimental operation, it is recommended to use 75% alcohol to wipe the centrifuge clean, especially the top cover, to avoid the introduction of contaminants.
7. In the SISPROT process, the membrane needs to be kept moist to avoid sample loss.

Acknowledgments

This work is supported by grants from the China State Key Basic Research Program Grants (2021YFA1301601, 2021YFA1301602, 2021YFA1302603, 2020YFE0202200, and 2022YFC3401104), the National Natural Science Foundation of China (22125403, 22074060, 22150610470, and 92253304), the Shenzhen Innovation of Science and Technology Commission (JCYJ20200109140814408, JCYJ20210324120210029, and JCYJ20200109141212325), and Guangdong province (2019B151502050).

Conflict of Interest The authors have no conflicts of interest to declare that are relevant to the content of this chapter.

References

1. Consortium H (2019) The human body at cellular resolution: the NIH Human Biomolecular Atlas Program. Nature 574(7777):187–192
2. Dagogo-Jack I, Shaw AT (2018) Tumour heterogeneity and resistance to cancer therapies. Nat Rev Clin Oncol 15(2):81–94
3. Mao Y, Wang X, Huang P, Tian R (2021) Spatial proteomics for understanding the tissue microenvironment. Analyst 146(12): 3777–3798
4. Wilhelm M, Schlegl J, Hahne H, Gholami AM, Lieberenz M, Savitski MM, Ziegler E, Butzmann L, Gessulat S, Marx H, Mathieson T, Lemeer S, Schnatbaum K, Reimer U, Wenschuh H, Mollenhauer M, Slotta-Huspenina J, Boese JH, Bantscheff M, Gerstmair A, Faerber F, Kuster B (2014) Mass-spectrometry-based draft of the human proteome. Nature 509(7502):582–587
5. Kim MS, Pinto SM, Getnet D, Nirujogi RS, Manda SS, Chaerkady R, Madugundu AK, Kelkar DS, Isserlin R, Jain S, Thomas JK, Muthusamy B, Leal-Rojas P, Kumar P, Sahasrabuddhe NA, Balakrishnan L, Advani J, George B, Renuse S, Selvan LD, Patil AH, Nanjappa V, Radhakrishnan A, Prasad S, Subbannayya T, Raju R, Kumar M, Sreenivasamurthy SK, Marimuthu A, Sathe GJ, Chavan S, Datta KK, Subbannayya Y, Sahu A, Yelamanchi SD, Jayaram S, Rajagopalan P, Sharma J, Murthy KR, Syed N, Goel R, Khan AA, Ahmad S, Dey G, Mudgal K, Chatterjee A, Huang TC, Zhong J, Wu X, Shaw PG, Freed D, Zahari MS, Mukherjee KK, Shankar S, Mahadevan A, Lam H, Mitchell CJ, Shankar SK, Satishchandra P, Schroeder JT, Sirdeshmukh R, Maitra A, Leach SD, Drake CG, Halushka MK, Prasad TS, Hruban RH, Kerr CL, Bader GD, Iacobuzio-Donahue CA, Gowda H, Pandey A (2014) A draft map of the human proteome. Nature 509(7502):575–581
6. Jiang L, Wang M, Lin S, Jian R, Li X, Chan J, Dong G, Fang H, Robinson AE, GTEx Consortium, Snyder MP (2020) A quantitative proteome map of the human body. Cell 183(1):269–283
7. Mund A, Coscia F, Kriston A, Hollandi R, Kovács F, Brunner AD, Migh E, Schweizer L, Santos A, Bzorek M, Naimy S, Rahbek-Gjerdrum LM, Dyring-Andersen B, Bulkescher J, Lukas C, Eckert MA, Lengyel E, Gnann C, Lundberg E, Horvath P, Mann M (2022) Deep visual proteomics defines single-cell identity and heterogeneity. Nat Biotechnol 40(8):1231–1240
8. Chen W, Wang S, Adhikari S, Deng Z, Wang L, Chen L, Ke M, Yang P, Tian R (2016) Simple and integrated spintip-based technology applied for deep proteome profiling. Anal Chem 88(9):4864–4871

9. Xue L, Lin L, Zhou W, Chen W, Tang J, Sun X, Huang P, Tian R (2018) Mixed-mode ion exchange-based integrated proteomics technology for fast and deep plasma proteome profiling. J Chromatogr A 1564:76–84
10. Xu R, Tang J, Deng Q, He W, Sun X, Xia L, Cheng Z, He L, You S, Hu J, Fu Y, Zhu J, Chen Y, Gao W, He A, Guo Z, Lin L, Li H, Hu C, Tian R (2018) Spatial-resolution cell type proteome profiling of cancer tissue by fully integrated proteomics technology. Anal Chem 90(9):5879–5886
11. Huang P, Li H, Gao W, Cai Z, Tian R (2019) A fully integrated spintip-based approach for sensitive and quantitative profiling of region-resolved in vivo brain glycoproteome. Anal Chem 91(14):9181–9189
12. Huang P, Kong Q, Gao W, Chu B, Li H, Mao Y, Cai Z, Xu R, Tian R (2020) Spatial proteome profiling by immunohistochemistry-based laser capture microdissection and data-independent acquisition proteomics. Anal Chim Acta 1127: 140–148

Detailed Protocol for Expansion of Large Tissue Samples for Expansion Microscopy

Vibeke S. Dam, Amalie M. Grønning, Benjamin B. Green, Frédéric H. Login and Lene N. Nejsum

Abstract

Expansion microscopy (ExM) is a powerful technique that enhances optical resolution by physically enlarging biological samples. The enlargement increases the distances between fluorophores and makes the sample transparent. Here, we present an ExM protocol optimized for tissue biopsies with 2 mm diameter and 1 mm thickness from inner medulla from perfusion-fixed rat kidneys. Besides inner medulla kidney samples, the protocol may be utilized for other tissue types with minor modifications.

Keywords Expansion microscopy (ExM), Tissue biopsies, Protocol, Kidney, Optical resolution

1 Introduction

Immunofluorescence (IF) is a powerful technique that enables visualization of target molecules with high spatial resolution and sensitivity. A challenge in IF is the limitation in optical resolution, which is the ability to distinguish between two objects that are closely spaced. Optical resolution is limited by the diffraction limit of light, typically around ~200–250 nm in the XY plane and ~500 nm in the Z-axis, depending on the imaging modality. Thus, this limits the ability to distinguish closely spaced molecular structures. Super-resolution techniques, such as stimulated emission depletion microscopy (STED) [1] and photoactivated localization microscopy (PALM) [2], overcome the diffraction limit and achieve resolutions down to 10 nm or even lower. Another approach to increase optical resolution is enlargement of the sample, namely expansion microscopy (ExM) [3]. In ExM, the sample is physically enlarged, which increases the distances between fluorophores and thereby enables more detailed visualization of molecular structures without altering the optical imaging path. Moreover, ExM enhances

Timothy L. Frankel and Arvind Rao (eds.), *Cellular Spatial Characterization and Analysis*, Methods in Molecular Biology, vol. 2995, https://doi.org/10.1007/978-1-0716-5027-1_6,

sample transparency, which improves the signal-to-noise ratio and increases light penetration.

Since the initial development of ExM [3], multiple protocols for the expansion of cells and tissue have been published (e.g., [4–6]), each offering varying degrees of optical resolution improvement. However, it is important to note that higher expansion factors often lead to increased signal loss due to fluorophore dilution. Importantly, the expansion must maintain the highest possible degree of isotropy (equal expansion in all directions) to ensure accurate spatial representation after expansion. In the classical 4.5× ExM protocol for cells grown on glass coverslips [3], the cell samples are subjected to IF with increased concentration of antibodies compared to regular IF. Post-staining, samples are soaked in a gel-monomer solution. Gel polymerization is initiated and a swellable polymer gel mesh where proteins are anchored to the acrylamide network is formed within and around the sample. The sample is homogenized via a partial digestion with proteinase K that facilitates sample expansion while maintaining sample integrity. Lastly, the hydrogel containing the stained and homogenized sample is immerged in water, which induces swelling.

When working with tissue, ExM can be applied to thin paraffin or cryostat sections [4, 6, 7]. Applying ExM to larger tissue samples provides a more comprehensive view of tissue architecture, preserving structural context across functional tissue units and reduces bias inherent of analyzing only thin sections.

Based on the original protocol for expanding cells, we have optimized expansion of tissue biopsies with 2 mm diameter and 1 mm thickness from the inner medulla of perfusion fixed rat kidneys (*see* Fig. 1 for a schematic overview and Fig. 2 for examples of images generated). We have also successfully applied the protocol to other tissues; thus, the protocol should be applicable to a wide range of tissue biopsies.

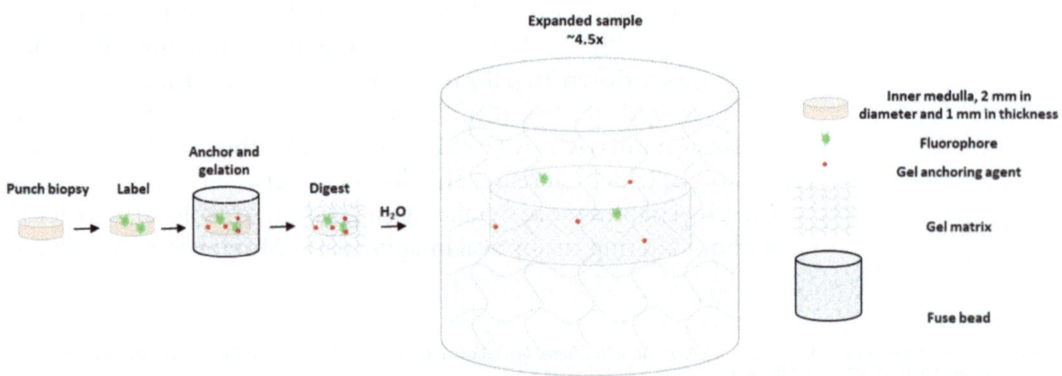

Fig. 1 Schematic of the different steps of the expansion protocol

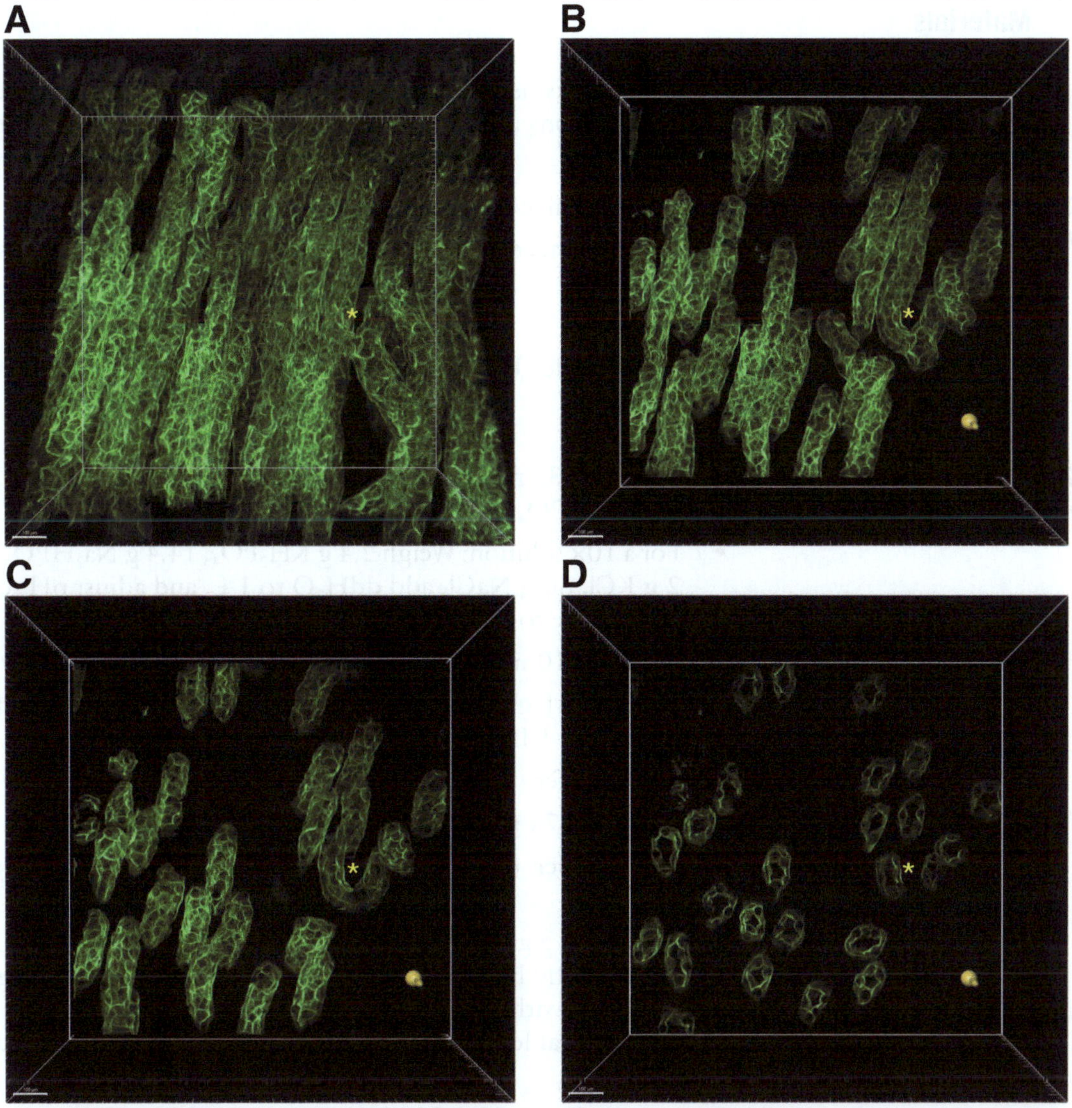

Fig. 2 Expansion microscopy of a rat inner medulla punch biopsy labeled for aquaporin-2. A rat inner medulla punch biopsy was labeled for aquaporin-2 (AQP2), a water channel expressed in renal collecting ducts, and then subjected to expansion microscopy. Images were acquired using an Andor BC43 confocal microscope (10× objective, 0.5 μm z-stack increments) and deconvolved using the Fusion software from Andor. Image analysis was performed in Imaris 10.1.0. Images are presented as 3D maximum intensity projections of the indicated number of slices. (A) Image of the complete acquisition corresponding to 665 μm thickness (1330 z-stacks) of the expanded tissue sample. Panels B, C, and D show 200, 100, and 10 μm sections of panel A, respectively. Asterisks point to merging collecting ducts. Note the difference in information between images representing different thicknesses. The rat was injected with saline 30 min before euthanasia and perfusion fixation. All procedures were conducted in accordance with the Danish animal welfare act. The 3D image can be viewed on our webpage nejsumlab.au.dk/bioimaging under "Expansion Microscopy." Scale bars are 100 μm (note this is post-expansion). Yellow arrows indicate directions. The experimental protocol was approved by the national ethical review committee (Danish Animal Experiments Inspectorate) and carried out in compliance with the Project License (No. 2024-15-0201-01798)

2 Materials

Prepare all solutions using analytical-grade reagents and ultrapure water. Store solutions at room temperature (RT) unless otherwise indicated.

2.1 Tissue Preparation

1. Formaldehyde fixed tissue stored in PBS at 4°C (*see* **Note 1**).
2. Punch biopsy needle, 2 mm in diameter (Pfm medical, cat# 48201).
3. Razor blades.
4. Microscope slide, 1 mm in thickness (*see* **Note 2**).
5. Tape.

2.2 Immunofluorescence Staining

1. PBS buffer (137 mM NaCl, 2.7 mM KCl, 15 mM Na_2HPO_4, 1.5 mM KH_2PO_4, pH 7.4).
   - For a 10× solution: Weigh 2.4 g KH_2PO_4, 14.4 g Na_2HPO_4, 2 g KCl, 80 g NaCl, add ddH_2O to 1 L, and adjust pH to 7.4. Dilute to 1× before use.
2. TEG buffer (10 mM Tris, 0.5 mM EGTA, pH 9).
   - Weigh 1.21 g of Tris-base and 0.19 g of EGTA, and add ddH_2O to 1 L. Adjust pH to 9 if necessary.
3. Shielding buffer (50 mM NH_4Cl in PBS).
   - Weigh 2.674 g of NH_4Cl and dissolve in 1 L of PBS.
4. Blocking buffer (1% BSA, 0.2% gelatin, 0.05% saponin in PBS).
   - Weigh 0.1 g gelatin and 0.025 g saponin, and add ~30 mL PBS. Gently heat to ~50°C to dissolve the gelatin. Bring to 50 mL with PBS and add 0.5 g BSA. Store at 4°C. Prepare fresh at least every 14 days or if the solution has gone cloudy.
5. Staining buffer (0.1% BSA, 0.3% Triton X-100 in PBS).
   - Weigh 0.05 g of BSA and add 150 μL of Triton X-100 to 50 mL of PBS. Store at 4°C.
6. Wash buffer (0.1% BSA, 0.2% gelatin, and 0.05% saponin in PBS).
   - Weigh 0.05 g of BSA and 10 g of gelatin, and add 2.5 μL of saponin to 50 mL of PBS. Store at 4°C.
7. Primary antibodies of interest (*see* **Note 3**).
8. Secondary antibodies with fluorescent dyes suitable for expansion (*see* **Note 4**).
9. Nuclear stain suitable for expansion (e.g., Hoechst 33342 10mg/mL (Thermo Fisher Scientific, Cat#H3570). Make

a 10× dilution in H_2O for working stock of 1mg/mL. Use stock 1:500 for final concentration of 2 μg/mL).

10. Oven set at 37°C.
11. Oven set at 65°C.
12. Anchor 100× stock solution (35.4 mM Acryloyl-X (AcX) (ThermoFisher Scientific, Cat# A20770) in DMSO).
    - Weigh 10 mg and add to 1 mL DMSO. Dilute to 1× in PBS before use.

2.3 Gel Embedding

1. Inhibitor solution (0.5% 4-Hydroxy-TEMPO (4-HT)(Sigma-Aldrich, Cat# 176141) in H_2O).
   - Weigh 50 mg and add to 10 mL H_2O.
2. Ammonium peroxodisulfate (APS, 10% in H_2O).
3. NaCl (5 M).
4. Sodium acrylate (7 M).
5. Acrylamide (4 M).
6. N,N′-methylenebisacrylamide (2%).
7. PBS buffer (137 mM NaCl, 2.7 mM KCl, 15 mM Na_2HPO_4, 1.5 mM KH_2PO_4, pH 7.4).
   - For a 10× solution: Weigh 2.4 g KH_2PO_4, 14.4 g Na_2HPO_4, 2 g KCl, 80 g NaCl, add H_2O to 1 L, and adjust pH to 7.4. Dilute to 1× before use.
8. Monomer solution (1.7 M Sodium Acrylate, 0.2 M Acrylamide, 0.32% N,N′-methylenbis(acrylamide), 1.9 M NaCl in 1× PBS).
   - Add 2.3 mL of 7 M sodium acrylate, 0.5 mL of 4 M acrylamide, 1.5 mL of 2% N,N′-methylenbis(acrylamide), 3.6 mL of 5 M NaCl, and 1.0 mL of 10× PBS, add H_2O to a total volume of 9.4 mL (0.5 mL), and store at −20°C.
9. Parafilm.
10. Fuse beads cut in half (e.g., Hama beads, Cat# 201-00).
11. Button probe 145 mm (Hounisen DK, Cat# 0017.0218).
12. Coverslips 5 mm in diameter.

2.4 Digestion

1. Digestion buffer (800 mM NaCl, 50 mM Tris-Base, 25 mM EDTA, 0.5% Triton-X, pH 7.5).
   - Weigh 606 mg Tris-base, 730,6 mg EDTA, and 4680 mg NaCl, and add 0.5 mL Triton-X, add H_2O to a total volume of 100 mL. Adjust pH to 7.5.
2. Proteinase K (800 U/mL) (Sigma Aldrich, cat #3115828001).
3. Oven set at 60°C.

3 Methods

3.1 Tissue Preparation (see Fig. 3A–F)

1. Place the tissue on a microscope slide and make a punch biopsy from the fixed tissue using a 2 mm punch biopsy needle (*see* **Notes 1 and 5**).
2. Using razorblades, cut a 1 mm slice from the tissue biopsy and place the slice in the well of a 96-well plate or in a microtube and overlay with PBS. Be careful that the tissue does not dry. The below protocol is performed using a 96-well plate where each well can hold one tissue biopsy. All volumes are indicated for one well of the 96-well plate. The volumes can be adjusted to a microtube (*see* **Note 2**).

3.2 Immunofluorescence Staining

1. For target retrieval, aspirate the PBS from the tissue biopsies by pipetting and add 100 μL TEG buffer. Place the 96-well plate in a preheated oven at 65°C and incubate for 1 h.
2. Place the 96-well plate at RT and let it cool to RT for approximately 30 min.
3. Aspirate the TEG buffer from the tissue by pipetting and add 100 μL shielding buffer and incubate for 30 min at RT.
4. Rinse 3× in blocking buffer and leave the tissue biopsies in the final round of blocking buffer for 30 min.
5. Incubate with primary antibodies diluted in staining buffer at 37°C for 7 days (*see* **Note 3**).
6. Move the 96-well plate to RT and let it cool to RT for approximately 30 min.
7. Rinse 3× for 10 min in wash buffer.
8. Incubate with secondary antibodies (1:100, *see* **Note 4**) and Hoechst 33342 (2 μg/mL) diluted in staining buffer at 37°C for 96 h.
9. Rinse 3× for 2 min in PBS.

3.3 Anchoring-Treatment

1. Aspirate all PBS from the tissue by pipetting. Add 50 μL AcX anchoring solution and incubate overnight at RT.

3.4 Gelation

1. Place monomer solution, APS, and 4-HT on ice.
2. Wash tissue biopsies 3× for 2 min in PBS.
3. Incubate with 20–50 μL monomer solution (enough to cover the tissue biopsy) and incubate for 1 h at RT.
4. Place the tissue biopsy on parafilm and carefully place half a fuse bead over the tissue so that the tissue is centered within the bead (*see* Fig. 3G).

5. Mix individual components of the gelation solution on ice (*see* **Note 6**) by adding 1 μL of 0.5% 4-HT, 0.2 μL of TEMED, and 2 μL of 10% APS to 196.8 μL of monomer solution. Add gel solution and seal the incubation chamber by placing a 5 mm coverslip on top of the fuse bead as a lid.
6. Incubate at RT for 1.5 h to allow gelation.
7. Carefully remove the lid/coverslip and gently push the gel embedding the tissue out of the bead using a button knob.

3.5 Digestion

1. Make 500 μL digestion solution with 1:100 proteinase K per tissue slide. Use either a microtube or a 48-well plate.
2. Place the microtube or 48-well plate in a preheated oven at 60°C and incubate for 24 h (*see* **Note 7**).
3. Wash the gel 2× for 2 min in PBS. Store the gel in tubes at 4°C until expansion. Do not add buffer but store "dry" (*see* **Note 8**).

3.6 Expansion

1. Place the gel in the well of a 6-well plate.
2. Add approximately 4 mL of H_2O to the well (the gel should be covered) and expand the gel 2× for 30 min in H_2O at RT with gentle rocking.
3. Remove H_2O, add H_2O containing Hoechst 33342 (2 μg/mL), and incubate for 30 min at RT with gentle rocking.
4. Repeat Step 2.

3.7 Imaging

1. Trim the gel, e.g., under a fluorescence stereo microscope, using a scalpel to remove excess gel.
2. Place the gel on a poly-L-lysine coated coverslip or similar surface within an imaging chamber and capture images using your preferred microscope for imaging (*see* **Notes 9 and 10**).

4 Notes

1. For rodent kidney tissue, perfusion fixation is recommended to preserve the open structure of the tubules.
2. To cut the tissue biopsy into 1 mm in thickness, place two razor blades around a 1 mm objective glass and secure with tape as in Fig. 3B. Use the device to carefully cut the biopsy into 1 mm thickness.
3. The concentration of primary antibodies is routinely more than 5× higher than the concentration used for normal staining of sections. This must be optimized for each antibody.

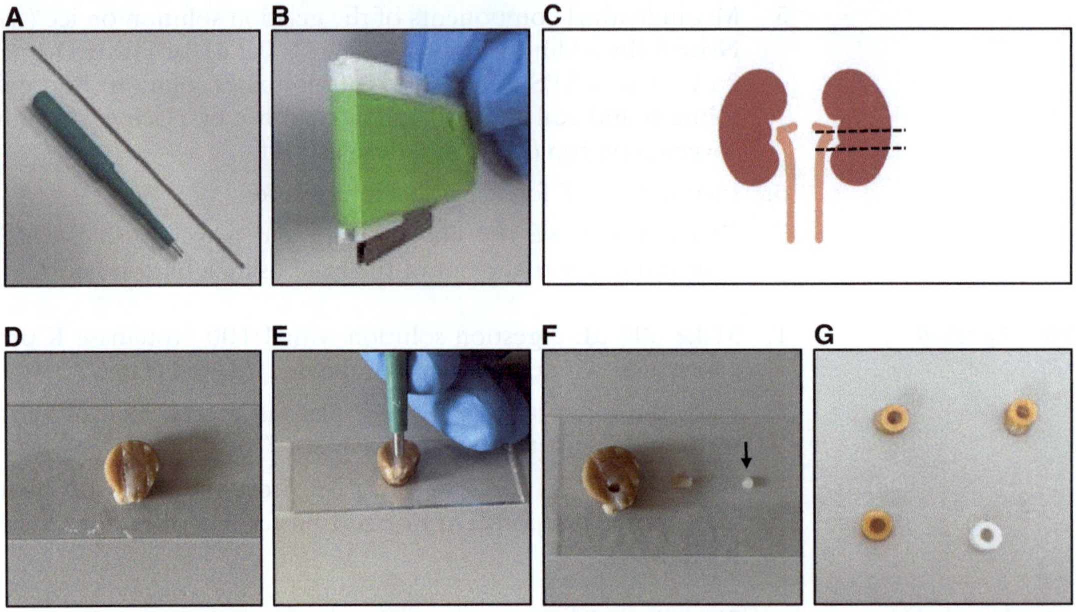

Fig. 3 Procedure for obtaining inner medulla punch biopsies from rat kidney. (**A**) Punch biopsy needle (2 mm diameter) and button probe (used in E). (**B**) Razor blade tool with two blades taped around a 1 mm object glass (used in F). (**C**) Schematic illustrating kidney slicing location before biopsy. (**D**) Thick kidney slice. (**E**) Punch biopsy performed in the inner medulla. (**F**) Biopsy cut into 1 mm sections using the razor blade tool. (**G**) Fuse beads used as gelation chambers. The schematic in (**C**) was created with BioRender.com

The incubation time and temperatures in this protocol were optimized for biopsies from the inner medulla from rat kidneys with a diameter of 2 mm and a thickness of 1 mm so that the antibody penetrates to the core of the biopsy. Incubation time and temperature should be optimized for each tissue type, tissue size, and/or antibodies used in this application.

4. Some fluorescent dyes may not be compatible with ExM, as the expansion protocol can diminish their fluorescent signal. We routinely use the following secondary anti-mouse and anti-rabbit antibodies at 1:100 dilution for ExM: Donkey anti-Mouse IgG (H+L) Highly Cross-Adsorbed Secondary Antibody, Alexa Fluor™ Plus 594 (ThermoFisher Scientific, cat# A32744); Donkey anti-Mouse IgG (H+L) Highly Cross-Adsorbed Secondary Antibody, Alexa Fluor™ 488 (ThermoFisher Scientific, cat# A21202); Donkey anti-Rabbit IgG (H+L) Highly Cross-Adsorbed Secondary Antibody, Alexa Fluor™ 488 (ThermoFisher Scientific, cat# A21206); Donkey anti-Rabbit IgG (H+L) Highly Cross-Adsorbed Secondary Antibody, Alexa Fluor™ 594 (ThermoFisher Scientific, cat# A21207); and Donkey anti-Rabbit IgG (H+L) Secondary Antibody DyLight 549 (Novus, Cat# NBP1-72967). In the far-red spectrum we have used two

drop-n-stain antibodies: Drop-n-stain CF640 Donkey anti-rabbit (Biotium, cat# BIT-20962) and Drop-n-stain CF640 Donkey anti-mouse (Biotium, cat# Bit-20963).

5. Make sure to punch toward a hard support, e.g., a clean microscope slide. If the tissue gets trapped in the punch needle, carefully use a button probe or similar to push the tissue out.
6. Make the gel solution by adding the components in the order stated in the protocol. Keep the solution cold by placing it on ice. 4-HT is an inhibitor of the gelation process and will slow the gelation process. This is beneficial for two reasons; it provides time to add the solution to the tissue before the solution start polymerizing and the slower polymerization results in improved embedding of the tissue. Bis-acrylamide cross-links the acrylamide chains, which progress to the formation of the porous gel matrix. The level of cross-linking, and therefore the pore size and consequent expansion size of the gel, can be controlled by varying the ratio of acrylamide to bis-acrylamide. Ammonium persulfate (APS) initiates polymerization of the acrylamide and bis-acrylamide, and TEMED catalyzes free radical formation of the APS. Gelation begins immediately upon adding these two components.
7. The time and temperature should be optimized for the specific tissue type for optimal digestion of the tissue. The digestion process is crucial for achieving uniform tissue expansion. Incomplete digestion causes the tissue to break apart during expansion, while overdone digestion leads to complete tissue destruction.
8. The gel can be stored at 4°C for several weeks before expansion, with no noticeable loss of signal or change in sample quality.
9. Coating coverslips with poly-L-lysine helps the gel to adhere, thus preventing drift. Make sure that there is no excess fluid which can make the gel drift.
10. The ability to image deep into the gel depends on your microscope setup. For the images in Fig. 2, we used a BC43 spinning disk microscope from Andor Technology—Oxford Instruments, imaging with the 10× objective.

Acknowledgments

Thanks to Simon Skovbo Lassen for help with color adjustments. Expansion microscopy of renal tissue in the laboratory was supported by the Novo Nordisk Foundation via a Hallas-Møller Ascending Investigator Grant (NNF20OC0059487 to Lene N. Nejsum) and an Interdisciplinary Synergy Grant (NFF20OC0063808, Lene N. Nejsum as co-applicant).

Conflict of Interest Expansion microscopy of renal tissue in the laboratory was supported by the Novo Nordisk Foundation via a Hallas-Møller Ascending Investigator Grant (NNF20OC0059487 to Lene N. Nejsum) and an Interdisciplinary Synergy Grant (NFF20OC0063808, Lene N. Nejsum as co-applicant).

References

1. Hell SW, Wichmann J (1994) Breaking the diffraction resolution limit by stimulated emission: stimulated-emission-depletion fluorescence microscopy. Opt Lett 19(11):780–782
2. Betzig E, Patterson GH, Sougrat R, Lindwasser OW, Olenych S, Bonifacino JS et al (2006) Imaging intracellular fluorescent proteins at nanometer resolution. Science 313(5793):1642–1645
3. Chen F, Tillberg PW, Boyden ES (2015) Optical imaging. Expansion microscopy. Science 347(6221):543–548
4. Chang JB, Chen F, Yoon YG, Jung EE, Babcock H, Kang JS et al (2017) Iterative expansion microscopy. Nat Methods 14(6):593–599
5. Truckenbrodt S, Maidorn M, Crzan D, Wildhagen H, Kabatas S, Rizzoli SO (2018) X10 expansion microscopy enables 25-nm resolution on conventional microscopes. EMBO Rep 19:9
6. Damstra HGJ, Mohar B, Eddison M, Akhmanova A, Kapitein LC, Tillberg PW (2022) Visualizing cellular and tissue ultrastructure using Ten-fold Robust Expansion Microscopy (TREx). Elife 18(11):e73775
7. Zhao Y, Bucur O, Irshad H, Chen F, Weins A, Stancu AL et al (2017) Nanoscale imaging of clinical specimens using pathology-optimized expansion microscopy. Nat Biotechnol 35(8):757–764

Check for updates

Chapter 7

Current Methods in CODEX High-Multiplex Microscopy to Describe Spatial Relationships in the Tissue Microenvironment

Joseph Nichols, Amina Nurmammadova, Yannick Palmowski, Alexander Rochwarger, Ahmad Makky, Mohammed Zidane, Annika Jäger, Jing Zhao, Yizheng Zhang, Lanzhu Li, Nastassja Lehmann, Karen Greif, Saumya Manmadhan, Christine Beschorner and Christian M. Schürch

Abstract

Illuminating mechanisms at the tissue and cellular levels using indexed oligonucleotide-conjugated antibodies has further increased the resolution necessary to study pathological disease at microscopic levels. CO-Detection by indEXing (CODEX) is a high-multiplex microscopy method that uses up to 100 unique conjugated antibodies to elucidate which cell types and cellular neighborhoods are present in the imaged tissue, to determine their positions relative to each other and their functional states for physiologically-based mechanistic derivations. The first part of these procedures describes how to conjugate antibodies to their assigned oligonucleotide. Then, these conjugates are all optimized for either formalin-fixed paraffin-embedded (FFPE) or fresh-frozen (FF) tissues. In the third part, the conjugate-stained tissue section undergoes the CODEX multicycle reaction where fluorescently labeled oligonucleotides complementary to conjugates are periodically added and removed to aid in the capture of images. Lastly, the collected images are processed to set the stage for cell type and cellular neighborhood mapping on the imaged tissue for further spatial analysis work. This method has advanced basic antibody research and translational pathology workflows as well as refining new clinical treatments by providing bioinformatic support to clinicians to help patients with various diseases, especially cancer.

Keywords CODEX, High-multiplex microscopy, Tissue microenvironment, Cancer immunology, Personalized therapy

1 Introduction

The structure and position of a group of cells relative to other cells or groups of cells in tissue denote its physiological effector functions. And observing how these structures spatially and morphologically change in the context of disease has aided in personalized clinical diagnostics and inspired campaigns to uncover, image, and collect

Timothy L. Frankel and Arvind Rao (eds.), *Cellular Spatial Characterization and Analysis*, Methods in Molecular Biology, vol. 2995, https://doi.org/10.1007/978-1-0716-5027-1_7,

pathological tissue architectures. This effort at the cellular and tissue microenvironment levels is catalyzed by the CO-Detection by indEXing (CODEX) technology, where tissue-associated antigens are targeted and imaged to ultimately define the boundaries of all cellular groups or neighborhoods [1–7].

To visualize a cellular neighborhood with CODEX, four different sets of procedures must be executed (Fig. 1). The first set involves conjugating antibodies to unique DNA oligonucleotides and verifying the conjugation. Then, each conjugate's optimal dilution and exposure time is elucidated with the tissue of interest culminating in a captured, microscopic image that supports the set parameters. In the third set of this protocol, all defined conjugates are stained onto tissue, a CODEX multicycle reaction is then performed, and a classical hematoxylin and eosin stain is done post-reaction, to utilize established morphological features when mapping the tissue.

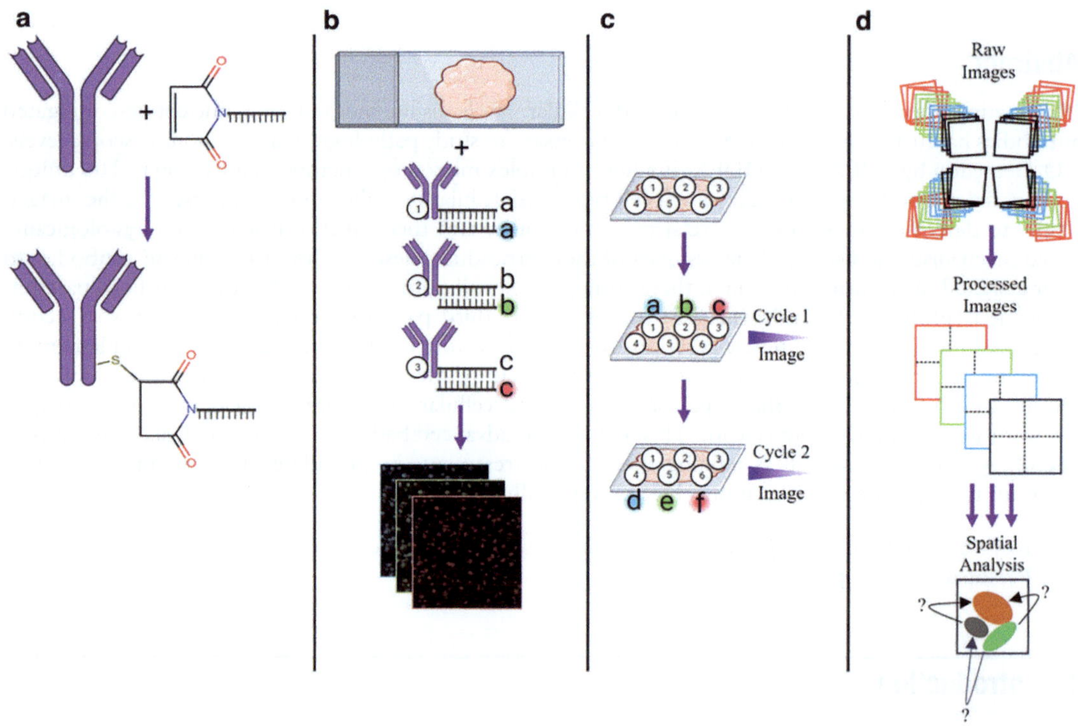

Fig. 1 The CODEX protocol. (**a**) Antibodies are conjugated to maleimide-modified DNA oligonucleotides through the creation of a thioether covalent bond. (**b**) Conjugates 1, 2, and 3 are optimized using the tissue of interest, complementary fluorescently labeled oligonucleotides *a*, *b*, and *c*, are introduced, and images are collected to support the set dilution and exposure time. (**c**) All conjugates are stained onto the tissue, oligonucleotides *a*, *b*, and *c* bind to conjugates during the first cycle, and an image is captured. Cycle 1 oligonucleotides are then removed and during the second cycle, a different set of oligonucleotides (*d*, *e*, *f*) are injected. Another image is captured, and the process is repeated for the rest of the conjugates. (**d**) Raw images are processed and cell segmentation and cell type mapping follow, setting the stage for defining the cellular neighborhoods and performing spatial analysis

In the final procedural set, the captured and collected raw images are processed to superimpose the identified cell types and cellular neighborhoods onto the imaged tissue using computer languages such as R or Python.

In the past few years, we have contributed methods and algorithms necessary to increase the resolution of the cellular neighborhoods as done in part four in addition to expanding and tailoring parts one to three. Creating more oligonucleotides to simultaneously observe more antigens, refining the bleaching procedures for conjugate facilitated images, and restructuring CODEX antibody panels used in past multicycle reactions are some examples of how we have furthered our endeavors and the protocol we present describes how.

2 Materials

The materials described below are presented both in order of their appearance and preparation.

2.1 The Creation and Assessment of Conjugates for CODEX (Part 1)

1. Activated maleimide-modified oligonucleotides (Biomers).
2. Inactivated maleimide-modified oligonucleotides (TriLink BioTechnologies).
3. Thermomixer (Eppendorf, 5382000023).
4. Analytical Balance (Sartorius, 674015).
5. Syringe (B Braun, 4606027V) and Needle (BD, 304100s).
6. Anhydrous Toluene (Sigma-Aldrich, 244511).
7. 100% Ethanol (VWR, 20821330).
8. 5 M NaCl Solution: 500 ml ddH_2O, 146.1 g NaCl (Sigma-Aldrich, S7653), 100 mg NaN_3 (Sigma-Aldrich, S8032).
9. Buffer C Solution: 966 ml ddH_2O, 30 ml 5 M NaCl Solution, 2 ml 0.5 M EDTA (pH 8.0) (Sigma-Aldrich, AM9261), 1 ml 1 M Tris-HCl (pH 7.5) (Teknova, T1075), 1 ml 1 M Tris-HCl (pH 7.0) (Teknova, T1070), 200 mg NaN_3.
10. NanoDrop 2000 (ThermoFisher Scientific, ND-2000).
11. PCR Tubes with domed caps (BRAND, BR781327).
12. Long Forceps (Zulco, XC01THUS).
13. Isothermal Transport Vessel (KGW Isotherm, 1214).
14. Lyophilizer Fast-Freeze Flask (Labconco, 7540900).
15. Lyophilizer (Labconco, 700202015).
16. Disposable Wipes (Carl Roth, 7558).
17. PCR Tubes with flat caps (BRAND, BR781326).
18. Drierite Desiccant (W A Hammond, 23001).

19. PCR Carboard Freezer Box (Argos, 10987067).
20. 10× DPBS (Sigma-Aldrich, D1408).
21. 1× DPBS Solution: Dilute the 10× DPBS (1:10) with ddH_2O (e.g., 900 ml ddH_2O, 100 ml 10× DPBS).
22. 0.1% DPBS-Tween Solution: 100 ml 1× DBPS Solution, 100 μl Tween 20 (Sigma-Aldrich, P1379).
23. Centrifugal Filter Units (Sigma-Aldrich, UFC505096).
24. 0.5 M TCEP Solution: 2.5 ml ddH_2O, 717 mg TCEP (Sigma-Aldrich, C4706), adjust pH to 7.0 with NaOH (Sigma-Aldrich, S8263), dilute to 5 ml with ddH_2O.
25. 2.5 mM TCEP Solution: 990 μl 1× DPBS, 5 μl 0.5 M EDTA (pH 8.0), 5 μl 0.5 M TCEP Solution.
26. High-Salt Buffer C Solution: 380 μl Buffer C Solution, 20 μl 5 M NaCl.
27. Metal Block (80/20, 2148).
28. High-Salt DPBS Solution: 180 ml ddH_2O, 45 ml 5 M NaCl Solution, 25 ml 10× DPBS, 50 mg NaN_3.
29. Stock Antibody Stabilizer Solution: 10 ml Antibody Stabilizer PBS (Candor, 131125), 2 mg NaN_3.
30. CODEX Antibody Stabilizer Solution: 9 ml Stock Antibody Stabilizer Solution, 1 ml 5 M NaCl Solution, 100 μl 0.5 M EDTA (pH 8.0).
31. Fluorescence Activated Cell Sorting (FACS) Tubes (Falcon, 352058).
32. Staining Solution 1 (S1): 445 mL ddH_2O, 50 ml 10× DPBS, 5 ml 0.5 M EDTA (pH 8.0), 2.5 g BSA (BIO&SELL, PF0100), 100 mg NaN_3.
33. 1 M Na_2HPO_4: 500 ml ddH_2O, 70.98 g Na_2HPO_4 (Sigma-Aldrich, S7907), 100 mg NaN_3.
34. 1 M NaH_2PO_4: 500 ml ddH_2O, 69.0 g NaH_2PO_4 (Sigma-Aldrich, S9638), 100 mg NaN_3.
35. Staining Solution 2 (S2): 250 ml S1, 175 mL ddH_2O, 30.5 ml 1 M Na_2HPO_4, 25 ml 5 M NaCl, 19.5 ml 1 M NaH_2PO_4, adjust pH to 7.0 with NaOH.
36. UltraComp eBead Compensation Beads (ThermoFisher Scientific, 01222242).
37. Stock Bottom Oligonucleotide (Integrated DNA Technologies).
38. Bottom Oligonucleotide: Dilute the Stock Bottom Oligonucleotide (1:10) with TE Buffer (e.g., 270 μl TE Buffer, 30 μl Stock Bottom Oligonucleotide).
39. Staining Solution 4 (S4): 450 ml S1, 50 ml 5 M NaCl.

40. Flow Cytometer (BD Biosciences, 642221).
41. Cell Engine (https://cellengine.com/#/).

2.2 The Optimization of the Created Conjugate (Part 2)

1. TOMO IHC Adhesive Glass Slide (Matsunami, TOM-1190).
2. Microscope Slide Rack (DWK Life Sciences, 10061392).
3. Staining Dishes (DWK Life Sciences, 10633533).
4. Xylene (VWR, 28975325).
5. 95% Ethanol: 95 ml 100% Ethanol, 5 ml ddH_2O.
6. 80% Ethanol: 80 ml 100% Ethanol, 20 ml ddH_2O.
7. 70% Ethanol: 70 ml 100% Ethanol, 30 ml ddH_2O.
8. Pressure Cooker (Rommelsbacher, MD1000)
9. Target Retrieval Solution, pH 9 (10×) (Agilent, S2367).
10. Antigen Retrieval Solution: Dilute the Target Retrieval Solution (1:10) with ddH_2O (e.g., 45 ml ddH_2O, 5 ml Target Retrieval Solution).
11. Coplin Jar (DWK Life Sciences, 900470).
12. Coverslip Forceps (Dumont, 1125133).
13. 1 M NaOH (Sigma-Aldrich, 283010)
14. Bleaching Solution: 100 ml 1× DPBS, 18 ml 30% Hydrogen Peroxide (Supelco, 1072101000), 3.2 ml 1 M NaOH.
15. Light Pads (Aibecy, 3131/107928648244335 4112/55).
16. 10x TBS IHC Buffer with Tween (Cell Signaling Technology, 9997S).
17. 1× Tris-Buffered Saline Tween (TBST): Dilute 10× TBS IHC Buffer with Tween (1:10) with ddH_2O (e.g., 90 ml ddH_2O, 10 ml 10× TBS IHC Buffer with Tween).
18. UV Light Repair Pen (BONDIC, SK8024).
19. Blocking Reagent 1 (B1): 10 ml S2, 10 mg mouse IgG (Sigma-Aldrich, I5381).
20. Blocking Reagent 2 (B2): 10 ml S2, 10 mg rat IgG (Sigma-Aldrich, I4131).
21. Blocking Reagent 3 (B3): Salmon Sperm DNA (Sigma-Aldrich, AM9680). Aliquots are stored at −20°C for later use.
22. TE Buffer: 98.8 ml ddH_2O, 1 ml 1 M Tris-HCl (pH 8.0) (Teknova, T1080), 200 μl 0.5 M EDTA (pH 8.0), 20 mg NaN_3.
23. Blocking Component 4 (BC4): A mixture of all 57 non-fluorescently labeled bottom oligonucleotides each concentrated to 0.5 mM using TE Buffer [1].

24. Blocking Solution with BC4: 390 µl S2, 25 µl B1, 25 µl B2, 25 µl B3, 35 µl BC4.
25. Conjugated Antibody Solution for Part 2: One conjugate from each channel (Alexa488, ATTO550, Alexa647) is combined with respect to their individual dilutions and then Blocking Solution with BC4 is added to yield a final volume of 100 µl.
26. 1.6% Paraformaldehyde S4 Fixative Solution: 225 µl S4, 25 µl Paraformaldehyde, 16% w/v aq (Alfa Aesar, 43368).
27. 100% Methanol (Honeywell, 32213).
28. 10× H2 Buffer: 960 ml ddH_2O, 30 ml 5 M NaCl, 10 ml 1 M Tris (pH 7.5), 0.943 ml Triton X-100 (Carl Roth, 30513), 2.03 g $MgCl_2(6H_2O)$ (Carl Roth, 21891), 200 mg NaN_3.
29. 1x H2 Buffer: Dilute the 10× H2 Buffer (1:10) with ddH_2O (e.g., 900 ml ddH_2O, 100 ml 10x H2 Buffer).
30. Rendering Buffer (R1): 40 ml DMSO (Carl Roth, 70294), 160 ml 1× H2 Buffer (20% DMSO, 80% 1× H2 Buffer).
31. Stripping Buffer (R2): 40 ml DMSO, 10 ml 1× H2 Buffer (80% DMSO, 20% 1× H2 Buffer).
32. CODEX Detection Solution: 90 µl R1, 7 µl B3, 1 µl of bottom oligonucleotide (for Alexa488), 1 µl of bottom oligonucleotide (for ATTO550), and 1 µl of bottom oligonucleotide (for Alexa647).
33. Razor (Personna, 610045).
34. Cytoseal (Epredia, 83124).
35. 24 × 50 mm Coverslip (Epredia, BB02400500AC13MNZ0).
36. Keyence Microscope (BZ-X810).

2.3 The CODEX Multicycle Reaction (Part 3)

1. 100% Acetone (neoFroxx, LC49162).
2. VECTABOND Reagent (VECTABOND, SP18007).
3. VECTABOND Solution: 125 ml Acetone, 2.5 ml VECTABOND Reagent.
4. 22 × 22 Coverslips (Electron Microscopy Sciences, 7220401).
5. Coverslip Jars (DWK Life Sciences, 02912637).
6. Six–well culture plates (Corning, 353046).
7. Conjugated Antibody Solution for Part 3: All optimized conjugates are combined with respect to their individual dilutions and then Blocking Solution with BC4 is added to yield a final volume of 100 µl. If the solution is prepared with 50 conjugates or more, the amount of blocking solution remains at 50 µl (e.g., 70 µl of Conjugates + 50 µl of Blocking Solution

with BC4). However, this solution must then be reconcentrated as described in step 4 of Sect. 3.21.

8. Bissulfosuccinimidyl Suberate (BS3) (ThermoFisher Scientific, 21580).
9. BS3 Solution: 250 μl DMSO, 50 mg BS3.
10. BS3 Fixative Solution: 1000 μl 1× DPBS, 20 μl BS3 Solution.
11. Plate Buffer: 50 ml 1× H2 Buffer, 2.5 ml B3, 83.3 μl Hoechst 33342 (ThermoFisher Scientific, 62249).
12. Black 96-well Plate (Akoya Biosciences, 7000006).
13. DRAQ5 (ThermoFisher Scientific, 650880).
14. Aluminum sealing (Corning, PCRAS200).
15. PhenoCycler (Akoya Biosciences).
16. Coverslip gaskets (Akoya Biosciences, 7000010).
17. Hoechst Solution: 999 μl 1× H2 Buffer, 1 μl Hoechst.
18. Hematoxylin (Agilent, S3309302).
19. Eosin G (Merck, 1170811000).

2.4 The Analysis of CODEX Data (Part 4)

1. Computer Specifications: Current computer has 128 GB of RAM, an 8 GB NVIDIA Quadro RTX 4000, and 45 terabytes of storage.
2. https://github.com/SchurchLab
3. https://github.com/bmyury
4. https://github.com/will-yx

2.5 Working with Fresh-Frozen Tissue

1. Cryomold (Sakura, 4557).
2. Optimal Cutting Temperature (OCT) Compound (Sakura, 4583).
3. Cryostat (Leica, CM3050S).
4. SuperFrost Plus Microscope Slide (NOVOGLAS, 030060).
5. 1.6% Paraformaldehyde S1 Fixative Solution: 900 μl S1, 100 μl Paraformaldehyde, 16% w/v aq.
6. Blocking Solution without BC4: 390 μl S2, 25 μl B1, 25 μl B2, 25 μl B3.
7. Conjugated Antibody Solution for Part 2: One conjugate from each channel (Alexa488, ATTO550, Alexa647) is combined with respect to their individual dilutions and then Blocking Solution without BC4 is added to yield a final volume of 100 μl.
8. Poly-l-lysine (Sigma-Aldrich, P8920).

3 Methods

The entire CODEX protocol is organized into four different parts. First, the CODEX Panel (Sect. 3.1) organizes to which oligonucleotide each antibody will conjugate (Sects. 3.2–3.9), and then FACS is used to test the conjugation (Sects. 3.10–3.12). Next, a manual procedure involving staining, fixative, and microscopy-based techniques (Sects. 3.13–3.19) is executed to optimize the dilution and exposure times of each conjugate for the tissue of interest. In the third part, all optimized conjugates are stained onto a tissue-loaded coverslip which is then introduced into the PhenoCycler to commence the multicycle reaction (Sects. 3.20–3.26). Lastly, the raw images generated from the reaction will be processed and further analyzed to yield mechanistic insights at both tissue and individual cell level (Sects. 3.27–3.32).

3.1 Create the CODEX Panel

1. Open Microsoft Excel, list all the antigens, ensure they accurately correspond to the tissue of interest, and assign each to one of three channels (Alexa488, ATTO550, Alexa647) (*see* **Note 1**).
2. For each antigen identify the antibody it will be targeted by as well as the unique DNA oligonucleotide that will be conjugated to the antibody (*see* **Note 2**).
3. Next, based on prior or published data, predefine the cycle number (the cycle where each antigen will be imaged), dilution of the conjugate, and the appropriate exposure time in milliseconds for all listed antigens. This information will later be entered into the CODEX Instrument Manager computer software program (Sect. 3.23, step 6) (*see* **Note 3**).

3.2 Activate the Oligonucleotide Listed on the Panel

1. Activated oligonucleotides are purchased from Biomers (https://www.biomers.net/). If activated oligonucleotides have been purchased, skip to Sect. 3.5. If maleimide-modified oligonucleotides need to be activated, complete steps 2 to 11 below as well as Sects. 3.3 and 3.4.
2. Move a thermomixer into the fume hood and pre-heat it to 90°C for later use in step 6.
3. Use an analytical balance to tare a 2.0 ml Eppendorf tube and transfer the lyophilized oligonucleotide into the tared tube.
4. Record the mass of the oligonucleotide.
5. Use a syringe and needle to transfer 1 ml of Anhydrous Toluene into the tared Eppendorf tube containing oligonucleotide.
6. Use the thermomixer to heat the tube for 2 h at 90°C.
7. Use a pipette to gently remove the 1 ml of Anhydrous Toluene from the Eppendorf tube without disturbing the pellet.

8. Repeat steps 5, 6, and 7 one time.
9. Repeat steps 5 and 7 one time.
10. Transfer 1.5 ml of 100% Ethanol into the Eppendorf tube and carefully invert the tube three times. After the pellet reforms at the bottom of the tube, remove all the ethanol.
11. Repeat step 10 three times.
12. Transfer Buffer C to the Eppendorf tube, making sure to dissolve the pellet by pipetting the solution up and down (1 mg Oligonucleotide: 50 μl Buffer C).

3.3 Measure the Concentration of the Oligonucleotide

1. We currently use the NanoDrop 2000 from Thermo Fisher Scientific to measure the concentration.
2. The settings selected are "Classic" and "Nucleic Acid."
3. The instrument is blanked with 1 μl of Buffer C Solution and the oligonucleotide concentration is measured in μg/μl.

3.4 Lyophilize the Oligonucleotide

1. Calculate the volume of Oligonucleotide-Buffer C Solution needed to yield 100 μg in a PCR tube and transfer it.
2. Obtain a domed PCR cap, pierce it with two holes using the purple needle, and cap the PCR tube containing the Oligonucleotide-Buffer C Solution (*see* **Note 4**).
3. Grip the PCR tube with long forceps and dip the bottom portion of the tube into liquid nitrogen but do not submerge it completely (*see* **Note 5**).
4. Then, place the PCR tube in a box filled with dry ice.
5. Remove a Lyophilizer Fast-Freeze Flask from the −80°C freezer (*see* **Note 6**).
6. Wrinkle three disposable wipes, put them within the flask, place the PCR tube on top of the wipes, connect the flask to the lyophilizer, and let it run overnight (*see* **Note 7**).
7. On the next day, replace the needle-pierced PCR cap with a flat cap. Place drierite desiccant on the base of a PCR Cardboard Freezer Box and put the PCR tube inside. Store the box at a temperature of −20°C for up to 2 years or more.

3.5 Measure the Concentration of the Antibody Listed on the Panel

1. The NanoDrop 2000 is used here to measure concentration as well.
2. The settings selected are "Classic" and "Protein A280."
3. The instrument is blanked with 1 μl of 1× DPBS Solution and the antibody concentration is measured in mg/ml.

3.6 Prepare the Antibody

1. Calculate the mass of the antibody and oligonucleotide needed. The ratio of antibody to oligonucleotide must be 1:2.

2. Calculate the volume of antibody needed for the conjugation.
3. Obtain a centrifugal filter column and collecting tube and assemble them together to form the centrifugal filter unit.
4. Transfer 500 μl of 0.1% DPBS-Tween Solution into the centrifugal filter unit.
5. Centrifuge the unit at 12 000 × *g* for 2 min at room temperature.
6. Discard the contents from both the filter column and collecting tube.
7. Vortex the tube containing the antibody.
8. Determine whether the antibody needs to be diluted with 1× DPBS Solution (*see* **Note 8**).
9. Transfer the appropriate amount of antibody volume to the unit.
10. Centrifuge the unit at 12 000 × *g* for 8 min at room temperature.
11. Only discard the contents from the bottom collecting tube.

3.7 Reduce the Antibody

1. Transfer 360 μl of 2.5 mM TCEP Solution to the centrifugal filter unit.
2. Vortex the unit and incubate it for 30 min at room temperature (*see* **Note 9**).
3. Centrifuge the unit at 12 000 × *g* for 8 min at room temperature.
4. Only discard the contents from the bottom collecting tube.
5. Transfer 400 μl of Buffer C to the unit.
6. Centrifuge the unit at 12 000 × *g* for 8 min at room temperature (*see* **Note 10**).
7. Only discard the contents from the bottom collecting tube.
8. Repeat steps 5, 6, and 7 one time.

3.8 Conjugate the Antibody to the Assigned Oligonucleotide

1. Prepare 400 μl of 1× DPBS Solution in a 1.5 ml Eppendorf tube (*see* **Note 11**).
2. In the presence of liquid nitrogen gas, transfer 150 μl of 1× DPBS from the 400 μl preparation to the PCR tube containing the oligonucleotide (*see* **Note 12**).
3. Transfer all contents from the PCR tube to the Eppendorf tube. The volume of the Eppendorf tube should return to 400 μl of 1× DPBS in addition to having the dissolved oligonucleotide.
4. Calculate the volume of oligonucleotide needed for conjugation (200 μg Oligonucleotide: 400 μl 1× DPBS).
5. Transfer the corresponding volume of resuspended oligonucleotide to its respective antibody within the centrifugal filter unit that was prepared in step 8 of Sect. 3.7.

6. Vortex the unit and incubate it for 2 h at room temperature to facilitate antibody–oligonucleotide conjugation.

3.9 Stabilize the Conjugate

1. Centrifuge the centrifugal filter unit at 12 000 × *g* for 8 min at room temperature.
2. Only discard the contents from the bottom collecting tube.
3. Transfer 450 μl of High-Salt DPBS Solution to the unit.
4. Centrifuge the unit at 12 000 × *g* for 8 min at room temperature.
5. Only discard the contents from the bottom collecting tube.
6. Repeat steps 3, 4, and 5 two times.
7. Calculate the volume of CODEX Antibody Stabilizer Solution needed (100 μg Antibody: 200 μl Stabilizer).
8. Remove the filter column from the bottom collecting tube.
9. Transfer the appropriate amount of Stabilizer volume onto the white membranes that line the inner walls of the filter column. Pipette the entire solution up and down along the membranes several times (*see* **Note 13**).
10. Acquire, label, and invert a new collecting tube and "cap" the filter column (column down, tube up).
11. Flip the capped filter column upside-down such that the contents fall into the new collecting tube.
12. Centrifuge the capped unit in the upside-down (column up, tube down) position at 3000 × *g* for 2 min at room temperature.
13. Only discard the filter column.
14. The collecting tube contains the conjugate. Refrigerate the conjugate at 4°C. The conjugate can survive at 4°C for up to 2 years or more.

3.10 Prepare the Conjugate for the Flow Cytometer

1. Label FACS tubes for the conjugate and its corresponding negative control. Label one FACS tube for the positive control (*see* **Notes 14** and **15**).
2. Transfer 200 μl of Staining Solution 2 (S2) to all FACS tubes.
3. Obtain the UltraComp eBeads reagent and vortex it for 2 s.
4. Transfer 1 drop (50 μl) of UltraComp eBeads to all FACS tubes.
5. Select a positive control (*see* **Note 16**).
6. Prepare each FACS tube with the appropriate contents: 0 μl for the negative control, 1 μl for the selected positive control, and 1 μl of the conjugate.
7. Vortex all FACS tubes for 2 s and incubate them in the dark for 5 min at room temperature.

8. Transfer 1 ml of S2 to all FACS tubes.
9. Centrifuge all FACS tubes at 500 × *g* for 5 min at room temperature.
10. For each FACS tube, inspect the bottom of the tube for pellets and quickly invert the tube over a waste container to discard the supernatant.
11. Refrigerate the decanted positive control FACS tube at 4°C until step 16 of this section.
12. Prepare each FACS tube with the appropriate contents: 1 μl of bottom oligonucleotide complementary to conjugate for both the negative control and conjugate labeled FACS tubes (*see* **Note 17**).
13. Except for the positive control, incubate all other FACS tubes in the dark for 5 min at room temperature.
14. Except for the positive control, transfer 1 ml of Staining Solution 4 (S4) to all other FACS tubes.
15. Repeat steps 9 and 10 one time.
16. Transfer 250 μl of S4 to all FACS tubes including the retrieved positive control.
17. If the experiment will be delayed, refrigerate all FACS tubes at 4°C for up to 1 day, and make sure to vortex the tubes before continuing. Otherwise, proceed to Sect. 3.11.

3.11 Prepare, Clean, and Collect Data from the Flow Cytometer

1. The BD Biosciences LSR II Flow Cytometer is used in these steps.
2. The instrument is considered clean when the threshold rate decreases to around 0 to 8 evt/s.
3. Data is collected and recorded between a threshold rate of 3000 to 10,000 evt/s. When finished, export the data as Flow Cytometry Standard (FCS) files.

3.12 Analyze Flow Cytometry Data

1. Cell Engine is a currently used subscription-based online software in our group (https://cellengine.com/#/).
2. Briefly, FCS files are uploaded to Cell Engine and gated. Axes are adjusted and each FCS file is inspected. If two populations are observed, the antibody is considered conjugated (Fig. 2) (*see* **Note 18**).

The second part of the CODEX protocol (Sects. **3.13–3.19**) focuses on optimizing each conjugate's dilution and exposure time for the tissue of interest in preparation for a future multicycle run.

3.13 Create the FFPE Tissue Block and Section the Block

1. Use an Embedding Center Module to create an FFPE Tissue Block using the tissue of interest.

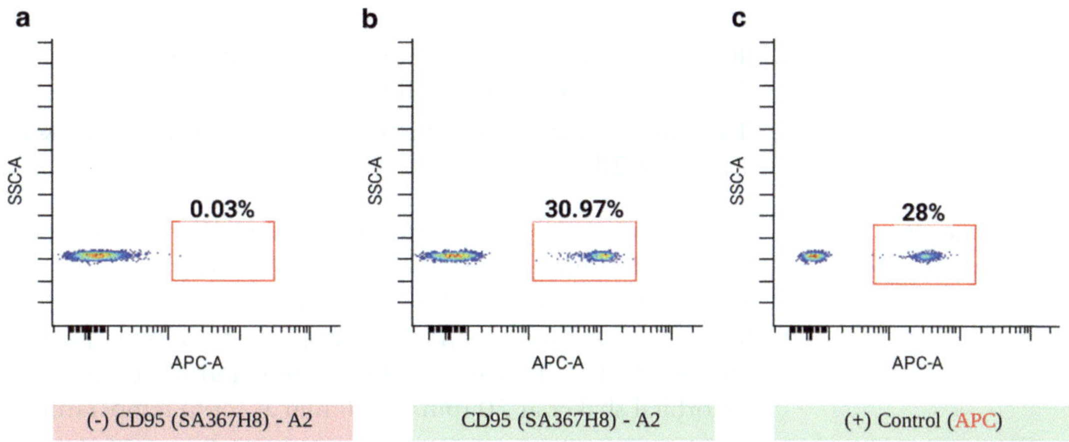

Fig. 2 Conjugation Results. The antibody being evaluated is CD95 (SA367H8) from BioLegend conjugated to oligonucleotide A2. (**a**) The negative control for the experiment. (**b**) The CD95 conjugate. (**c**) The positive control

2. With a microtome create a 4 μm thick section from the tissue block, load it onto a TOMO IHC Adhesive Glass Slide, and air dry the slide (*see* **Note 19**).
3. If the experiment will continue on the same day, proceed to step 1 of Sect. 3.14.
4. If the experiment will continue on a different day, bake the slide at 37°C overnight and store it at 4°C. When ready, proceed to step 1 of Sect. 3.14 (*see* **Note 20**).

3.14 Deparaffinization

1. Bake the tissue loaded microscope slide for 1 h at 70°C (*see* **Note 21**).
2. Load the slide onto a microscope slide rack and submerge the rack in different staining dish solutions, at the indicated times and temperatures, in this order: Xylene (10 min, Room Temperature), Xylene (10 min, RT), Xylene (10 min, RT), 100% Ethanol (3 min, RT), 100% Ethanol (3 min, RT), 95% Ethanol (3 min, RT), 95% Ethanol (3 min, RT), 80% Ethanol (3 min, RT), 70% Ethanol (3 min, RT), ddH_2O (3 min, RT), and ddH_2O (3 min, RT).

3.15 Antigen Retrieval

1. Partly fill the pressure cooker with ddH_2O.
2. Transfer Antigen Retrieval Solution into a Coplin jar and place the jar inside the cooker without submerging it completely. If necessary, remove water from the cooker. Then, turn the pressure cooker on.
3. Heat at the following settings: 30 to 60 min, 65°C (*see* **Note 22**).
4. Insert the microscope slide into the Coplin jar. Heat at the following settings: 10 min, 95°C.

5. Heat at the following settings: 30 min, 60°C.
6. Remove the Coplin jar from the pressure cooker. Cool at the following settings: 30 min, RT.
7. Determine whether bleaching the tissue section is necessary (*see* **Note 23**).

3.16 Conjugate Staining

1. Retrieve the microscope slide from the Coplin jar filled with Antigen Retrieval Solution or 1× DPBS Solution. Gently tap off the excess solution onto a disposable wipe.
2. Place the microscope slide in a Coplin jar filled with 1× Tris-Buffered Saline Tween (TBST) Solution and place the jar on an orbital shaker at 20 rpm for 10 min at room temperature.
3. Retrieve the microscope slide from the Coplin jar filled TBST Solution. Gently tap off the excess solution onto a disposable wipe.
4. With a disposable wipe, dry the perimeter of the tissue section located on the microscope slide and use a UV Light Repair Pen to encircle it with gel and to harden the gel with light (*see* **Note 24**).
5. Place the microscope slide onto the humified pipette box and apply 100 μl of Blocking Solution with BC4 in a drop-by-drop fashion. Close the humified pipet box and incubate it on an orbital shaker at 20 rpm for 30 to 60 min at room temperature (*see* **Note 25**).
6. Retrieve the microscope slide and gently tap off the excess solution onto a disposable wipe.
7. Place the microscope slide onto the humified pipet box and apply 100 μl of Conjugated Antibody Solution in a drop-by-drop fashion. Close the humified pipet box and incubate it on an orbital shaker at 20 rpm overnight at 4°C (*see* **Note 26**).

3.17 Conjugate Fixation

1. Retrieve the microscope slide and gently tap off the excess solution onto a disposable wipe.
2. Place the microscope slide in a Coplin jar filled with Staining Solution 2 (S2) for 2 min at room temperature and then repeat step 1.
3. Repeat step 2, one time with a fresh solution.
4. Place the microscope slide onto a humified pipette box and apply 100 μl of 1.6% Paraformaldehyde S4 Fixative Solution in a drop-by-drop fashion. Close the humified pipet box and incubate it for 10 min at room temperature and then repeat step 1.
5. Place the microscope slide in a Coplin jar filled with 1× DPBS Solution for 1 min at room temperature and then repeat step 1.

6. Repeat step 5 two more times with fresh solutions.
7. Place the microscope slide in a Coplin jar filled with cold 100% Methanol for 5 min at 4°C and then repeat step 1.
8. Repeat steps 5 and 6, one time (*see* **Note 27**).
9. Determine whether bleaching the tissue section is necessary. Please *see* **Note 23** for more information.
10. Place the microscope slide in a Coplin jar filled with Staining Solution 4 (S4). If the experiment will continue on the same day, proceed to Sect. 3.18. Otherwise, refrigerate the jar at 4°C for up to two weeks.

3.18 Complementary Bottom Oligonucleotides Binding to Conjugates

1. Retrieve the microscope slide and gently tap off the excess solution onto a disposable wipe.
2. Place the microscope slide in a Coplin jar filled with Rendering Buffer (R1) for 1 min at room temperature and then repeat step 1.
3. Place the microscope slide in a Coplin jar filled with Stripping Buffer (R2) for 10 min at room temperature and then repeat step 1.
4. Repeat step 2 one time with a fresh solution.
5. Place the microscope slide onto the humified pipette box and apply 100 μl of CODEX Detection Solution in a drop-by-drop fashion. Close the humified pipette box, store it in the dark, incubate it for 10 min at room temperature, and then repeat step 1.
6. Place the microscope slide in a Coplin jar filled with Rendering Buffer (R1) for 30 s at room temperature and then repeat step 1.
7. Place the microscope slide into a Coplin jar filled with Staining Solution 4 (S4) for 1 min at room temperature and then repeat step 1.
8. Repeat step 7 one time with a fresh solution.
9. Gently, remove the hardened gel that is encircling the section from the microscope slide with forceps or a razor blade.
10. Rinse the microscope slide by dipping it in a Coplin jar filled with Staining Solution 4 (S4). Then, dry the perimeter of the microscope slide with a disposable wipe while making sure to not touch the tissue section.
11. Add cytoseal to the slide and carefully place a 24 × 50 mm coverslip over the cytoseal. Gently press the coverslip with long tweezers to remove any bubbles within the cytoseal.
12. Let the microscope slide dry in the dark for 30 min at room temperature.

13. After incubation, remove any excess cytoseal from the perimeter of the microscope slide with a disposable wipe.
14. Rinse the microscope slide by dipping it in a Coplin jar filled with ddH_2O. Then, dry the microscope slide with a disposable wipe.

3.19 Inspect, Capture, and Save Images

1. Use the BZ-X810 Microscope from Keyence to center and to auto-focus the tissue section image. Then, use the navigation feature to get a zoomed-out overview of the image (*see* **Note 28**).
2. Depending on the bottom oligonucleotide used, inspect the section in either channel Alexa488, ATTO550, or Alexa 647.
3. Capture and save the image (Fig. 3).
4. Type the conjugate name, dilution, and exposure time as the file name of the image.

The third part of the CODEX protocol consists of staining tissue-loaded coverslips with all optimized conjugates (Sects. **3.20** and **3.21**), creating a 96-well Bottom Oligonucleotide Plate complementary to those conjugates (Sect. **3.22**), configuring the PhenoCycler (Sect. **3.23**) and microscope (Sect. **3.24**), and transferring all imaging data (Sect. **3.25**) as well as performing a post-reaction hematoxylin and eosin stain (Sect. **3.26**).

3.20 Prepare Coverslips with VECTABOND

1. Place new coverslips into a large, glass-made petri dish (*see* **Note 29**).
2. Fill the petri dish with ddH_2O and incubate the dish for 5 min at room temperature.

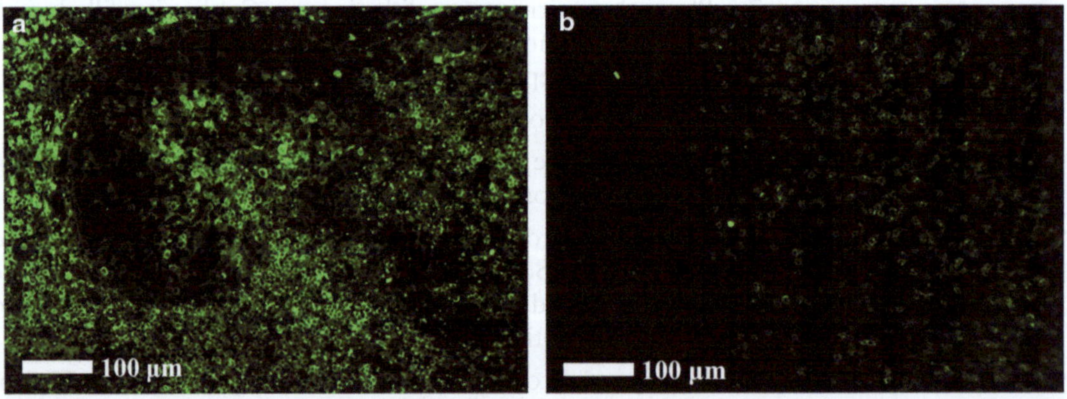

Fig. 3 Conjugate facilitated images. (**a**) Human tonsil tissue was stained with CCR6 antibody from BD Biosciences (11A9) at a 1:100 dilution (1 μl) with 500 ms of exposure time in the ATTO550 channel (conjugated to oligonucleotide A53). (A53) (**b**) Skin tissue from a patient with cutaneous T-cell lymphoma stained with CD8 antibody from Cell Marque (C8144B) at a 1:50 dilution (2 μl) with 500 ms of exposure time in the ATTO550 channel (conjugated to oligonucleotide A8)

3. Discard the ddH_2O, fill the petri dish with 100% Acetone, and incubate the dish for 5 min at room temperature.
4. Remove and dry each coverslip with a disposable wipe.
5. Discard the 100% Acetone, return the coverslips to the petri dish, fill it with VECTABOND solution, put the lid on, and incubate the dish for 30 min at room temperature.
6. Discard the VECTABOND solution, fill the petri dish with 100% Acetone, and incubate the dish for 30 s at room temperature.
7. Repeat step 4.
8. Bake all coverslips in the oven for 1 h at 70°C and then store them at room temperature for later use.

3.21 Variations with the FFPE Multicycle Reaction

1. Create the FFPE Tissue Block and Section the Block. The steps here remain the same as described in Sect. 3.13 (*see* **Note 30**).
2. Deparaffinization. The steps here remain the same as described in Sect. 3.14. To save solution material throughout Sect. 3.21, we recommend using coverslip jars instead of staining dishes and Coplin jars.
3. Antigen Retrieval. The steps here remain the same as described in Sect. 3.15. We recommend using a six-well culture plate during the 45-min bleaching process and coverslip jars during the subsequent washes with 1× DPBS solutions.
4. Conjugate Staining. The steps here remain the same as described in Sect. 3.16. Please reference the methods section to learn how the Conjugated Antibody Solution is prepared differently. Also note, if the Conjugated Antibody Solution is prepared with 50 conjugates or more, the solution must be reconcentrated. (1) Prepare the Antibody Conjugated Solution the same way as described in the methods for part 3 of CODEX (e.g., 70 μl of Conjugates + 50 μl of Blocking Solution with BC4). (2) Transfer 500 μl of 0.1% DPBS-Tween Solution into a new centrifugal filter unit. (3) Centrifuge the unit at 12 000 × *g* for 8 min at room temperature. (4) Discard the contents from both the filter column and collecting tube. (5) Transfer 100 μl of Conjugation Antibody Solution into the centrifugal filter unit. (5) Repeat step (3). (6) Only discard the contents from the bottom collecting tube. (7) Remove the filter column from the collecting tube. (8) Transfer 100 μl of Blocking Solution with BC4 onto both white membranes that line the inner walls of the filter column. (9) Acquire, label, and invert a new collecting tube and "cap" the filter column (column down, tube up). (10) Flip the capped filter column upside-down such that the contents fall into the new collecting tube. (11) Centrifuge the capped unit in the upside-down

(column up, tube down) position at 3000 × *g* for 2 min at room temperature. (12) Only discard the filter column. (13) The collecting tube contains the new Conjugation Antibody Solution. Transfer the entire volume of the solution onto the tissue loaded coverslip.

5. Conjugate Fixation. The steps here remain the same as described in Sect. 3.17 except for two additional steps. After completing steps 1 to 8 of Sect. 3.17, place the coverslip onto the humified pipet box and apply 100 μl of BS3 Fixative Solution in a drop-by-drop fashion and repeat steps 5 and 6 one time. Proceed to steps 9 and 10 of Sect. 3.17 (*see* **Note 31**).
6. Complementary Bottom Oligonucleotides binding to Conjugates. Skip Sect. 3.18.
7. Inspect, Capture, and Save Images. Skip Sect. 3.19.
8. Proceed to Sect. 3.22.

3.22 Create the Bottom Oligonucleotide Plate

1. Create the Plate Buffer (PB) in a falcon tube, wrap it in aluminum foil, and store it at 4°C if it will be used later.
2. Create the Bottom Oligonucleotide Plate using a black-colored 96-well plate. Each well represents one cycle from the multicycle reaction. Here are some rules to keep in mind. Rule 1, the volume of each well is 250 μl (e.g., A1–A12). Rule 2, the first (A1) and last wells (A12) must be blank (250 μl PB). Rule 3, the second to last well (A11) must contain DRAQ5 (2.5 μL), only two bottom oligonucleotides (10 μL each), and PB (227.5 μl). Rule 4, all other wells (A2–A10) must contain 10 μl of each bottom oligonucleotide associated with the cycle in question and these wells must be diluted to 250 μl with PB.
3. Next, seal the row(s) of the well plate with aluminum sealing film. If the experiment will be delayed, refrigerate the plate at 4°C for up to one day. Otherwise, proceed to Sect. 3.23.

3.23 Configure the PhenoCycler

1. Prepare all four canisters and connect them to the PhenoCylcer. Fill the DI Water canister with ddH_2O. Fill the amber glass canister with DMSO. Empty the vacuum waste canister. Fill the 1× H2 Buffer canister.
2. Properly align and load the 96-well Bottom Oligonucleotide Plate into the PhenoCycler and make sure the four translucent troughs to the left of the plate are empty and dry.
3. Turn on the instrument using the switch on the back right.
4. Assemble the Stage Assembly located on the left of the PhenoCycler. The Stage Assembly is comprised of the Stage Plate and the Stage Insert. First, place a blank coverslip on the center of the black Stage Plate. Then, put a black coverslip gasket on top of the coverslip. Finally, put the silver Stage

Insert on top and twist both knobs at the same time to secure the coverslip.

5. Double left-click on the CODEX Instrument Manager desktop icon.
6. Select New Template and transfer the information from the CODEX Panel into the program (*see* **Note 32**).
7. Input an Operator name, select Start Experiment, and the Experiment Start Wizard will pop up.
8. Click Next in the Check List section.
9. Click Next in the Load Buffers section.
10. Click Next in the Check Fluidics section and then click OK.
11. Click Prime Instrument and wait for 6 to 10 min. Do NOT click Next.
12. Disassemble and then reassemble the Stage Assembly with the conjugate-stained coverslip. First, pipette out any fluid from the well located on the Stage Plate. Disassemble the Stage Assembly and remove the blank coverslip. Next, remove the gel that was applied to the stained coverslip with either forceps or a razor blade. Finally, reassemble the Stage Assembly with the stained coverslip. The tissue should be facing upwards.
13. Click Next in the Prime Instrument section.
14. Do NOT click anything in the Prepare Sample section.
15. Create the Hoechst Staining Solution in a 1.5 ml Eppendorf tube, wrap the tube in aluminum foil, and store it at 4°C if it will be used later. Transfer 700 μl of Hoechst Staining Solution directly to the coverslip. Wait 1 min.
16. Click Immediate Wash Tissue in the Prepare Sample section.
17. Do NOT click anything in the Microscope Precheck section.

3.24 Configure the Microscope and Start the Multicycle Reaction

1. Turn on the BZ-X810 Keyence Microscope by pressing the button on the bottom right of the instrument and wait for the blue light to stop blinking.
2. Elevate the Stage Assembly to moisten the bottom with a ddH_2O wet disposable wipe. Insert the Stage Assembly onto the microscope's stage. Make sure all wires coming from inside the microscope are centered on the outside. This will prevent them from getting crushed when the microscope's lid closes.
3. Double left-click the BZ-X800 Viewer desktop icon and click Login.
4. Click Filter Cube and the Filter Cube window will pop up.
5. Open the bottom portion of the microscope and inspect the filter cube. Click on "CH1" and the CH1 filter cube will

appear on the bottom of the microscope. Physically grip the sides of the cube and check if it is secured and not loose. Repeat this process for filter cubes CH2, CH3, and CH4.

6. Click OK, Capture Still Images, select Versatile, OK, and the Capture Still Images window will pop up.
7. Select the Measure tab and deselect Scale. Return to the Microscope tab.
8. Select the X2 lens, turn on the Excitation Light and Low Photobleach, set the camera setting to Mono, select the CH1 Fluor DAPI channel, and select Auto-Focus. Adjust the Brightness (Exposure) as needed.
9. Select Navigation (top left) and a small navigation window will pop up. Add ten navigation images by simply clicking Add and Stop multiple times. On the tenth navigation image, select Save as Image and create the folder where all multicycle images will be stored.
10. Return to the navigation window and remain on the tenth navigation image and center on a region of interest by simply clicking on it. Return to the Capture Still Images window, go to Stage View, make the Point Memo one (1:), and click Set.
11. Return to the navigation window and remain on the tenth navigation image and center on another region of interest by simply clicking on it. Return to the Capture Still Images window, go to Stage View, make the Point Memo two (2:), and click Set.
12. Continue repeating the process described in steps 11 and 12 to organize all regions of interest.
13. Select the ×20 lens, select Stitching, and adjust the number of image tiles in the x and y directions (*see* **Note 33**).
14. Return to Stage View, select Point Memo one (1:), click Go, and Auto-Focus. Then go to the Navigation window and select the first navigation image (1:), click Delete, OK, and Add.
15. Return to Stage View, select Point Memo two (2:), click Go, and Auto-Focus. Then go to the Navigation window and select the second navigation image (2:), click Delete, OK, and Add.
16. Continue repeating the process described in steps 15 and 16 to set all the regions associated with the multicycle reaction.
17. Return to the navigation window and delete all navigation images that are not being used. Inspect each navigation image that was configured to make sure everything is in order as well as to Auto-Focus each image.

18. Select Z-Stack and use the Set buttons to assign the proper z-stack number (*see* **Note 34**).
19. Turn on Multicolor and click ON for each channel and turn off Overlay.
20. Click Start Capture (bottom right corner) and in the Root Path box, select the folder created in step 9. Click OK, Yes, Cancel the run, and select Yes. Check if some images were saved in the correct computer folder using File Explorer.
21. Click Live Image (bottom right corner), Menu (top left corner), Capture Setting, Save, OK, and OK.
22. Return to the navigation window, select the first created navigation image (1:), auto-focus the image, and make sure the first channel selected is CH1 Fluor DAPI.
23. Return to the CODEX Start Wizard.
24. Click Microscope Pre-check in the Microscope Precheck section (*see* **Note 35**).
25. If successful, select Yes, and Next.
26. Before clicking Start in the Start Run section, make sure all computer-related tasks of interest are finished or any work-related files are exported. The computer should NOT be used during the run as it can interfere with the reaction.
27. Click Start (*see* **Note 36**).

3.25 Transfer the Data Associated with the Multicycle Reaction

1. When the reaction has finished a window will appear titled Experiment finished. Select Finish experiment and click OK.
2. Return to the CODEX Instrument Manager window and select the Transfer Data tab.
3. Select the name of the experiment under Available Experiments, click on Verify, and on the Destination Folder icon.
4. Select Copy and a Transfer Data window will appear, revealing how much time the transfer will take.
5. Open the microscope lid, remove the Stage Plate, and set it on the Stage Mount located to the left of the PhenoCycler.
6. With a pipette, remove extra liquid from the well located at the center of the Stage Plate.
7. Pick up the Stage Assembly and invert it quickly. The silver Stage Insert will drop on your hand. The attached coverslip and gasket will be on the back.
8. With forceps, "tug" on the top and bottom tips of the gasket. This will loosen the coverslip enough for it to be removed. Moistening the area with water may also help.

9. Store the coverslip in a coverslip jar filled with Staining Solution 4 (S4) and refrigerate the jar at 4°C for later use in Sect. 3.26.
10. Clean the instrument by selecting the Maintenance tab on the CODEX Instrument Manager window to begin the process with a blank coverslip.
11. Dry the Stage Assembly with a disposable wipe.
12. Remove the 96-well Bottom Oligonucleotide Plate, empty and dry the four troughs, and prepare all canisters.
13. Turn off the PhenoCycler and microscope.

3.26 Perform a Hematoxylin and Eosin Stain

1. Assemble the Stage Assembly. First, place a gasket on the Stage Plate. Second, place the conjugate-stained coverslip on top of the gasket. Then, put another gasket on top of the coverslip. Finally, put the Stage Insert on top and twist both knobs at the same time to secure the coverslip (*see* **Note 37**).
2. Transfer 700 μl of each solution onto the coverslip, at the following times, in this order: 100% Ethanol (20s), 100% Ethanol (20s), 70% Ethanol (20s), ddH_2O (20s), Hematoxylin (120s), Warm Tap Water (20s), 70% Ethanol (20s), Eosin (90s), 70% Ethanol (20s), 95% Ethanol (20s), 100% Ethanol (20s), and 100% Ethanol (20s).
3. Transfer a third wash of 100% Ethanol to clean the coverslip. Dry the plate with disposable wipes.
4. Load the Stage Assembly into the microscope and turn it on.
5. Click on the BZ-X800 Viewer desktop icon and click Login.
6. Click Filter Cube and the Filter Cube window will pop up.
7. Open the bottom portion of the microscope and inspect the filter cube. Click on "CH1" and the CH1 filter cube will appear on the bottom of the microscope. Physically remove this DAPI filter cube while making sure to never touch the lenses. Store the cube in bubble wrap.
8. Return to the Filter Cube window and change the CH1 illumination setting to Brightfield. Click OK, Capture Still Images, select Versatile, OK, and the Capture Still Images window will pop up.
9. Click Menu, Capture Setting, Open, From a Setting File, open the folder where all images are stored, select the .bzc file, and click OK. The microscope will return to the original configured settings before the multicycle reaction started (Sect. 3.24, step 22).
10. Click on the CH1, Auto-Focus, and adjust Brightness (Exposure).

11. Set the Camera Setting to Color. Click Yes to adjust the white balance. A White Balance window will appear along with a black colored square border that appears in the image. Place the square to the desired position, select Small for the Area, and click Set. The image of the tissue should change.
12. In Stage View, select Point Memo one (1:), click Go, and Auto-Focus.
13. Search the folder created in step 9 of Sect. 3.24 for the desired captured image and make sure it matches the live image. Aligning the captured image to the live image may be necessary.
14. Continue repeating the process described in steps 12 and 13 for all regions of interest. After all regions of interest are selected and aligned, capture and save the H&E images. This step can take up to 20 min to complete depending on the number of images being captured.

The fourth and final part of the CODEX protocol concentrates on mechanism derivation by way of analyzing images collected from the multicycle reaction. The images are first processed (Sect. **3.27**), cells are then segmented (Sect. **3.28**), and clustered to identify cell types (Sect. **3.29**), cell windows are created and clustered and the cellular neighborhoods that result are mapped on imaged tissue (Sect. **3.30**) to lay the foundation for spatial analysis (Sect. **3.31**) (Fig. 4). Each step described below is not limited to one computational pipeline to complete the analysis successfully. Established and new software is currently being optimized for CODEX by many different laboratories and for other multiplexed imaging technologies. Hence, each step will briefly describe the overall goal.

3.27 Processed Images

1. The tissue section is imaged in tiles and each tile is imaged at multiple levels (z-stack). The image processor deconvolutes, removes background noise, and determines the best focus level for each tile. Then these tiles are registered, aligned to the same coordinate and orientation, and stitched together to yield processed images for cell segmentation.
2. There are several image processors available, such as the processor provided by Akoya Biosciences, the one created by the Garry Nolan Laboratory at Stanford University, and the Convolutional Registration of Images at Sub-Pixel resolution (CRISP) for CODEX [8] (*see* **Note 38**).

3.28 Cell Segmentation

1. Cell boundaries are identified based on nucleus segmentation.
2. There are many programs available to accomplish this task, such as the software developed by Akoya Biosciences, CellSeg, and the program associated with CRISP [8].

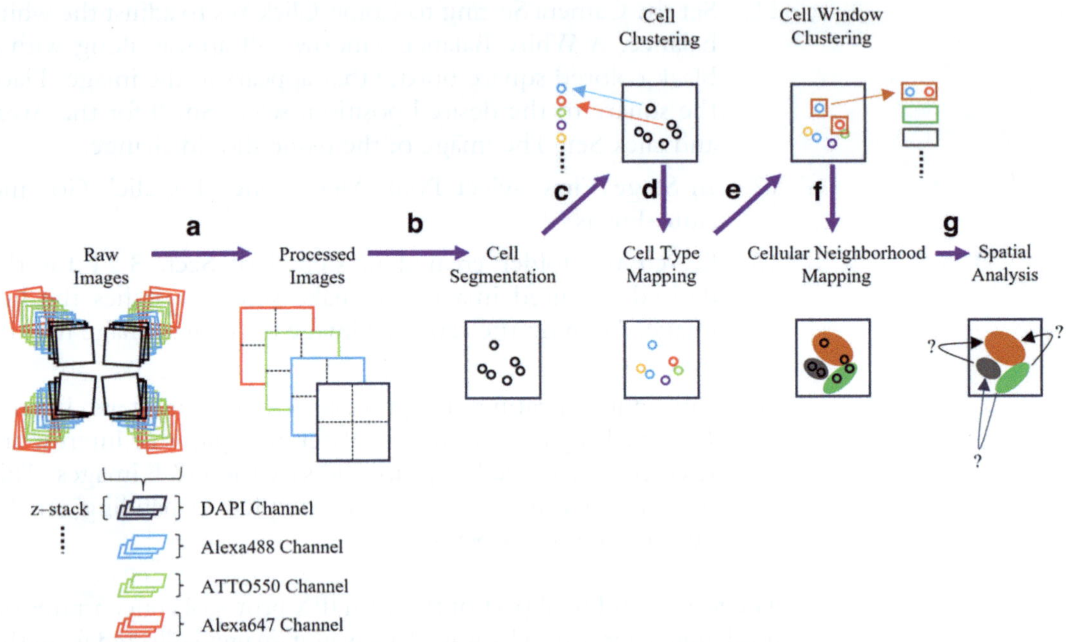

Fig. 4 CODEX Data Analysis Overview. (**a**) Raw, captured, and collected images must drift compensated, deconvoluted, and undergo background subtraction through processing. The best focal plane from the z-stack associated with the DAPI channel for each cycle is applied to all other markers. (**b**) Processed images then undergo cell segmentation which creates a comma-separated values (CSV) file. The file contains the details of each single cell. (**c**) Cell clustering and (**d**) cell type mapping then follows with the use of a CSV file. (**e**) Clustered cell windows aid in (**f**) defining the cellular neighborhoods, and (**g**) neighborhood interactions are analyzed at the tissue and cellular levels

3. By the end of cell segmentation, a CSV file is created that includes data for each single cell, such as x and y coordinates and all associated protein marker expressions.

3.29 Cell Clustering and Cell Type Mapping

1. Typically, the data used to accomplish this analysis step is a CSV file. Segmented cells are clustered based on their protein expression and then, their cell type is identified on the imaged tissue using ImageJ or other software such as Enable Medicine, an online, subscription based, visualization software.
2. We use in-house developed tools to overlay the clusters onto the hyperstack images using Fiji/ImageJ. These tools are available here: https://github.com/bmyury.

3.30 Cell Window Clustering and Cellular Neighborhood Mapping

1. Computational steps are applied to define the cellular neighborhoods based on the resulting cellular window clusters.

3.31 Spatial Analysis

1. Infer cell-cell and neighborhood interactions based on their position to one another.

Fresh Frozen (FF) tissue may also undergo all four parts of the CODEX protocol albeit with differences as described below.

3.32 CODEX Variations with Fresh Frozen (FF) Tissue

1. Part 1 of CODEX. The preparation of the CODEX Panel (Sect. 3.1), the creation of conjugates (Sects. 3.2–3.9), and their evaluation (Sects. 3.10–3.12) remain the same (*see* **Note 39**).
2. Part 2 of CODEX. The differences are described in steps 3 to 9 of this section.
3. Create the FF Tissue Block and Section the Block. The steps here are different to those described in Sect. 3.13. An FF tissue block is made with OCT compound and sectioned with a cryostat. (1) Place the tissue sample into a cryomold, apply the optimal cutting temperature (OCT) compound to the mold, and store the mold in dry ice for 5 min at room temperature. (2) Set the chamber temperature to −24°C and the specimen disc holder temperature to −18°C. (3) Put the loaded specimen disc onto the quick-freeze shelf and pivot and lower the stationary heat extractor onto the block to promote better adherence. (4) Retrieve the specimen disc and insert it into the holder. (5) Create a 7 μm section, load it onto a SuperFrost Microscope Slide, and let the slide air dry for 10 min outside of the cryostat. (6) If the experiment will continue on a different day, store the slide at −80°C. (7) If the experiment will continue on the same day, no temperature incubation is necessary (*see* **Note 40**).
4. Deparaffinization. Skip Sect. 3.14.
5. Antigen Retrieval. Skip Sect. 3.15.
6. Conjugate Staining. Some steps remain the same as described in Sect. 3.16. (1) First, empty a pipet box and lay a thin layer of drierite desiccant to the base, and create a humified pipet box as previously described (*see* **Note 25**). (2) Also, prepare the 1.6% Paraformaldehyde S1 Fixative Solution, Blocking Solution without BC4, and the Conjugated Antibody Solution. (3) Place the microscope slide onto a bed of drierite desiccant and close the pipet box and incubate it for 2 min at room temperature. (4) Place the microscope slide in a Coplin jar filled with 100% Acetone for 10 min at room temperature. (5) Retrieve the microscope slide and gently tap off the excess solution onto a disposable wipe. (6) Place the microscope slide onto the humified pipet box's stage and close the pipet box and incubate for 2 min at room temperature. (7) Place the microscope slide in a Coplin jar filled with Staining

Solution 1 (S1) for 2 min at room temperature and then tap off the excess solution onto a disposable wipe. (8) Repeat step (7), one time with a fresh solution. (9) With a disposable wipe, dry the perimeter of the tissue section located on the microscope slide and use a UV Light Repair Pen to encircle it with gel and harden the gel with light. (10) Place the microscope slide onto the humified pipet box and apply 100 μl of 1.6% Paraformaldehyde S1 Fixative Solution in a drop-by-drop fashion. Close the humified pipet box and incubate it for 10 min at room temperature. (11) Repeat steps (7) and (8), one time. (12) Place the microscope slide in a Coplin jar filled with Staining Solution 2 (S2) for 5 min at room temperature and then tap off the excess solution onto a disposable wipe. (13) Place the microscope slide onto the humified pipet box and apply 100 μl of Blocking Solution without BC4 in a drop-by-drop fashion. Close the humified pipette box and incubate it on an orbital shaker at 20 rpm for 30 to 60 min at room temperature and then tap off the excess solution onto a disposable wipe. (14) Place the microscope slide onto the humified pipet box and apply 100 μl of Conjugated Antibody Solution in a drop-by-drop fashion. Close the humified pipet box and incubate it on an orbital shaker at 20 rpm for 1.5 to 3 h at room temperature (*see* **Note 41**).

7. Conjugate Fixation. The steps here remain the same as described in Sect. 3.17. The tissue section is not treated with BS3 Fixative Solution. FF tissue can be bleached only during step 9 of Sect. 3.17.
8. Complementary Bottom Oligonucleotides binding to Conjugates. The steps here remain the same as described in Sect. 3.17 except for one step. Since the blocking solution was prepared without BC4, stripping buffer is not necessary and thus, step 3 of Sect. 3.18 may be skipped.
9. Inspect, Capture, and Save Images. The steps here remain the same as described in Sect. 3.19.
10. Part 3 of CODEX. The differences are described in steps 11 to 20 of this section.
11. Prepare Coverslips with Poly-l-lysine. The steps here are different to those described in Sect. 3.20. First, coverslips are treated with Poly-l-lysine before being loaded with an FF tissue section. (1) Pour 15 mL of Poly-l-lysine Solution into a 10-cm diameter, glass-made, petri dish. (2) Submerge 10 to 15 coverslips in the dish for 5 min at room temperature. (3) Retrieve the coverslips and tap off the excess solution onto a disposable wipe. (4) "Sandwich" all coverslips in disposable wipes and let them dry for 2 h at room temperature. (4) Store the treated coverslips at −80°C.

12. Create the FF Tissue Block and Section the Block. The steps are the same as described in step 5 of this section except for one step. While the microscope slide may remain outside the cryostat chamber at room temperature before being loaded with tissue, the coverslips should be placed inside the chamber to cool before section loading.
13. Deparaffinization. Skip Sect. 3.14.
14. Antigen Retrieval. Skip Sect. 3.15.
15. Conjugate Staining. The steps here are the same as described in step 6 of this section except for the preparation of two solutions. The Blocking Solution is now prepared with BC4. The Conjugated Antibody Solution is prepared differently as well and note to reconcentrate the solution if it is prepared with 50 conjugates or more. Also, to save solution material substitute Coplin jars for coverslip jars.
16. Conjugate Fixation. The steps here remain the same as described in Sect. 3.17 except for two additional steps. After completing steps 1 to 8 of Sect. 3.17, place the coverslip onto the humified pipet box and apply 100 µl of BS3 Fixative Solution in a drop-by-drop fashion and repeat steps 5 and 6, one time. Proceed to steps 9 and 10 of Sect. 3.17.
17. Complementary Bottom Oligonucleotides Binding to Conjugates. Skip Sect. 3.18.
18. Inspect, Capture, and Save Images. Skip Sect. 3.19.
19. Create the Bottom Oligonucleotide Plate. The steps here remain the same as described in Sect. 3.22.
20. The steps associated with the configuration of the PhenoCycler (Sect. 3.23) to the hematoxylin and eosin stain (Sect. 3.26) remain unchanged.
21. Part 4 of CODEX. The final analytical part (Sects. 3.27–3.31) remains the same.

4 Notes

1. Antigens with a low concentration should be assigned to channels ATTO550 or Alexa647, and those with a high concentration should use channel Alexa488. Intranuclear antigens should appear as early as possible in the multicycle reaction.
2. Originally, one panel targeted only 57 antigens. This limit has been raised to 79 due to newly validated DNA oligonucleotides in our laboratory.

3. This panel will help in remaining organized throughout the CODEX procedure and incorporate other data such as immunohistochemistry (IHC), immunofluorescence (IF), hematoxylin and eosin (H&E) stains, and more, to aid in the refinement of the panel.
4. Gently tap the PCR tube onto the laboratory bench to ensure the contents fall to the bottom of the tube. Also, perform steps 1 to 3 of Sect. 3.4 as quickly and safely as possible.
5. Liquid nitrogen is stored in an isothermal transport vessel to better facilitate this step.
6. The Lyophilizer Fast-Freeze Flask is stored for 1 to 2 h at −80°C before use.
7. Make sure the PCR tube is always in the upright position during the overnight lyophilization process.
8. If the calculated antibody volume is below 50 μL then dilute the volume to 100 μl with 1× DPBS. If the volume is equal to or greater than 50 μl then no dilution is necessary.
9. A 15- or 20-min incubation time could also be acceptable depending on the antibody being conjugated.
10. During this centrifugation step, please finish steps 1 to 4 of Sect. 3.8 to resuspend the oligonucleotide. Once centrifugation has finished, transfer the resuspended oligonucleotide to its respective antibody as described in step 5 of Sect. 3.8.
11. 1× DPBS is used during the first round of conjugation. High-Salt Buffer C is used during the second round of conjugation if the antibody failed to conjugate to oligonucleotides in the first round. Steps 1 to 3 of Sect. 3.8 may be substituted with High-Salt Buffer C.
12. Create the gas by pouring liquid nitrogen from one isothermal transport vessel into a different vessel that contains a metal block. When the liquid is carefully poured onto this metal block, the gas forms, and then 1× DPBS gets transferred in the presence of this gas.
13. Do not puncture the membrane with the pipette tip.
14. The negative control contains beads and fluorescently labeled oligonucleotides. The positive control contains beads and a selected positive control. Please *see* **Note 16** for more information regarding positive controls. The conjugate labeled FACS tubes contain beads, the conjugate, its complementary fluorescently labeled oligonucleotide.
15. Both S2 and S4 solutions used in Sect. 3.10 may be substituted with 1× DPBS solutions.
16. We typically use one of the following positive controls: Fluorescein Isothiocyanate (FITC), Phycoerythrin (PE), or Allophycocyanin (APC) antibodies.

17. A "top oligo" is the oligonucleotide conjugated to the antibody. A "bottom oligo" is the fluorescent oligonucleotide complementary to the top oligo on the antibody.
18. Sometimes conjugations fail, and not all commercially available antibodies work well for tissue. Furthermore, for some antigens, multiple antibody clones must be tested to find the optimal one (which results in higher costs).
19. The water bath used after tissue section loading has a temperature ranging from 45°C to 52°C.
20. If the experiment will be delayed for 1 to 6 months, dip the tissue loaded microscope or coverslip in paraffin and store it at 4°C. When you are ready to resume, bake the sample for 3 hours at 70°C. Then, proceed to step 2 of Sect. 3.14.
21. We recommend to also start steps 1 and 2 of Sect. 3.15 to save time.
22. This step may run longer than 30 min depending on how long it takes to complete the deparaffinization process in step 2 of Sect. 3.14.
23. There are three options to choose from concerning tissue section bleaching. (1) If no bleaching is necessary, then skip all bleaching steps and proceed to Sect. 3.16. (2) If bleaching is necessary, start the process here (Sect. 3.15, step 7). (3) You may also choose to bleach the tissue in step 11 of Sect. 3.17. The bleaching procedure starts with submerging the microscope slide in a large petri dish filled with the freshly made bleaching solution and "sandwiching" the petri dish in light pads for 45 min at room temperature. After repeating this 45-min step with a fresh solution, place the microscope slide in a Coplin jar filled with 1× DPBS Solution for 3 min at room temperature. Repeat this wash three more times with fresh 1× DPBS solutions.
24. The washing steps throughout the CODEX procedure can partly or completely remove the gel. Simply, repeat this step to reapply fresh gel.
25. To create a humified chamber, we wet a paper towel with tap water and place it on the base of a pipette box. The pipette box is reassembled, the slide is placed on the stage, and the lid is placed down.
26. It is highly recommended that the chamber incubates on a shaker at 4°C. However, as a last resort, you may simply refrigerate the chamber overnight at 4°C without an orbital shaker.
27. In our laboratory, we do not regularly fixate with BS3 Fixative Solution during part 2 of CODEX for the manual staining. However, it certainly can be implemented. After completing

steps 1 to 8 of Sect. 3.17, place the microscope slide onto the humified pipet box and apply 100 μl of BS3 Fixative Solution in a drop-by-drop fashion and repeat steps 5 and 6, one time. Proceed to steps 9 and 10 of Sect. 3.17.

28. Other inverted microscopes can be used.
29. Steps 1 to 7 of Sect. 3.20 should be done under a fume hood.
30. It is highly recommended that two coverslips are simultaneously prepared as one could break during the procedures described in Sect. 3.21.
31. Our laboratory always fixates with BS3 Fixative Solution for part 3 of CODEX for both FFPE and FF tissues.
32. Our "DAPI Exposure" time is set to 6.667.
33. We recommend capturing the images in odd numbered tiles such as 3 × 3 or 5 × 5. With these patterns, a middle tile is always created and ultimately used to find the best focal plane in the z-stack associated with the DAPI channel.
34. The z-stack number typically ranges from 7 to 21. We recommend using only odd numbers.
35. The computer will automatically switch between different windows for around 60 seconds during the microscope configuration process. Do not click on anything as this is going on.
36. One cycle typically takes around 90 to 120 min. Also, the canisters attached to the PhenoCycler must be monitored. If the multicycle reaction is running for a long time (>1 week), the waste container can overflow, or a different canister can run out of reagent. Make sure to either monitor the canisters or simply split the CODEX Panel in half to perform two different multicycle reactions.
37. We highly recommend purchasing a new Stage Assembly for the H&E stain and not using the same equipment used during the multicycle run.
38. We currently use CRISP in our laboratory. Please visit https://github.com/will-yx for information on how to install and run CRISP.
39. The blue Alexa488 channel works better with FF tissue than FFPE tissue.
40. If it is later discovered that the morphology of the tissue is of poor quality, then try incubating the cryomold with liquid nitrogen. First, put a metal block into an isothermal transport vessel and then carefully pour liquid nitrogen inside. Make sure the metal block is not completely submerged in liquid nitrogen. Once the tissue is placed in the cryomold with OCT compound, put the mold on top of the metal block, seal the vessel, and let it incubate for 5 min. This promotes

faster freezing and better tissue morphology. Both the cryostat chamber and holder temperatures are lowered to −16°C as well during this process. Fresh-frozen tissue is infectious. Please section with caution.

41. When working with FF tissue, BC4 is removed from the blocking solution only in part 2 of CODEX. BC4 is reintroduced into the blocking solution in part 3 of CODEX.

Conflicts of Interest

C.M.S. is a cofounder and shareholder of Vicinity Bio GmbH, and is a scientific advisor to and has received research funding from Enable Medicine Inc. The other authors declare that no competing interests exist.

References

1. Schürch CM, Bhate SS, Barlow GL, Phillips DJ, Noti L, Zlobec I et al (2020) Coordinated cellular neighborhoods orchestrate antitumoral immunity at the colorectal cancer invasive front. Cell 182:1341–1359
2. Kennedy-Darling J, Bhate SS, Hickey JW, Black S, Barlow GL, Vazquez G et al (2021) Highly multiplexed tissue imaging using repeated oligonucleotide exchange reaction. Eur J Immunol 51:1262–1277
3. Black S, Phillips D, Hickey JW, Kennedy-Darling J, Venkataraaman VG, Samusik N et al (2021) CODEX multiplexed tissue imaging with DNA-conjugated antibodies. Nat Protoc 16:3802–3835
4. Phillips D, Schürch CM, Khodadoust MS, Kim YH, Nolan GP, Jiang S (2021) Highly multiplexed phenotyping of immunoregulatory proteins in the tumor microenvironment by CODEX tissue imaging. Front Immunol 12:687673
5. Mayer AT, Holman DR, Sood A, Tandon U, Bhate SS, Bodapati S et al (2023) A tissue atlas of ulcerative colitis revealing evidence of sex-dependent differences in disease-driving inflammatory cell types and resistance to TNF inhibitor therapy. Sci Adv 9:eadd1166
6. John WH, Winston RB, Stephanie AN, Aaron H, Almudena Espin P, Roxanne C et al (2021) High resolution single cell maps reveals distinct cell organization and function across different regions of the human intestine. bioRxiv 2021:469203. https://doi.org/10.1101/2021.11.25.469203
7. Schürch CM (2022) Characterization of the tumor microenvironment by highly multiplexed microscopy. Pathologie (Heidelb) 43:21–24
8. Yu Xin W, Colin AH, James NH, Jasmin G, Mohsen A, Shiqi S et al (2022) A single cell spatial temporal atlas of skeletal muscle reveals cellular neighborhoods that orchestrate regeneration and become disrupted in aging. bioRxiv 2022:494732. https://doi.org/10.1101/2022.06.10.494732

Check for updates

Chapter 8

Mapping the Tumor Microenvironment with Integrative Single-Cell RNA Sequencing and Spatial Proteomics: Uncovering Mechanisms of Disease and Therapeutic Resistance

Ashley P. Tsang, Ahmed M. Elhossiny, Marina Pasca Di Magliano and Arvind Rao

Abstract

Understanding complex diseases such as cancer requires insight into both the intrinsic properties of individual cells and their interactions within the tumor microenvironment. Integrating single-cell RNA sequencing (scRNA-seq), which captures transcriptional states, with spatial proteomics, which provides spatially resolved protein expression data, offers a powerful opportunity to unravel disease mechanisms. In this protocol, we describe a framework that unifies scRNA-seq and spatial proteomics into a joint graph-based representation. This approach enables accurate prediction of disease pathologies and reveals critical cell–cell interactions that drive disease progression.

Keywords Spatial proteomics, Single-cell RNA sequencing, Multimodal integration, Deep learning, Cell–cell communication, Spatial statistics, Graph networks, Tumor microenvironment

1 Introduction

The tumor microenvironment (TME) is a spatially structured ecosystem of malignant, immune, and stromal cells, whose interactions drive tumor progression and therapy resistance. Understanding how these cells communicate within tissue architecture is essential to uncovering cancer mechanisms [1–3]. scRNA-seq captures transcriptional heterogeneity but lacks spatial resolution. Spatial proteomics—via technologies like multiplex immunofluorescence (mIF), imaging mass cytometry (IMC), and co-detection by indexing (CODEX) [4]—addresses this gap by measuring protein expression in situ at subcellular resolution [5]. Together, these modalities reveal both cell-intrinsic states and spatially organized signaling that underlie disease progression.

Timothy L. Frankel and Arvind Rao (eds.), *Cellular Spatial Characterization and Analysis*, Methods in Molecular Biology, vol. 2995,
https://doi.org/10.1007/978-1-0716-5027-1_8,

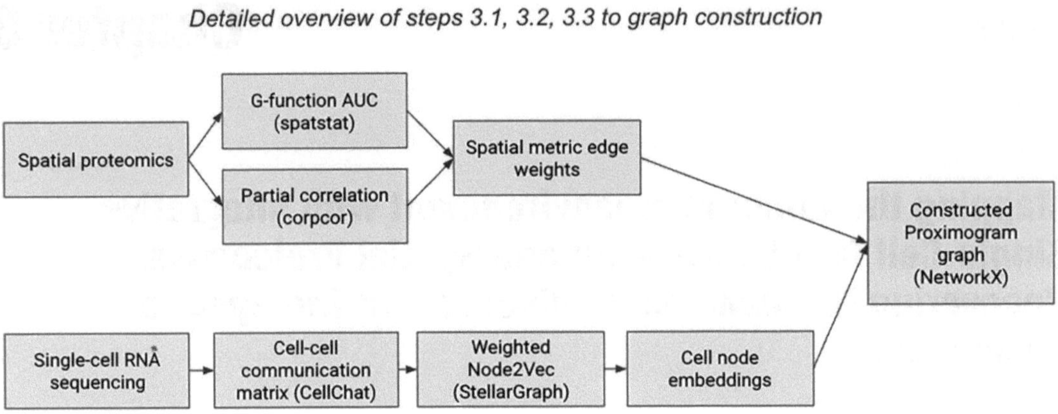

Fig. 1 Detailed framework overview of graph construction

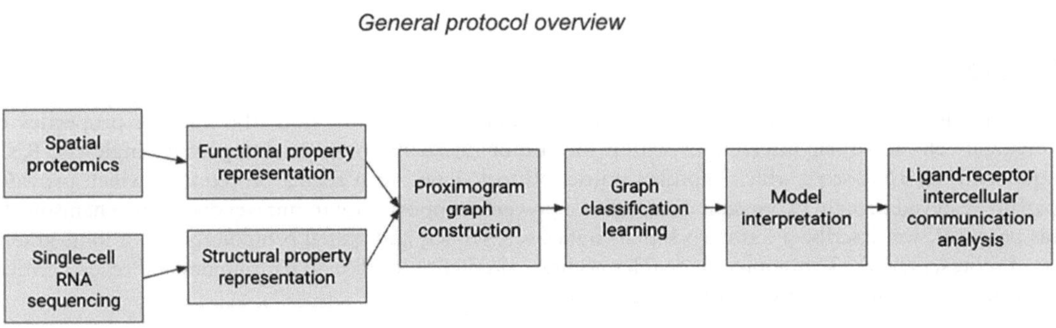

Fig. 2 General framework overview

To effectively integrate both structural and functional information from these complementary data, Proximogram models the TME as a graph where cells are nodes, spatial proximity defines edges, and molecular attributes such as cell signaling from scRNA-seq are encoded as node features [6]. Unlike traditional spatial statistics, Proximogram integrates spatial topology with molecular and phenotypic information, enabling multi-resolution analysis of cellular neighborhoods and their influence on signaling programs. In this protocol, we describe how to construct a unified graph from scRNA-seq and mIF data (Fig. 1) and detail the model training and interpretation steps used to identify cell–cell communication patterns linked to disease outcomes (Fig. 2).

2 Materials

2.1 Software

1. R: For spatial statistics and cell–cell communication analyses:
   (a) spatstat (https://spatstat.org/)
      (i) spatstat is an R package for conducting spatial statistical analyses [7].

(b) corpcor (https://cran.r-project.org/web/packages/corpcor/index.html)

(i) corpcor is an R package for the estimation of covariance and partial correlation [8].

(c) CellChat (https://github.com/jinworks/CellChat)

(i) CellChat is a tool for inference and analysis of intercellular communication [9].

(ii) Refer to the tutorial directory for detailed instructions and example input formats. You may also refer to the published protocol [10].

(d) LIANA (https://saezlab.github.io/liana/)

(i) LIANA is a tool for cell–cell communication inference [11].

(ii) Refer to the tutorial section for detailed instructions.

(e) NicheNet (https://github.com/saeyslab/nichenetr)

(i) NicheNet is a tool for predicting ligand–receptor links for interacting cells [12].

(ii) Refer to the tutorial section for detailed instructions.

2. Python: For graph construction, embedding, and classification:

(a) NetworkX (https://networkx.org/documentation/stable/index.html)

(i) NetworkX is a Python package for complex networks [13].

(b) StellarGraph (https://github.com/stellargraph/stellargraph)

(i) StellarGraph is a Python library for machine learning on graphs [14].

(ii) Refer to this tutorial for implementing weighted Node2Vec: https://stellargraph.readthedocs.io/en/v1.0.0rc1/demos/node-classification/node2vec/stellargraph-node2vec-weighted-random-walks.html

(iii) Refer to this tutorial for loading in NetworkX graphs: https://stellargraph.readthedocs.io/en/stable/demos/basics/loading-networkx.html

(iv) Refer to this tutorial for implementing and training a graph classification network (GCN): https://stellargraph.readthedocs.io/en/stable/demos/graph-classification/gcn-supervised-graph-classification.html

2.2 Datasets

1. Spatial proteomics dataset:

(a) This can originate from any spatial proteomics source (e.g., mIF, IMC) as long as the data matrix contains the following information: cell coordinates, cell type annotation, sample information.

(b) Samples should be labeled with a binary outcome (e.g., disease vs. control, subtype-A vs. subtype-B, responder vs. non-responder).

2. Single-cell RNA sequencing (scRNA-seq) dataset:

   (a) This should be pre-processed and annotated with cell types, overlapping with the cell types in the spatial proteomics dataset.

   (b) An example dataset can be found here: https://figshare.com/projects/Example_data_for_cell-cell_communication_analysis_using_CellChat/157272

3 Methods

3.1 Compute Cell Node Embeddings

1. Input scRNA-seq data into CellChat to infer a cell–cell communication probability matrix (*see* **Note 1**). Refer to Materials (2.1 Software, 1c) for detailed instructions and examples. The result is a communication probability matrix (P) and associated p-values (p_val).

2. To account for the significance of the communication scores, scale each pairwise communication probability using the transformation:
   For each pair of cell types (i, j):

```
scaled_score[i][j] = -log(p_val[i][j])
```

3. Symmetrize the matrix by computing the geometric mean of the directional communication probabilities for each cell–cell pair.
   For each pair of cell types (i, j):

```
symmetrized_score[i][j] = sqrt(scaled_score[i][j]
    * scaled_score[j][i])
```

4. Construct a cell–cell communication (CCC) graph using NetworkX (*see* **Note 2**), where:

   (a) Nodes are cell types.

   (b) Edges are weighted by the symmetrized communication probabilities computed above.

```
Initialize graph G
For each cell type:
     Add node to G
For each pair of cell types (i, j):
     Add weighted edge between node i and node j with
weight = symmetrized_score[i][j]
```

5. Generate cell node embeddings by applying a weighted Node2Vec model implemented in StellarGraph. Refer to the

tutorial in Materials (2.1 Software, 2b(ii)) for detailed instructions and examples.

```
rw = BiasedRandomWalk(G)
weighted_walks = rw.run(
 nodes=G.nodes(),
 length=walk_length,
 n=10,
 p=0.5,
 q=2.0,
 weighted=True,
 seed=42,
)
weighted_model = Word2Vec(
   weighted_walks, size=128, window=5, min_count=0,
sg=1, workers=1, iter=1
)
# extract embedding for a given "node_id"
emb = weighted_model.wv["node_id"]
```

These CCC node embeddings will be used as node features in the Proximogram model in subsequent steps.

3.2 Compute Cell Spatial Metrics

1. Using the spatial proteomics data input, compute the following cell spatial metrics across all combinations of cell type pairs:
   (a) Compute G-function area under the curve (AUC) using spatstat package. Refer to Materials (2.1 Software, 1a) for detailed instructions and examples.
   (b) Compute pairwise correlation using corpcor package. Refer to Materials (2.1 Software, 1b) for detailed instructions and examples.

```
 Input:
  spatial_proteomics_data (cell coordinates + cell
  type labels)
  cell_types = list of unique cell types
  R_distance = 30 # microns
Initialize:
  G_function_AUC_matrix
  correlation_matrix
For each sample:
  For each cell_type_A in cell_types:
    For each cell_type_B in cell_types:
      Subset coordinates for A and B
      Compute G-function between A and B up to
      R_distance
      Store AUC in G_function_AUC_matrix[A, B]
      Compute pairwise spatial correlation between
      A and B
      Store correlation in correlation_matrix[A, B]
Output:
 G_function_AUC_matrix
 Correlation_matrix
```

These metrics will be used as edge weights in the Proximogram model in subsequent steps.

2. Since G-function is not symmetric (i.e., G_function_AUC_matrix[A, B] ≠ G_function_AUC_matrix[B, A]), symmetrize the matrix by computing the geometric mean.
   For each pair of cell types (i, j):

```
G_function_AUC_matrix_sym[i][j] = sqrt(G_function_
AUC_matrix[i][j] * G_function_AUC_matrix[j][i])
```

3.3 Construct Proximogram Graphs

1. Use NetworkX to construct multigraphs (*see* **Notes 2 and 4**):
   (a) Nodes are unique cell types (*see* **Note 3**). Node features are the associated node embeddings computed as a result from Section 3.1.
   (b) Edges are undirected and are spatial metrics between the nodes/cell types. One edge is weighted by the G-function AUC, and the other edge is weighted by the pairwise correlation, computed as a result from Section 3.2.

```
G = nx.MultiGraph()
for cell_type in cell_types:
  G.add_node(cell_type, features=node_embeddings
  [cell_type])
for (type_a, type_b) in cell_type_pairs:
  G.add_edge(type_a, type_b, metric='G_AUC', weight=
  G_function_AUC_matrix_sym[type_a][type_b])
  G.add_edge(type_a, type_b, metric='Pcor', weight=
  Correlation_matrix[type_a][type_b])
```

3.4 Train Graphical Classification Network

1. Load the graph objects from NetworkX into StellarGraph (*see* **Notes 2 and 4**). Refer to the tutorial in Materials (2.1 Software, 2b(iii)) for detailed instructions and examples.

```
sg_graph = StellarGraph.from_networkx(G)
```

2. Use StellarGraph to train a supervised graph classification model. Refer to the tutorial in Materials (2.1 Software, 2b(iv)) for detailed instructions and examples (*see* **Note 5**).

```
model = GCNModel()
model.train(training_graphs, labels)
```

3. Report performance: accuracy, F1, precision, and recall.

```
metrics = model.evaluate(test_graphs, test_labels)
```

3.5 Edge Ablation Analysis

1. To determine the most influential edges/cell–cell interactions, iteratively remove one edge type (e.g., the (T-cell,Tumor) edge) (*see* **Note 6**). Retrain the model on the ablated graphs and compare performance metrics to baseline.

```
Input:
  graphs = list of proximogram graphs (one per
  sample)
  edges = list of all unique cell-type pairs (edges)
Initialize:
  results = empty list
```

```
For each edge in edges:
  Create a copy of graphs
  For each graph_copy in graphs:
    Remove edge from graph_copy
      Train the graph classification model on the
      modified graphs
      Evaluate model performance (accuracy, F1,
      precision, recall)
      Save evaluation metrics associated with the
      ablated edge to results

Output:
  results = list of tuples (edge, evaluation_metrics)
```

2. Identify edges whose removal most significantly reduces performance. These are the edges most influential on the model decision making and will be assessed in more detail in the next section.

```
# sort edges by performance impact (i.e., how much
performance drops when removed)
baseline_score = get_baseline_score() # e.g., per-
formance with all edges present
# compute performance drop for each edge
performance_drop = []
for edge_id, score in results:
  drop = baseline_score - score
  performance_drop.append((edge_id, drop))

# sort by highest performance drop
performance_drop.sort(key=lambda x: x[1], reverse=
True)

# Identify top N most impactful edges
top_N = 3
top_edges = performance_drop[:top_N]

Output:
      top_edges = list of top_edges with most
      significant impact on performance
```

3.6 Identify Ligand–Receptor Interactions

1. Use LIANA (LIgand–receptor ANalysis frAmework) to identify candidate ligand–receptor interactions. Refer to Materials (2.1 Software, 1d) for detailed instructions and examples.
   (a) LIANA aggregates ranks across multiple cell–cell communication inference methods to generate a robust consensus list of candidate interactions.
   (b) For downstream analysis, retain only ligand or receptor genes expressed in at least 10% of sender or receiver cell subpopulations, respectively.

```
liana_results <- run_liana(expression_data)
filtered_liana <- filter_by_expression(liana_results,
threshold=0.1)
```

2. Apply NicheNet to predict ligand–receptor pairs that are most likely responsible for driving the observed differential gene expression between two cell types of interest. Refer to Materials (2.1 Software, 1e) for instructions on running NicheNet.

```
nichenet_results <- run_nichenet(sender_expression,
receiver_expression)
```

3. Consider only the candidate ligands and receptors filtered in the previous step. Identify the intersection between:
   (a) The high-confidence ligand–receptor interactions ranked by LIANA, and
   (b) The ligand–receptor pairs functionally implicated by NicheNet.

```
prioritized_interactions <- intersect(filtered_
liana, nichenet_results)
```

This consensus set represents the prioritized sustained ligand–receptor interactions most likely involved in the cell–cell interaction influencing pathology.

4 Notes

1. CellChat does not have to be used; other tools such as CellCall [15] can also be used to generate the CCC matrix.
2. Graph construction can also be conducted in R if preferred, using the igraph package [16].
3. All graphs constructed should have the same number of nodes, which is the number of unique cell types across the entire dataset.
4. It is recommended to save the constructed graphs to a compatible file type (e.g., GraphML) to circumvent the need to reconstruct the graphs each time.
5. The model and training hyperparameters may need to be modified depending on the data you are working with. Some data/learning tasks may be more difficult than others, requiring hyperparameter tuning.
6. Retraining the model for every possible edge that is removed can be very time consuming, especially depending on the number of cell types in the dataset. To address this, consider focusing only on one/few cell types or several cell–cell pairs of interest.

Acknowledgment

This work was supported by NIH T32 GM141746 to A.P.T.

Conflict of Interest A.R. serves as a member for Voxel Analytics LLC and consults for Genophyll LLC, Tempus Inc, Telperian, and serves as faculty advisor to TCS Ltd. He also serves as an Affiliate Investigator for the Fred Hutch Cancr Center, and a Satish Dhawan Visiting Chair Professor at the Indian Institute of Science Bangalore, India. All other authors have no conflicts of interest to declare.

References

1. Yuan Y (2016) Spatial heterogeneity in the tumor microenvironment. Cold Spring Harb Perspect Med 6(8):a026583
2. Mi H, Ho WJ, Yarchoan M, Popel AS (2022) Multi-scale spatial analysis of the tumor microenvironment reveals features of cabozantinib and nivolumab efficacy in hepatocellular carcinoma. Front Immunol 13:892250
3. Hunter MV, Moncada R, Weiss JM, Yanai I, White RM (2021) Spatially resolved transcriptomics reveals the architecture of the tumor-microenvironment interface. Nat Commun 12(1):6278
4. Black S, Phillips D, Hickey JW, Kennedy-Darling J, Venkataraaman VG, Samusik N et al (2021) CODEX multiplexed tissue imaging with DNA-conjugated antibodies. Nat Protoc 16(8):3802–3835
5. Lundberg E, Borner GHH (2019) Spatial proteomics: a powerful discovery tool for cell biology. Nat Rev Mol Cell Biol 20(5):285–302
6. Krishnan SN, Ji S, Elhossiny AM, Rao A, Frankel TL, Rao A (2024) Proximogram—a multi omics network-based framework to capture tissue heterogeneity integrating single-cell omics and spatial profiling. Comput Biol Med 182:109082
7. Baddeley A, Rubak E, Turner R (2015) Spatial point patterns: methodology and applications with R, 1st ed. Chapman & Hall, New York
8. Schafer J, Opgen-Rhein R, Zuber V, Ahdesmaki M, Silva APD, Strimmer K (2021) corpcor: efficient estimation of covariance and (partial) correlation [Internet]. 2021 [cited 2025 May 2]. Available from: https://cran.r-project.org/web/packages/corpcor/index.html
9. Jin S, Guerrero-Juarez CF, Zhang L, Chang I, Ramos R, Kuan CH et al (2021) Inference and analysis of cell-cell communication using CellChat. Nat Commun 12(1):1088
10. Jin S, Plikus MV, Nie Q (2025) CellChat for systematic analysis of cell–cell communication from single-cell transcriptomics. Nat Protoc 20(1):180–219
11. Dimitrov D, Türei D, Garrido-Rodriguez M, Burmedi PL, Nagai JS, Boys C et al (2022) Comparison of methods and resources for cell-cell communication inference from single-cell RNA-Seq data. Nat Commun 13(1):3224
12. Browaeys R, Saelens W, Saeys Y (2020) NicheNet: modeling intercellular communication by linking ligands to target genes. Nat Methods 17(2):159–162
13. Hagberg AA, Schult DA, Swart PJ (2008) Exploring network structure, dynamics, and function using NetworkX. In Pasadena, California; 2008 [cited 2025 May 2]. pp 11–15. Available from: https://doi.curvenote.com/10.25080/TCWV9851
14. CSIRO's Data61 (2018) StellarGraph machine learning library [Internet]. GitHub; 2018 (GitHub Repository). Available from: https://github.com/stellargraph/stellargraph
15. Zhang Y, Liu T, Hu X, Wang M, Wang J, Zou B, Tan P, Cui T, Dou Y, Ning L et al (2021) CellCall: integrating paired ligand–receptor and transcription factor activities for cell–cell communication. Nucleic Acids Res 49(15):8520–8534
16. Csardi G, Nepusz T (2006) The igraph software package for complex network research. InterJournal. 2006; Complex Systems: 1695

Part III

Spatial Genomics

Check for updates

Chapter 9

Single-Molecule Fluorescence In Situ Hybridization (smFISH) for RNA Localization Relative to a DNA Locus in Bacteria

Juan Echeverry, Yu-Huan Wang and Sangjin Kim

Abstract

When studying the localization of RNA within a cell, it is important to probe RNA relative to a subcellular landmark, such as a gene locus (transcription site). In this chapter, we describe a single-molecule fluorescence in situ hybridization (smFISH) protocol for labeling target RNAs and their DNA loci in bacteria. This is a versatile protocol applicable to various genes and species, providing valuable insights into RNA localization in bacterial cells.

Keywords smFISH, DNA FISH, FROS, DNA loci, Bacteria, RNA localization

1 Introduction

Understanding the cellular mechanisms that regulate RNA metabolism requires a method for precise measurement of RNA copy number and their spatial distribution within a cell. Fluorescence in situ hybridization (FISH) is a powerful technique for these measurements in RNA research [1]. FISH is based on the hybridization of fluorescently labeled single-stranded oligonucleotides to the DNAs and RNAs of interest, enabling the visualization of specific nucleic acid sequences at their native locations within cells [2]. Here, we will use the term FISH to refer to the labeling of target RNA while DNA FISH refers to the labeling of target DNA [3]. Despite the limitation of FISH methods to fixed cells, they exhibit superior target specificity based on the sequence complementarity. Also, FISH can detect a single RNA molecule (single-molecule FISH or smFISH) [4, 5] suitable for measuring both low-copy and high-copy RNA species

Sangjin Kim designed the original protocol. Juan Echeverry detailed the protocol and generated scripts. Yu-Huan Wang optimized the analysis protocol. All authors read and approved the final version of the manuscript.

Timothy L. Frankel and Arvind Rao (eds.), *Cellular Spatial Characterization and Analysis*, Methods in Molecular Biology, vol. 2995, https://doi.org/10.1007/978-1-0716-5027-1_9,

[6–8]. FISH can be combined with super-resolution microscopy for higher spatial resolution beyond the diffraction limit of light [9, 10]. There are high-throughput implementations of FISH that allow the visualization of many gene transcripts from the same cells [11–14]. Different transcripts can be visualized simultaneously by using probes of spectrally distinct fluorophores [15] or successively from multiple rounds of hybridization and washing steps [11, 12]. Subregions of an mRNA can be distinguished by using spectrally distinct fluorophores for their probes to show the presence or absence of the subregions due to transcription elongation and mRNA degradation [16–19] or splicing in eukaryotic cells [20]. Unlike traditional bulk RNA analysis methods (e.g., Northern blot [21] or real-time PCR [22]), FISH is a single-cell method, providing cell-to-cell variations within a population.

In recent years, FISH has been widely used to study gene expression kinetics [16–19] and subcellular localization of RNAs in bacteria [23–28]. In a model bacterium, *Escherichia coli*, many mRNAs are expressed to an average copy number of less than 1 [7]. Therefore, the single-molecule sensitivity of FISH is critical for accurately counting the number of RNAs. Furthermore, the FISH technique has allowed researchers to view the complex organization of the bacterial transcriptome in cells. Based on the diffusion of RNA in the cytoplasm, RNAs were expected to be present at random locations within a cell [23, 29]. However, a study showed that several mRNAs in *Caulobacter crescentus* and *lacZ* mRNA in *E. coli* localize near the site of transcription [23]. Another study reported that *E. coli* mRNAs localize to where their encoded proteins localize for their cellular functions [24]. Later, a high-throughput super-resolution FISH study in *E. coli* showed that mRNAs encoding inner-membrane proteins localize near the membrane while other mRNAs are distributed in the cytoplasm [14, 27]. The extensive variations observed in mRNA localization have attracted considerable attention from the scientific community [30]. In eukaryotic cells, mRNA localization in distinct membrane-bound organelles is a well-established mechanism for spatially restricting protein synthesis [31]. However, in bacteria, the mechanisms and functional significance of mRNA localization are still being elucidated.

Considering the life cycle of an RNA from birth (transcription) to death (mRNA degradation), RNA can be present at the gene locus during transcription, before releasing for free diffusion (Fig. 1a). In FISH images, RNAs being transcribed (nascent RNAs) should exhibit colocalization with the DNA (Fig. 1a). In contrast, released RNAs are more likely to localize away from the gene locus [17] unless there are other mechanisms in play to keep the released transcripts near the locus [17, 23]. Marking a gene locus during FISH enables distinguishing nascent and released RNAs and measuring how far certain RNAs are from their site of transcription.

Previously, we published a smFISH protocol focusing on counting mRNAs in bacteria based on tiling probes and an array probe (Fig. 1b, c) [19]. In this chapter, we describe a FISH procedure to study

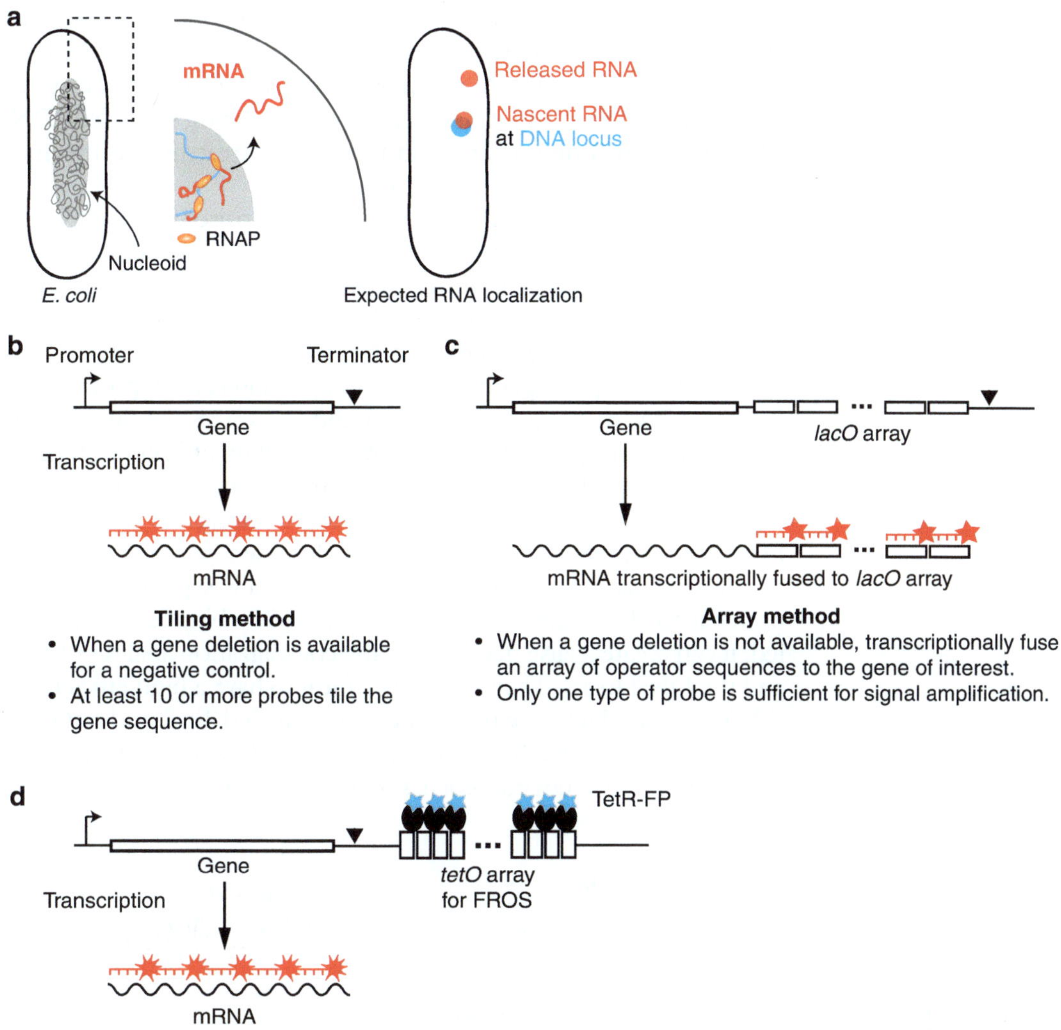

Fig. 1 Overview of FISH in bacteria. (**a**) Expected RNA localization relative to gene loci in bacterial cells. (**b**) and (**c**) Two different probe designs for smFISH in bacteria. (**d**) Gene loci labeling by FROS together with RNA FISH

mRNA localization relative to the transcription site. Chromosomal DNA loci can be visualized either by DNA FISH or fluorescence repressor-operator system (FROS), and the FISH procedure is modified accordingly to accommodate DNA labeling steps.

To perform DNA FISH together with smFISH, an additional step of heating the sample at 95°C is required to denature the DNA double helix at the beginning of the probe hybridization step [32]. DNA FISH probes may target the gene of interest itself or the region outside the gene via the tiling method (like RNA FISH shown in Fig. 1b). DNA FISH can also be done to an array of repeated sequences (Fig. 1c). In all cases, the probes should be designed to hybridize to the template strand of the DNA, so that they do not label transcripts.

Also, any potential antisense transcription should be checked to avoid labeling antisense transcripts. It is important to confirm that the DNA FISH signal is from DNA, not from any transcripts, by treating the sample with DNase and RNase after the last washing step. True DNA FISH signal will disappear upon the DNase treatment but remain unaffected upon the RNase treatment.

Although DNA FISH has been successfully paired with RNA FISH in bacteria [23], we prefer using the FROS method because of the guaranteed specificity and fewer steps to optimize and troubleshoot. FROS is based on fluorescently labeled repressor proteins bound to an array of its binding sites on the DNA (Fig. 1d) [33, 34]. Unlike DNA FISH, FROS requires genome engineering to insert the repressor binding sites close to the gene of interest and to express the fluorescently labeled repressor proteins. However, the labeling efficiency (% of loci visualized) is much higher than DNA FISH, as long as careful attention is made to minimize the loss of fluorescence during the fixation [35], hybridization, and washing steps. Example images are shown in Fig. 2.

A gene can exist in multiple copies (spatially separated) within a bacterial cell due to chromosome replication [36]. If not all loci are labeled, it can create a false negative for the colocalization analysis of RNA and the DNA locus. Therefore, it is critical to have a high efficiency of DNA labeling. Here, we use fluorescently labeled TetR and *tetO* array as an example of FROS for the chromosomal *lacZ* loci in *E. coli* (Figs. 1d and 2a). The same protocol has been applied to LacI-based FROS in

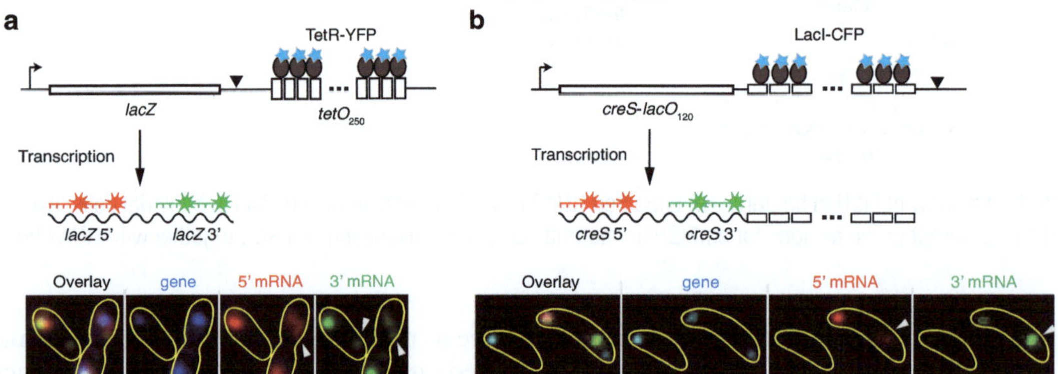

Fig. 2 Example images of FROS and FISH. (**a**) Visualization of *lacZ* mRNA and chromosome loci in *E. coli*. The 5' and 3' mRNA subregions were hybridized with 24 tiling probes labeled with Cy5 and Cy3B, respectively. DNA loci were marked with TetR-YFP bound to a *tetO* array. TetR-YFP was expressed from a pBAD plasmid. 0.02% arabinose was used for induction for 15 min, and cells were washed into fresh media to remove arabinose. *lacZ* mRNA was induced with 0.05 mM IPTG for 15 min before fixation. (**b**) Visualization of *creS* mRNA and chromosome loci in *C. crescentus*. The 5' and 3' mRNA subregions were hybridized with 18 tiling probes labeled with Cy5 and Cy3B, respectively. DNA loci were marked with LacI-CFP bound to a *lacO* array. LacI-CFP was expressed from the xylose locus on the chromosome and induced with 0.03% xylose for 1 h before fixation. In both cases, the majority of the mRNA signal co-localized with FROS (gene loci), with a few mRNA spots found outside the gene loci (white arrows). Scale bar = 1 μm

C. crescentus (Fig. 2b). We will explain strain engineering for FROS and a FISH procedure, which minimizes the loss of FROS signal at the end. Lastly, we will explain ways to analyze data for spatial localization within the cell coordinates. We will also comment on modifications needed for different species and genes in the Notes section.

2 Materials

2.1 Bacterial Cell Culture

1. A strain of interest with FROS capability (*see* **Note 1**).
2. A negative control strain for testing nonspecific binding of probes (*see* **Note 2**).
3. Growth media.

2.2 Fluorescent Probes

1. Unlabeled DNA oligonucleotides with a C6 amino modification at the 5' end.
2. Cy3B NHS ester and Cy5 NHS ester.
3. Cold ethanol.
4. 0.1 M sodium bicarbonate (pH 8.5). Prepare fresh right before usage.
5. 3 M sodium chloride.
6. RNase-free TE buffer: 10 mM Tris-HCl pH 8.0 with 1 mM EDTA.

2.3 smFISH

1. DEPC water: MilliQ water with 0.1% diethyl pyrocarbonate (DEPC). Mix DEPC with water and incubate the bottle (covered) at 37°C overnight and autoclave it the next day.
2. DEPC PBS: Dissolve 80 g NaCl, 2 g KCl, 14.2 g Na_2HPO_4, and 2.7 g NaH_2PO_4 in 1 L MilliQ water. Filter (0.22 μm) into a glass bottle and add 0.1% DEPC. Follow the process shown for the DEPC water. This is 10× stock, which should be diluted to 1×.
3. 4× formaldehyde fix: mix 5 ml of 20% formaldehyde with 0.75 ml of 1 M DEPC sodium phosphate buffer and 0.5 ml of DEPC water. Store at 4°C.
4. 70% ethanol.
5. Wash solution: 25% formamide and 2× saline-sodium citrate (SSC).
6. Prehybridization solution: 20% formamide, 2× SSC, 2 mM Vanadyl ribonucleoside complexes (VRC), 0.1% Bovine serum albumin (BSA).
7. Probe hybridization solution: 20% formamide, 2× SSC, 2 mM VRC, 0.1% BSA, 0.4 mg/ml *E. coli* tRNA, 10% dextran sulfate, fluorescent probes (*see* **Notes 3** and **4**).
8. Picodent silicone dental gum.

2.4 Coverslip and Glass Slide Preparation

1. Coverslips: 24 × 60 No. 1 or 22 × 50 No. 1.5.
2. Glass slides: 25.4 mm × 76.2 mm × 1 mm.
3. Ethanol.
4. MilliQ water.
5. 0.1% poly-l-lysine.
6. Hydrophobic marker.

2.5 Equipment

1. UV–vis spectrophotometer.
2. Refrigerated centrifuge.
3. Counter-top heat block.
4. Incubated shaker.
5. Incubator or oven for 30°C.
6. Vacuum aspirator.
7. Nitrogen gas.
8. Forceps.
9. Coplin jars.
10. Ultrasonic cleaner.
11. Pipettes and multichannel pipettes.
12. Reagent reservoir.
13. Empty pipette tip box.

2.6 Imaging and Analysis

1. Nikon Eclipse Ti-2 Epi-fluorescence microscope.
2. Nikon Phase-contrast 100× objective (Plan Apochromat NA 1.45).
3. SOLA-E fluorescence excitation source from Lumencor.
4. Hamamatsu ORCA II-ER CCD camera.
5. Filter sets for YFP, Cy3, and Cy5.
6. Nikon Elements software.
7. MATLAB.
8. Oufti (compiled version) [37].
9. U-Track (version 2.3) [38].

3 Methods

To avoid RNA degradation due to environmental RNase, wear gloves and wipe out the bench surface and apparatus (e.g., pipettes) with 70% ethanol before experiments. Use RNase-free plastic consumables and filtered pipette tips. Lastly, prepare solutions using DEPC water as much as possible.

3.1 Construction of a FROS Strain (Before FISH Experiments)

1. Amplify a *tetO* array with an antibiotic cassette by PCR from a template strain or a plasmid. The PCR primers should have 50 bp overhang, targeting the chromosome insertion site.
2. Integrate the *tetO* array into the chromosomal locus of interest via lambda red recombination method based on pKD46 plasmid [39].
3. Remove the antibiotic cassette by the Flp recombination based on pCP20 plasmid [40].
4. Transform the plasmid expressing TetR fused to a fluorescent protein (FP). To adjust the expression level of TetR-FP, use an inducible promoter. To reduce the unbound TetR-FP, which creates a high background signal, use a low-copy plasmid or insert the gene into the chromosome. Also, the FP should be chosen to be spectrally separated from organic dyes used for the FISH probes. We have used YFP or CFP for FROS together with Cy3 and Cy5 for FISH (Fig. 2).
5. Image the live cells and confirm that FROS signal is bright and cellular background is low. If the cellular background is high, TetR-FP expression should be lowered. To determine the cellular background, image a strain without any FP to judge the autofluorescence level under the same imaging condition.
6. Analyze the images and determine the number of FROS foci per cell. The distribution of the number of FROS foci in live cells serves as a benchmark for judging the loss of FROS signal over FISH procedure. Hence, imaging should be carefully performed using the same cell culture to be used for FISH.

3.2 Labeling of Probes (Before FISH Experiments)

1. Design probe sequences using Stellaris Probe Designer online tool in the Biosearchtech website.
2. Perform ethanol precipitation of DNA oligos to remove any impurities.
3. Dissolve the DNA oligos in MilliQ water to a final concentration of 1 mM.
4. Dissolve ~1 mg of dye in DMSO to a final concentration of 20 mM.
5. Mix 25 μl of freshly prepared 0.1 M sodium bicarbonate, 5 μl of 1 mM DNA, and 5 μl of dye stock in an Eppendorf tube. Cover the tube with aluminum foil to avoid exposure to light.
6. Incubate the mixture for 6 h at room temperature with gentle mixing.
7. Add 87.5 μl of cold 100% ethanol and 3.5 μl of 3 M sodium chloride to the mixture. Store the tube at −80°C for at least 30 min to overnight.
8. Centrifuge at 21 000 × *g* for 30 min at 4°C.

9. Remove the supernatant carefully using a pipette. Add cold ethanol and spin the tube again at 21 000 × *g* for 3 min at 4°C. Repeat this washing step three times and remove most of the ethanol by pipette.
10. Leave the tube open to dry the DNA pellet in the air. Ethanol will evaporate. Make sure to block light during this step.
11. Dissolve the pellet in DEPC water or DEPC TE buffer.
12. Check the labeling efficiency by comparing the absorption of the DNA (260 nm) and the conjugated dye. When the absorption is converted to molar concentration, the ratio of DNA to dye should be 1, indicating 100% labeling efficiency. If the efficiency is lower than 0.9, repeat the labeling reaction with a new dye stock. If the efficiency is higher than 1, repeat the ethanol precipitation. In either case, one can run additional purification such as denaturing polyacrylamide gel electrophoresis to separate the labeled and unlabeled DNA as well [41].

3.3 Preparation of the Bacterial Cell Cultures

1. Decide the strains to use for FISH. We always include a strain for negative control, which does not contain target sequences for the FISH probes (e.g., a gene deletion strain).
2. Inoculate colonies in a liquid medium of choice and grow overnight in a temperature-controlled shaker (220 rpm). Make sure to include appropriate antibiotics in case the strain includes plasmids.
3. Dilute the overnight culture with the fresh media of the same type at least 10^4 fold. Achieve the high dilution ratio by a serial dilution of 1/1000 and 1/100. Final volume can be 3 ml (in a culture tube) or 10–20 ml (in a flask), depending on the volume needed for FISH. Appropriate antibiotics should be included.
4. Shake the culture until the optical density at 600 nm becomes 0.2 for early exponential phase. During the growth, an inducer might be added to induce TetR-FP or to induce the gene of interest. Check the duration of induction.

3.4 Coverslip and Glass Slide Preparation (on the Day of FISH)

1. Use forceps to place coverslips and slides in a Coplin jar. Make sure that each coverslip and slide is separated from one another (*see* **Note 5**).
2. Fill the Coplin jar with 100% ethanol.
3. Place the jar in an ultrasonic cleaner and sonicate for 15–20 min.
4. Remove the ethanol into a waste container and rinse the jar three to four times with running MilliQ water.
5. Leave a little water in the jar and fill the rest with 100% ethanol (final ethanol concentration ~70%).
6. Repeat sonification (Step 3) and rinsing (Step 4).

7. Fill the jar with MilliQ water and perform sonication (Step 3).
8. Grab one cover slip or slide with forceps at a time. Apply nitrogen gas to the surface to remove any liquid. Store dried coverslips and slides in a clean covered plastic box, such as a pipette tip box. Slides will not be used until the end of the FISH protocol.
9. For dried coverslips, use a hydrophobic pen to draw circles on the glass surface. These circles serve as wells, in which individual samples will be applied (Fig. 3a). Wait 5–10 min for the ink to dry. This step should be done in a pipette tip box for 1 ml pipettes. If circles are drawn based on the circles in the plastic insert in the box, one can use a multichannel pipette to apply solutions to all wells simultaneously as the distance between wells matches the distance between tips in the multichannel pipette (Fig. 3b).

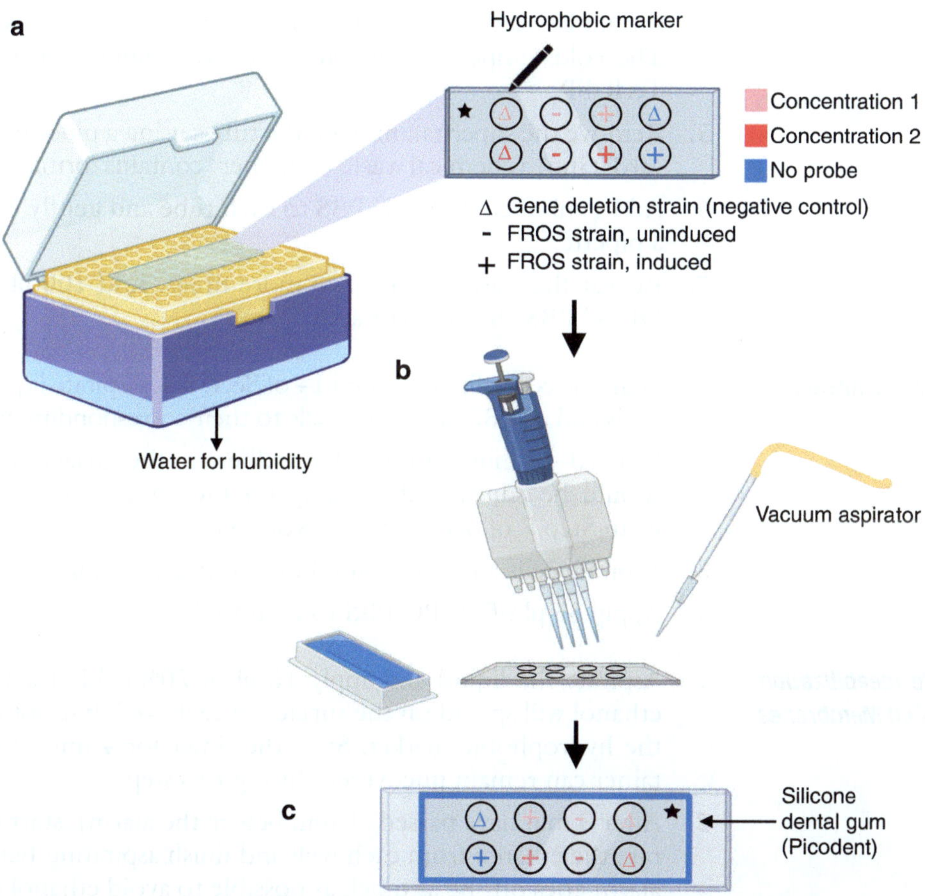

Fig. 3 Schematics of overall experimental procedure for smFISH. (**a**) Arrangement of wells on a cleaned coverslip. Wells are drawn with a hydrophobic marker. (**b**) Solution exchanges with a multi-channel pipette and a vacuum aspirator. (**c**) Mounting of the coverslip onto a cleaned glass slide and sealing with silicon dental gum

10. Apply 20 μl 0.1% poly-L-lysine to each well. If this volume does not cover the well area, apply a larger volume.
11. Wait 10 minutes and then aspirate the poly-L-lysine using a vacuum (*see* **Note 6**). A longer duration is also fine and does not affect the result.
12. Apply 20 μl DEPC water to each well.
13. Store in a closed environment to prevent evaporation.
14. Set aside until ready for use (*see* **Note 5**).

3.5 Cell Fixation and Washing

1. Prepare clean Eppendorf tubes with 300 μl of 4× fixatives.
2. Take 900 μl of cell culture and add it to the fixatives immediately. We do this right next to the shaker. There is no need to vortex or vigorously shake the tube.
3. Incubate at room temperature for 15 min and on ice for 30 min.
4. Centrifuge the tubes at 6500 g for 4 min at 4°C. The speed should be adjusted for different bacterial species (*see* **Note 7**). The cold temperature is critical to avoid fluorescence loss of TetR-FP.
5. Remove the supernatant from the tubes using a pipette and discard it into a chemical waste container (contains formaldehyde).
6. Add 1 ml of cold DEPC PBS to each tube and gently mix with a pipette.
7. Repeat the washing step two more times. Add 100 μl of cold DEPC PBS after the last spin.

3.6 Cell Adhesion

1. Grab the coverslip from Step 14 of Sect. 3.4. Aspirate liquid from wells and add 35 μl of fixed cells to their corresponding wells.
2. Wait 10–30 minutes for cells to adhere to the surface. The time should be adjusted depending on the concentration of cells from Step 7 of Sect. 3.5 (*see* **Note 8**).
3. Aspirate cells and remaining liquid using a vacuum.
4. Apply 35 μl of DEPC PBS to each well.

3.7 Permeabilization of the Cell Membranes

1. Aspirate the liquid and apply 15 μl of 70% cold ethanol. The ethanol will spread on the surface of each well, but not beyond the hydrophobic marker. Start the timer for 4 min. The container can remain uncovered during this step.
2. After 3 min have passed (1 min before the alarm), start to aspirate the ethanol from each well and finish aspirating before the alarm goes off. Be as quick as possible to avoid ethanol contact for more than 4 min. Also, leave the wells exposed to the air for one extra minute to completely dry the surface (*see* **Note 9**).
3. Add 35 μl of the wash solution to each well.

3.8 Prehybridization and Preparation of Hybridization Solution

1. Aspirate the liquid and apply 35 μl of the prehybridization solution to each well.
2. Cover the container and incubate at 30°C for 30 min. To provide humidity, add some water to the bottom of the container (Fig. 3a).
3. While waiting, prepare the hybridization solution and incubate it in a 37°C heat block until ready. Dextran sulfate is very viscous and requires a large orifice pipette tip (simply cut the end using a clean razor blade). Make sure the components are well mixed by gently pipetting up and down but avoid bubble formation. We also prepare no-probe control, which is simply the hybridization solution without any probes. For solutions with fluorescent probes, try to avoid light as much as possible.

3.9 Hybridization, Washing, and Mounting

1. Aspirate the prehybridization solution and add 25 μl of hybridization solution to each well.
2. Cover the container with aluminum foil and incubate at 30°C for 2 h (*see* **Note 10**).
3. Aspirate hybridization solutions. And apply the wash solution to each well.
4. Repeat aspiration and application of new wash solutions four times.
5. With the wash solution in each well, incubate the samples at 30°C for 15 min to help release nonspecifically bound probes to the wash solution.
6. Repeat the above Steps 4 and 5.
7. Repeat Step 4 only.
8. After removing the wash solution, apply 35 μl of DEPC PBS to each well.
9. Aspirate and apply 35 μl of DEPC PBS. Repeat this four times.
10. Leave 35 μl of DEPC PBS in each well until ready.
11. Have a cleaned glass slide ready from Step 8 in Sect. 3.4.
12. Aspirate PBS from each well and apply 3 μl of DEPC PBS to each well.
13. Grab the coverslip from a corner using forceps. Flip it upside down. Hold the coverslip at a 45-degree angle and gently place one edge onto the prepared slide. Slowly lower the other edge of the slide, allowing the PBS to spread and any air to escape.
14. Seal the edge of the coverslip with Picodent (Fig. 3c, *see* **Note 11**).
15. Store at 4°C until ready to image. We typically image the next 1–2 days.

3.10 Imaging

1. Turn on the widefield epifluorescence microscope and prepare imaging with filter sets needed for FROS and FISH labels. Example images are shown in Fig. 2.
2. Drop immersion oil in the middle of the sample and flip to mount on the inverted microscope. The star mark placed at the top left corner of the coverslip should now be oriented at the top left corner as well (Fig. 3a, c). Make sure the sample is flat on the stage. If the silicon seal prevents the sample from lying flat, use a razor blade to cut it out.
3. Raise the objective and find the focus in phase contrast.
4. Use the live mode of phase contrast imaging to look around each well.
5. Take images of regions with many cells. Manually raster scan in each well and try to avoid taking images from an adjacent area.
6. Try to take five to ten images for each well.
7. Save the images to a folder. The Nikon software saves files as nd2 format. Later, these files should be exported into TIFF images for each channel. Phase contrast and fluorescence images will be in separate TIFF files.
8. After imaging is done, the slide can be stored at −20°C.

3.11 Data Analysis

1. Sort image files. Phase contrast images from one well should be in one folder, and corresponding fluorescence images should be in another folder. Different fluorescence channels should be separated into folders (channel 1, channel 2, etc.). This process is done by a MATLAB script called FISHfilePrep.m.
2. Analyze cell meshes using Oufti (Fig. 4a):
   a. Run the compiled version of Oufti as Administrator. This version does not require MATLAB.
   b. Uncheck "stack" since we are loading individual TIFF images.
   c. Load phase contrast TIFF images by selecting the folder containing data of one well.
   d. Select "Independent frames" since we are looking at independent images instead of a time-lapse image.
   e. Select "Load parameters" to load the parameter file for cell detection analysis.
   f. Select "File" to set up the output file for cell detection analysis (test1.mat).
   g. Press "All frames" to run Oufti cell detection. The analysis details will show up in the command window.
   h. After the analysis is done, manually check the result and delete the erroneous detections.

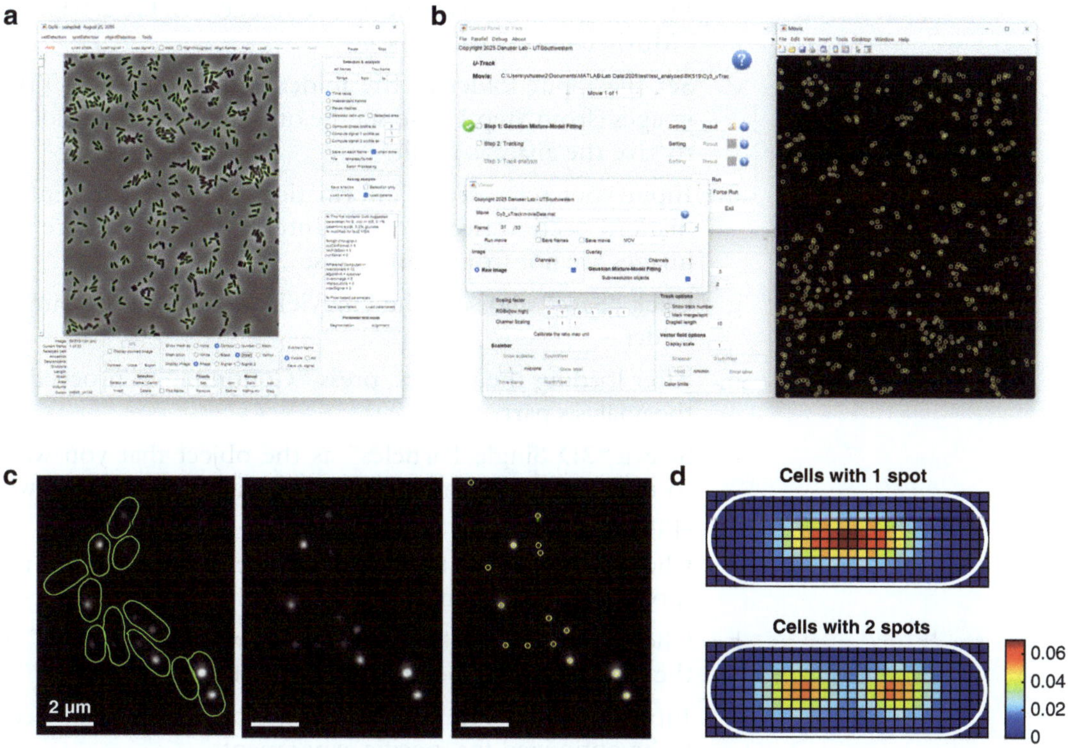

Fig. 4 Data analysis workflow and analysis result. (**a**) Cell detection from Oufti. (**b**) Spot detection from u-track. (**c**) A close-up view of a FISH image with analysis results. Left: with cell outlines from Oufti (green lines). Right: with spots identified by u-track (yellow circles). (**d**) 2D histogram (density heatmap) of spot localization in normalized cellular coordinates. The color represents the probability of finding a spot within a certain 2D bin location. The normalized localization was calculated in the first quartile and extended to the other three quartiles via mirror symmetry. The cell's short and long axes were divided into 10 and 30 bins, respectively. Cells with a single spot, likely due to having one gene copy (*top*), were separately analyzed from cells with two spots, possibly due to having two gene copies (*bottom*)

i. Rename the output file as "-mesh.mat" and select "Reuse meshes" and click "All Frames" to save the finalized result with parameters.

3. Identify spots in fluorescence images using u-track (Fig. 4b). This step requires MATLAB.

   a. Download "u-track" (version 2.3) from the GitHub site of DanuserLab/u-track and add the "u-track" folder and its subfolders into the MATLAB path.

   b. Change the directory to the folder that stores TIFF images.

   c. To launch u-track, enter "movieSelectorGUI" in the MATLAB command window. A GUI window "Movie Selection" will appear.

d. Press "New" to load the FISH images. A GUI window "Movie edition" will appear.

e. Set the input folder as the folder with fluorescent TIFF images (from Step 1) and set the output folder as the folder to save the analysis result.

f. Input your microscope information in the "Movie information" section (leave "Time Interval" as blank since the images are not from a time-lapse).

g. Click "Save" and save the "movieData.mat" in the output folder.

h. After loading the images, press "Continue" to proceed to the analysis part.

i. Select "2D Single Particles" as the object that you want to track. A GUI window "Control Panel – U-Track" will appear.

j. Click the "Setting" for "Step 1: Detection" to set up the spot detection parameters.

k. Choose the default "Gaussian Mixture-Model Fitting" as the detection method and click "Setting."

l. Input the following parameters (the parameters may need to be optimized for specific experiments).
   - Gaussian Standard Deviation: 1.28 pixels.
   - Alpha-value for Comparison with Local Background: 0.015 (The smaller the alpha value, the stricter the detection).

m. Click "Apply" to save the setup. The checkbox in front of "Step 1" will be automatically checked.

n. Click "Run" to launch the spot detection analysis. MATLAB command window is updated in real time while the program is running.

o. After the analysis is completed, click "Result" to check the analysis result.

p. Check the "Sub-resolution objects" to show the detected spots in each image. Optimize the detection parameters in Step 1 and repeat the analysis.

q. Click "Exit" to exit u-track.

r. Run the script "FISHdataAnalysis.m" to combine Oufti and u-track analysis results and perform further analysis, such as the subcellular position of spots (Fig. 4c, d and *see* **Note 12**).

4 Notes

1. Various FROS systems are available. In addition to TetR/*tetO*, LacR/*lacO* [33, 42] and MalI/*malO* [43] have been used to label gene loci in bacteria. For these, the intensity of the gene loci label is determined by the number of operator binding sites as well as the expression level of the repressor protein. Alternatively, ParB/*parS* requires a small insertion (~300 bp), but many ParB proteins can bind around the *parS* site [44, 45]. High fluorescence spot intensity can be achieved by increasing the expression level of ParB-FP. For all these methods, it is critical to have a high signal-to-background ratio in live cell imaging because the ratio may decrease during the FISH procedure. Excess free repressor proteins (excess compared to the number of binding sites) in the cytoplasm can create a high background in the FROS channel. Therefore, one needs to carefully adjust the expression level of FPs.
2. A negative control sample is from a strain lacking probe targets. In case the gene of interest is non-essential, its deletion mutant can be used [40]. If the gene is essential, one may knock down the gene expression by CRISPRi [46].
3. Prehybridization, hybridization and wash conditions can be optimized for each gene and probe sequences. We test 20–40% formamide and 5–50 nM probe concentrations (see Fig. 3a) to find an optimal condition based on the least non-specific binding in the negative control and the highest specific signal in the sample.
4. It is important to homogeneously mix the probes in the hybridization solution. Because the hybridization solution is viscous (due to dextran sulfate), one can employ up-down pipetting without creating bubbles to mix the solution (no vortex) and heating the hybridization solution in a 37–42°C heat block beforehand.
5. We recommend cleaning coverslips and glass slides on the day of the experiment. If they are cleaned and stored in water for too long (a few days), the surface becomes hydrophilic, and few cells remain adhered to the surface. Also, solutions spread over the boundary of wells created by the hydrophobic marker, creating cross-talk between wells.
6. Our protocol heavily relies on the vacuum aspirator to remove liquid from the coverslip surface. When the aspirator (glass pipette) is used, we make sure to use fresh pipette tips at the end and try to avoid any contamination between wells. We also keep the tip of the aspirator slightly above the coverslip

surface, primarily along the edge of each well, to avoid touching the center.

7. Different bacterial species may require different centrifugation speeds (Sect. 3.5). For example, 6500 × *g* is used for *E. coli*, and 4500 × *g* is used for *C. crescentus*.
8. It is important to have a good cell density in the well surface. If cells were lost during the washing step (Sect. 3.5), or if the surface adhesion was not long enough (Sect. 3.6), there can be fewer cells in the well, lowering the throughput. We recommend increasing the initial culture volume for fixation and concentrating them during the washing step (Sect. 3.5) to increase the concentration of cells. Also, the incubation can be extended to 1 h to increase the density.
9. The permeabilization of the cell membrane is extremely time sensitive. Allowing ethanol to be in contact with cells for more than 4 min leads to over-permeabilization, and cells will appear ghost-like in the phase contrast imaging. To be safe, we start the 4-min timer as soon as the first well is in contact with the ethanol. We start vacuuming the ethanol a minute before the 4-min timer is up, following the same order we applied the ethanol. Also, the surface should be completely dried. Otherwise, many cells appear floating or partially attached to the surface in the phase contrast images. The sample should be air-dried for 30–60 s before applying the next solution after the permeabilization.
10. It is well known that the fixation diminishes the intensity of the fluorescent proteins [35]. We have noticed that the formamide in the hybridization and washing steps has a similar effect. If the FROS signal does not look great after FISH, one can check the FROS signal after each step of the FISH procedure, by sealing the coverslip with a glass slide (i.e., jump to Step 12 in Sect. 3.9). We found that incubating the sample at 30°C, instead of 37°C, during prehybridization, hybridization, and washing helps to retain the FROS signal.
11. It is common to use a nail polisher to seal the coverslip [47]. We experienced that the fluorescence signal of Cy5 and Cy3B was much dimmer when the nail polisher was used for sealing [48]. The silicon-based dental sealant (Picodent) does not have this problem, and it is reversible. It can be cleanly removed using a razor blade and sealed again.
12. Representative images and smFISH analysis files are available for download from our GitHub site (https://github.com/sjkimlab/FISH2025).

Acknowledgments

We thank Dr. Christine Jacobs-Wagner and her lab members for various inputs on this method during its development. This work was supported by the NSF Center for Physics of Living Cells (1430124), NSF Science and Technology Center for Quantitative Cell Biology (2243257), and NIH (R35GM143203).

Conflict of Interest The authors have no conflicts of interest to declare that are relevant to the content of this chapter.

References

1. Singer RH, Ward DC (1982) Actin gene expression visualized in chicken muscle tissue culture by using in situ hybridization with a biotinated nucleotide analog. Proc Natl Acad Sci 79:7331–7335. https://doi.org/10.1073/pnas.79.23.7331
2. Young AP, Jackson DJ, Wyeth RC (2020) A technical review and guide to RNA fluorescence in situ hybridization. PeerJ 8:e8806. https://doi.org/10.7717/peerj.8806
3. Volpi EV, Bridger JM (2008) FISH glossary: an overview of the fluorescence in situ hybridization technique. BioTechniques 45:385–409. https://doi.org/10.2144/000112811
4. Femino AM, Fay FS, Fogarty K, Singer RH (1998) Visualization of single RNA transcripts in situ. Science 280:585–590. https://doi.org/10.1126/science.280.5363.585
5. Raj A, van den Bogaard P, Rifkin SA, van Oudenaarden A, Tyagi S (2008) Imaging individual mRNA molecules using multiple singly labeled probes. Nat Methods 5:877–879. https://doi.org/10.1038/nmeth.1253
6. So L, Ghosh A, Zong C, Sepúlveda LA, Segev R, Golding I (2011) General properties of transcriptional time series in *Escherichia coli*. Nat Genet 43:554–560. https://doi.org/10.1038/ng.821
7. Taniguchi Y, Choi PJ, Li G-W, Chen H, Babu M, Hearn J, Emili A, Xie XS (2010) Quantifying *E. coli* proteome and transcriptome with single-molecule sensitivity in single cells. Science 329:533–538. https://doi.org/10.1126/science.1188308
8. Jones DL, Brewster RC, Phillips R (2014) Promoter architecture dictates cell-to-cell variability in gene expression. Science 346:1533–1536. https://doi.org/10.1126/science.1255301
9. Beliveau BJ, Boettiger AN, Avendaño MS, Jungmann R, McCole RB, Joyce EF, Kim-Kiselak C, Bantignies F, Fonseka CY, Erceg J, Hannan MA, Hoang HG, Colognori D, Lee JT, Shih WM, Yin P, Zhuang X, Wu C (2015) Single-molecule super-resolution imaging of chromosomes and in situ haplotype visualization using oligopaint FISH probes. Nat Commun 6:7147. https://doi.org/10.1038/ncomms8147
10. Fei J, Singh D, Zhang Q, Park S, Balasubramanian D, Golding I, Vanderpool CK, Ha T (2015) Determination of in vivo target search kinetics of regulatory noncoding RNA. Science 347:1371–1374. https://doi.org/10.1126/science.1258849
11. Lubeck E, Coskun AF, Zhiyentayev T, Ahmad M, Cai L (2014) Single-cell in situ RNA profiling by sequential hybridization. Nat Methods 11:360–361. https://doi.org/10.1038/nmeth.2892
12. Eng C-HL, Lawson M, Zhu Q, Dries R, Koulena N, Takei Y, Yun J, Cronin C, Karp C, Yuan G-C, Cai L (2019) Transcriptome-scale super-resolved imaging in tissues by RNA seqFISH+. Nature 568:235–239. https://doi.org/10.1038/s41586-019-1049-y
13. Chen KH, Boettiger AN, Moffitt JR, Wang S, Zhuang X (2015) Spatially resolved, highly multiplexed RNA profiling in single cells. Science 348:aaa6090. https://doi.org/10.1126/science.aaa6090
14. Sarfatis A, Wang Y, Twumasi-Ankrah N, Moffitt JR (2025) Highly multiplexed spatial transcriptomics in bacteria. Science 387:eadr0932. https://doi.org/10.1126/science.adr0932
15. Lukumbuzya M, Schmid M, Pjevac P, Daims H (2019) A multicolor fluorescence in situ hybridization approach using an extended set of fluorophores to visualize microorganisms. Front Microbiol 10:1383. https://doi.org/10.3389/fmicb.2019.01383
16. Iyer S, Park BR, Kim M (2016) Absolute quantitative measurement of transcriptional kinetic

parameters in vivo. Nucleic Acids Res 44:e142. https://doi.org/10.1093/nar/gkw596
17. Wang M, Zhang J, Xu H, Golding I (2019) Measuring transcription at a single gene copy reveals hidden drivers of bacterial individuality. Nat Microbiol 4:2118–2127. https://doi.org/10.1038/s41564-019-0553-z
18. Kim S, Beltran B, Irnov I, Jacobs-Wagner C (2019) Long-distance cooperative and antagonistic RNA polymerase dynamics via DNA supercoiling. Cell 179:106–119. https://doi.org/10.1016/j.cell.2019.08.033
19. Kim S, Vaidya K (2020) Probing mRNA kinetics in space and time in *Escherichia coli* using two-color single-molecule fluorescence in situ hybridization. J Vis Exp 161:e61520. https://doi.org/10.3791/61520
20. Waks Z, Klein AM, Silver PA (2011) Cell-to-cell variability of alternative RNA splicing. Mol Syst Biol 7:506. https://doi.org/10.1038/msb.2011.32
21. Streit S, Michalski CW, Erkan M, Kleeff J, Friess H (2009) Northern blot analysis for detection and quantification of RNA in pancreatic cancer cells and tissues. Nat Protoc 4:37–43. https://doi.org/10.1038/nprot.2008.216
22. Nolan T, Hands RE, Bustin SA (2006) Quantification of mRNA using real-time RT-PCR. Nat Protoc 1:1559–1582. https://doi.org/10.1038/nprot.2006.236
23. Montero Llopis P, Jackson AF, Sliusarenko O, Surovtsev I, Heinritz J, Emonet T, Jacobs-Wagner C (2010) Spatial organization of the flow of genetic information in bacteria. Nature 466:77–81. https://doi.org/10.1038/nature09152
24. Nevo-Dinur K, Nussbaum-Shochat A, Ben-Yehuda S, Amster-Choder O (2011) Translation-independent localization of mRNA in *E. coli*. Science 331:1081–1084. https://doi.org/10.1126/science.1195691
25. Toran P, Smolina I, Driscoll H, Ding F, Sun Y, Cantor CR, Broude NE (2014) Labeling native bacterial RNA in live cells. Cell Res 24:894–897. https://doi.org/10.1038/cr.2014.47
26. Pilhofer M, Pavlekovic M, Lee NM, Ludwig W, Schleifer K-H (2009) Fluorescence in situ hybridization for intracellular localization of nifH mRNA. Syst Appl Microbiol 32:186–192. https://doi.org/10.1016/j.syapm.2008.12.007
27. Moffitt JR, Pandey S, Boettiger AN, Wang S, Zhuang X (2016) Spatial organization shapes the turnover of a bacterial transcriptome. eLife 5:e13065. https://doi.org/10.7554/eLife.13065
28. Dugar G, Svensson SL, Bischler T, Wäldchen S, Reinhardt R, Sauer M, Sharma CM (2016) The CsrA-FliW network controls polar localization of the dual-function flagellin mRNA in *Campylobacter jejuni*. Nat Commun 7:11667. https://doi.org/10.1038/ncomms11667
29. Golding I, Cox EC (2004) RNA dynamics in live *Escherichia coli* cells. Proc Natl Acad Sci 101:11310–11315. https://doi.org/10.1073/pnas.0404443101
30. Fei J, Sharma CM (2018) RNA localization in bacteria. Microbiol Spectr 6(5):10.1128/microbiolspec.rwr-0024-2018. https://doi.org/10.1128/microbiolspec.RWR-0024-2018
31. Chin A, Lécuyer E (2017) RNA localization: making its way to the center stage. Biochim Biophys Acta Gen Subj 1861:2956–2970. https://doi.org/10.1016/j.bbagen.2017.06.011
32. Jensen RB, Shapiro L (1999) The Caulobacter crescentus smc gene is required for cell cycle progression and chromosome segregation. Proc Natl Acad Sci 96:10661–10666. https://doi.org/10.1073/pnas.96.19.10661
33. Robinett CC, Straight A, Li G, Willhelm C, Sudlow G, Murray A, Belmont AS (1996) In vivo localization of DNA sequences and visualization of large-scale chromatin organization using lac operator/repressor recognition. J Cell Biol 135:1685–1700. https://doi.org/10.1083/jcb.135.6.1685
34. Viushkov VS, Lomov NA, Rubtsov MA, Vassetzky YS (2022) Visualizing the genome: experimental approaches for live-cell chromatin imaging. Cells 11:4086. https://doi.org/10.3390/cells11244086
35. Son JB, Kim S, Yang S, Ahn Y, Lee NK (2024) Analysis of fluorescent proteins for observing single gene locus in a live and fixed *Escherichia coli* cell. J Phys Chem B 128:6730–6741. https://doi.org/10.1021/acs.jpcb.4c01816
36. Klappenbach JA, Dunbar JM, Schmidt TM (2000) rRNA operon copy number reflects ecological strategies of bacteria. Appl Environ Microbiol 66:1328–1333. https://doi.org/10.1128/AEM.66.4.1328-1333.2000
37. Paintdakhi A, Parry B, Campos M, Irnov I, Elf J, Surovtsev I, Jacobs-Wagner C (2016) Oufti: an integrated software package for high-accuracy, high-throughput quantitative microscopy analysis. Mol Microbiol 99:767–777. https://doi.org/10.1111/mmi.13264
38. Jaqaman K, Loerke D, Mettlen M, Kuwata H, Grinstein S, Schmid SL, Danuser G (2008) Robust single-particle tracking in live-cell time-lapse sequences. Nat Methods 5:695–702. https://doi.org/10.1038/nmeth.1237
39. Sharan SK, Thomason LC, Kuznetsov SG, Court DL (2009) Recombineering: a homologous recombination-based method of genetic engineering. Nat Protoc 4:206–223. https://doi.org/10.1038/nprot.2008.227
40. Datsenko KA, Wanner BL (2000) One-step inactivation of chromosomal genes in *Escherichia coli* K-12 using PCR products. Proc

Natl Acad Sci 97:6640–6645. https://doi.org/10.1073/pnas.120163297
41. Joo C, Ha T (2012) Labeling DNA (or RNA) for single-molecule FRET. Cold Spring Harb Protoc 2012:pdb.prot071027. https://doi.org/10.1101/pdb.prot071027
42. Michaelis C, Ciosk R, Nasmyth K (1997) Cohesins: chromosomal proteins that prevent premature separation of sister chromatids. Cell 91:35–45. https://doi.org/10.1016/S0092-8674(01)80007-6
43. Wallden M, Fange D, Lundius EG, Baltekin Ö, Elf J (2016) The synchronization of replication and division cycles in individual *E. coli* cells. Cell 166:729–739. https://doi.org/10.1016/j.cell.2016.06.052
44. Rodionov O, Łobocka M, Yarmolinsky M (1999) Silencing of genes flanking the P1 plasmid centromere. Science 283:546–549. https://doi.org/10.1126/science.283.5401.546
45. Li Y, Sergueev K, Austin S (2002) The segregation of the *Escherichia coli* origin and terminus of replication. Mol Microbiol 46:985–996. https://doi.org/10.1046/j.1365-2958.2002.03234.x
46. Peters JM, Colavin A, Shi H, Czarny TL, Larson MH, Wong S, Hawkins JS, Lu CHS, Koo B-M, Marta E, Shiver AL, Whitehead EH, Weissman JS, Brown ED, Qi LS, Huang KC, Gross CA (2016) A comprehensive, CRISPR-based functional analysis of essential genes in bacteria. Cell 165:1493–1506. https://doi.org/10.1016/j.cell.2016.05.003
47. Donaldson JG (2015) Immunofluorescence staining. Curr Protoc Cell Biol 69:431–437. https://doi.org/10.1002/0471143030.cb0403s69
48. Raj A (2020) FAQ. In: Single molecule RNA FISH. https://sites.google.com/site/singlemoleculernafish/faq. Accessed 10 Mar 2025

Check for updates

Chapter 10

A Protocol for Spatial Transcriptomics Using the 10× Genomics Visium Platform

Jing Yi Lee, Bavani Kannan, Zhen Wei Neo, Vikneswari Rajasegaran, Jeffrey Chun Tat Lim, Joe Poh Sheng Yeong and Jason Yongsheng Chan

Abstract

Conventional transcriptomics analyzes a mixture of cells simultaneously either from tissue or single cells, for which the information on its in vivo or in situ position is lost. Although we can now perform cell type annotations for heterogenous samples using single-cell profiling, information on the spatially defined attributes that underpin the heterogeneous nature of the cells is lacking. Here, we describe a further optimized 10× Visium spatial transcriptomics protocol, a method that enables the deconvolution of heterogenous tissues while retaining its spatial information. The 10× Visium protocol allows the transcriptomic profiling of both fresh frozen and FFPE tissues while retaining their native spatial information. This protocol has wide potential applications to address the intricacies of the tumor microenvironment such as cellular interactions between the different tissue compartments and or with immune cells and elucidate how those interactions may contribute to tumorigenesis or disease progression. The 10× Visium spatial transcriptomics assay has been widely applied to study the spatial transcriptome of various tissue types across human and mouse samples such as lung, melanoma, and endometrial cancer to name a few. The entire protocol from tissue collection to final library preparation for fresh frozen samples takes about 5 days and for FFPE samples, about 3 days. Sequencing time ranges from 2 to 4 weeks and varies between different sequencing vendors.

Keywords Next generation sequencing, Spatial transcriptomics, Immunotherapy, Tumor microenvironment, Protocol

1 Introduction

The spatial distribution of unique cell populations within the tissue architecture contributes to the complexity of diseases such as cancer and their pathogenesis. Spatially resolved transcriptomics (SRT) has emerged as a valuable tool for comprehensively characterizing the intricate interplay between different cell types, biomolecules, and the microenvironment. This approach provides an opportunity for

The authors Jing Yi Lee and Bavani Kannan contributed equally.

Timothy L. Frankel and Arvind Rao (eds.), *Cellular Spatial Characterization and Analysis*, Methods in Molecular Biology, vol. 2995, https://doi.org/10.1007/978-1-0716-5027-1_10,

researchers to understand the heterogeneity inherent to tumor tissues [1–3], shedding light on their dynamic behavior and facilitating the identification of critical cellular interactions that drive tumorigenesis and disease progression [4].

An advantage of SRT over the conventional bulk transcriptomics is its ability to dissect the diverse cellular compositions and functional variations across different regions of a tissue with the use of on-site barcoding methods. By capturing the spatial organization of cells and the gene expression profiles unique to each tissue architectural compartment, researchers can potentially delineate the intricate network of cellular interactions, signaling pathways, and microenvironmental influences that contribute to tumor evolution and therapy resistance.

There are various spatial transcriptomics technologies available today, each with its own set of advantages and limitations. Here, we describe the methodology of 10× Visium, a technology which enables high-throughput spatial gene expression profiling at a near-single-cell resolution. Briefly, the 10× Visium technology entails a customized microscope slide that contains four capture regions (6.5× 6.5 mm) for mounting tissues (frozen or FFPE). Each capture region is printed with 4992 spots and each spot has a diameter of 55 μm that contains an array of DNA-based capture probes. Each capture probe contains a unique spot-specific spatial barcode, a unique molecular identifier as well as a poly (dT) tract that is used to capture mRNA containing poly (A) tail and potentially enables the profiling of the whole poly (dA)-tailed transcriptomes [5]. The workflow involves standard tissue-fixing for fresh frozen tissues and staining (hematoxylin & eosin or immunofluorescence) that is followed by image capture. For fresh frozen Visium gene expression assay, the tissue is permeabilized to release the mRNAs that are then captured by the poly (dT) tract of the nearest capture probes. The captured mRNAs are then reverse transcribed to cDNAs that have both the unique spatial barcode that provides the "address" of where the mRNAs originate from, as well as the unique molecular barcode from the corresponding capture probes. The cDNA libraries can then be generated and sequenced by a standard NGS XE "Next generation sequencing (NGS)" workflow. The gene expression information obtained can be mapped to specific locations within the tissue by aligning the image captured earlier in the workflow to known spatial barcode information [6]. The FFPE Visium gene expression assay offers human and mouse probe panels against the whole transcriptome. The panels consist of probe pairs that hybridize to their target mRNA and are then ligated to one another. The mRNA is degraded via RNase treatment and tissue permeabilization, releasing the ligated probes. The ligated products are then captured by the oligos consisting of a spatial barcode present on the Capture Area followed by library preparation and sequencing. By combining histological imaging with spatially barcoded RNA sequencing, 10× Visium technology allows the simultaneous visualization of tissue morphology and the transcriptomic landscape, enabling the comprehensive mapping of cell types, their spatial distributions, and the associated gene expression patterns within the tissue microenvironment, at near single-cell resolution.

The ability to spatially resolve transcriptomics of complex tissue architectures has a profound impact on how we understand the tumor immune microenvironment and its implications on immune surveillance. In a recent study by Loh et al., spatial transcriptomics profiling of Asian head and neck angiosarcoma (AS-HN) demonstrated how angiosarcomas classified as immune-hot based on bulk tumor profiling may in fact carry most of the immune signals away from the tumor compartment whereas immune-cold tumors may contain hotspots of inflammation within the tumor compartment, which could have easily been masked in bulk tumor profiling [4]. This finding implies that bulk gene expression may not be sufficient in determining inflammation scores that have been used in prediction of response to immune checkpoint inhibitors in cancers such as non-small cell lung cancer (NSCLC). Spatial transcriptomic profiling can also be applied to identify and characterize different tumor clones to delineate their respective tumor-specific pathways. In a study by Hwang et al. comparing treatment-naïve and neoadjuvant-treated pancreatic ductal adenocarcinoma (PDAC) patients, they found that basal-like PDAC cells promoted more immune cell infiltration than the classical-like PDAC cells. Additionally, the immune cell infiltrates associated with basal-like PDAC cells were enriched for lymphoid cells and were distinct from those associated with classical-like PDAC cells that were enriched for macrophages. This suggested that employing treatment strategies specific to the type of PDAC cells would be more effective, such as immune checkpoint inhibitors for basal-like PDAC and myeloid-directed therapies for classical-like PDAC [7].

Therefore, by deciphering the spatial relationships between cells, unraveling the molecular cues governing cell–cell interactions, and elucidating the spatial organization of gene expression programs, spatial transcriptomics serves as a powerful tool for uncovering novel biomarkers, therapeutic targets, and spatially guided treatment strategies that hold promise for improving cancer diagnosis and therapy.

2 Materials

Note: Refer to 10× Genomics website for a full list of alternative consumables and reagents.

Refer to Tables 1–11 for consumables and reagents required for this assay.

Table 1
Plastics and equipment for use throughout assay

General plastics and equipment		
Plastic	**Brand/Cat. No.**	**Notes**
DNA LoBind Tubes, 1.5 ml	Eppendorf/2231000945	To be used for storage of cDNA and libraries
50 ml Sterile Polypropylene Centrifuge Tubes	–	Brand of choice
15 ml Sterile Polypropylene Centrifuge Tubes	–	Brand of choice
Slide Mailer	–	50 ml tube could be used as alternative
Tips LTS 1ML Filter RT-L1000FLR	Rainin/30389213	–
Tips LTS 200UL Filter RT-L200FLR	Rainin/30389240	–
Tips LTS 20UL Filter RT-L10FLR	Rainin/30389226	–
ART Barrier, Filtered, LR, Sterile, Hinged Rack 1000 μl	Thermo Scientific™/ 2079-05-HR	To be used with any pipette of choice other than Rainin. ART tips have been shown to have lower retention compared to Rainin in our experience
ART 200 tips, Filtered, Sterile, Hinged Rack	Thermo Scientific™/2069-HR	
ART 20P tips, Filtered, Sterile, Hinged Rack	Thermo Scientific™/ 2149P-HR	
ART 10 REACH, Filtered, LR, Sterile, Hinged Rack	Thermo Scientific™/2140-05-HR	
Equipment	**Brand/Cat. No.**	**Notes**
Pipet-Lite LTS Pipette L-2XLS+	Rainin/17014393	For use with Rainin tips
Pipet-Lite LTS Pipette L-10XLS+	Rainin/17014388	
Pipet-Lite LTS Pipette L-20XLS+	Rainin/17014392	
Pipet-Lite LTS Pipette L-200XLS+	Rainin/17014391	
Pipet-Lite LTS Pipette L-1000XLS+	Rainin/17014382	

Table 2
Fresh frozen: embedding and sectioning

Cryosectioning materials		
Reagents and materials	**Brand/Cat. No.**	**Notes**
Dry ice/liquid nitrogen	–	–
OCT Compound	Sakura/ #4583	Maintain upside-down at 4°C before use
Visium Tissue Optimization Slide kit	10× Genomics/PN-1000191	–
Visium Spatial Gene Expression Slide kit	10× Genomics/PN-1000188	–
RNAse Away Reagent	Invitrogen/#10328-011	–
Absolute ethanol	Chemtech/H/G ETHANOL 99.9%	–
Glycerol	Merck/G5516-100ML	–
Equipment	**Brand/Cat. No.**	**Notes**
Cryovials	Fraction Technologies/CryoELITE Tissue Vials	–
Cryomolds – Disposable Base Molds (15 × 15 × 5 mm)	Electron Microscopy Sciences/ #62352-15	–
Microtome blade	Leica 818 High Profile/Microtome Blades	–
Microscope Slides	Thermo Scientific/AGAA000001##12E	For H&E QC
Autoclaved forceps	–	–
Cryostat	Leica/CM3050 S	–

Table 3
Fresh frozen: hemotoxylin and eosin staining

H&E staining materials		
Reagents and materials	**Brand/Cat. No.**	**Notes**
Methanol	Millipore Sigma/34860	Maintain fresh aliquots for assay at −20°C for at least 30 min
2-Propanol (Isopropanol), ≥99.5%	Millipore Sigma/l9516-25ML	–
Dako Mayer's Hematoxylin (Lillie's Modification)	Dako/S3309	–
Dako Eosin	Dako/CS701	–

(continued)

Table 3
continued

H&E staining materials		
Reagents and materials	**Brand/Cat. No.**	**Notes**
Dako Bluing Buffer	Dako/CS702	–
*Tris-Acetic Acid buffer (0.45M, pH 6.0)	–	Prepare ahead of time (see below for preparatory steps)
Milli-Q® EQ 7000 ultrapure water or equivalent	Millipore Sigma	–
KimWipes™ Delicate Task Wipes	Kimberly-Clark Professional™/34120	Preferred choice of laboratory wipe
Equipment	**Brand/Cat. No.**	**Notes**
Staining tray	–	–
Thermocycler Adaptor	10× Genomics	–
Bio-Rad T100 thermocycler	Bio-Rad/1861096	–
1 l glass beakers	–	Prepare four autoclaved glass beakers

*Preparation of Tris-Acetic Acid buffer (can be prepared beforehand and stored at room temperature):
1. Dissolve 11 g of Tris base in 100 ml nuclease-free water (NFW).
2. Adjust pH to 6.0 using 100% Acetic Acid.
3. Top volume up to 200 ml with NFW.
4. Filter through 0.2 μm filter unit.

Table 4
Fresh frozen/FFPE: coverslip mounting and imaging

Imaging materials		
Reagents and materials	**Brand/Cat. No.**	**Notes**
Microscope cover glass (24 × 50 mm)	Biomedia/BMH.880510	–
100% glycerol	Merck/G5516-100ML	–
Forceps	–	–
Absolute ethanol	Chemtech/H/G ETHANOL 99.9%	–
Equipment	**Brand/Cat. No.**	**Notes**
Imaging System	Carl Zeiss Axioscan 7 Microscope Slide Scanner	–

Table 5
Fresh frozen: tissue permeabilization optimization

Tissue permeabilization optimization materials		
Reagents and materials	**Brand/Cat. No.**	**Notes**
Visium Spatial Tissue Optimization Slide and Reagent Kit, 4 slides	10× Genomics/PN-1000193	–
SSC Buffer 20× Concentrate	Sigma-Aldrich/S66391L	–
Good quality RNA control	–	RIN ≥ 7, ≥500 ng/μl
Hydrochloric Acid Solution (HCl), 0.1N	Fisher Chemical/SA54-1	
Low TE Buffer (10 mM Tris-HCl pH 8.0, 0.1 mM EDTA)	Thermo Fisher Scientific/12090-015	–
Sodium Dodecyl Sulfate solution 10%	–	–
Visium Accessory Kit	10× Genomics/PN-1000194	–

Table 6
Fresh frozen: Visium gene expression assay

Visium gene expression assay materials		
Reagents and materials	**Brand/Cat. No.**	**Notes**
Visium Spatial Gene Expression Slide and Reagent Kit, 4 rxns	10× Genomics/PN-1000187	–
Nuclease-Free Water (NFW)	Invitrogen™/AM9932	–
MilliQ Water	Millipore Sigma	–
20× SSC Buffer	Sigma-Aldrich/S66391L	For preparation of 3× and 0.1× SSC. Mix well before using
SPRIselect Reagent Kit	Beckman Coulter/B23318	–
Ethyl Alcohol, Pure	Sigma	–
Buffer EB	Qiagen/19086	–
Potassium Hydroxide Solution, 8M	P4494-50ML	–
Tris 1M, pH 7.0, RNase-free	Thermo Fisher Scientific/AM9850G	–
KAPA SYBR FAST qPCR Master Mix	Millipore Sigma/KK4600	–
Agilent High Sensitivity DNA Kit	Agilent/5067-4626	–
Visium Accessory Kit	10× Genomics/PN-1000194	–
Equipment	**Brand/Cat. No.**	**Notes**
Real-Time qPCR System	Bio-Rad/CFX96 Real-time System	–
Bio-Rad T100 thermocycler	Bio-Rad/1861096	–
2100 Bioanalyzer Instrument	Agilent/G2939BA	–

Table 7
Fresh frozen: Visium spatial gene expression library construction

Visium spatial gene expression library construction materials		
Reagents and materials	**Brand/Cat. No.**	**Notes**
Library Construction Kit	10× Genomics/PN-1000190	–
Dual Index Kit TT Set A, 96 rxns	PN-1000215	–
Nuclease-free water (NFW)	Invitrogen™/AM9932	–
Buffer EB	Qiagen/19086	–
Visium Accessory Kit	10× Genomics/PN-1000194	–

Table 8
FFPE: tissue sectioning

Cryosectioning materials		
Reagents and materials	**Brand/Cat. No.**	**Notes**
Microscope slide	Thermo Scientific Mensel-Glaser AGAA000001##12E	For H&E QC
Microtome blade	Leica 818 High Profile Microtome Blades	–
RNAse Away Reagent	Invitrogen #10328-011	–
Absolute ethanol	Chemtech H/G ETHANOL 99.9%	–
Visium Spatial Gene Expression Slide	10× Genomics/2000233	–
Desiccant Drying Beads	–	–
Equipment	**Brand/Cat. No.**	**Notes**
Microtome	Leica RM2265	–
Leica Histocore Water Bath	Leica #140607020C0	–
Leica Histocore Slide Dryer	Leica#140607010C0	–
Histo-Tek Coolier Paraffin Block Cooling Plate	Histo-Tek REI-202	–
Room Temperature Water Bowl	–	Any container/dish can be used
Brightfield upright microscope	Olympus BX41	–
Biorad T100 Thermal cycler	Biorad #1861096	–

Table 9
FFPE: hemotoxylin and eosin staining

H&E staining materials		
Reagents and materials	**Brand/Cat. No.**	**Notes**
Xylene	Millipore Sigma/214736	–
Ethyl Alcohol, 200 Proof	Millipore Sigma/E7023	–
Dako Mayer's Hematoxylin (Lillie's Modification)	Dako/S3309	–
Eosin Y Solution (Modified Alcoholic)	Abcam/ab246824	Bottle should be replaced every 6 months to maintain quality
Dako Bluing Buffer	Dako/CS702	–
Hydrochloric Acid Solution (HCl), 0.1N	Fisher Chemical/ SA54-1	Or any equivalent HCl
Milli-Q® EQ 7000 ultrapure water or equivalent	Millipore Sigma	–
KimWipes™ Delicate Task Wipes	Kimberly-Clark Professional™/34120	Preferred choice of laboratory wipe
Equipment	**Brand/Cat. No.**	**Notes**
Staining tray	–	–
Thermocycler Adaptor	10× Genomics	–
Bio-Rad T100 thermocycler	Bio-Rad/1861096	–
1 l glass beakers	–	Prepare four autoclaved glass beakers

Table 10
FFPE: Visium gene expression assay

Visium gene expression assay materials		
Reagents and materials	**Brand/Cat. No.**	**Notes**
Visium Spatial for FFPE Gene Expression Kit, Human or Mouse transcriptome, 4 rxns	10× Genomics/PN-1000188 (Human) or PN-1000365 (Mouse)	–
Nuclease-Free Water (NFW)	Invitrogen™/AM9932	–
MilliQ Water	Millipore Sigma	–

(continued)

Table 10
continued

Visium gene expression assay materials		
Reagents and materials	**Brand/Cat. No.**	**Notes**
20× SSC Buffer	Sigma-Aldrich/S6639lL	For preparation of 2× SSC. Mix well before using
SPRIselect Reagent Kit	Beckman Coulter/B23318	–
Ethyl Alcohol, pure	Sigma	–
Buffer EB	Qiagen/19086	–
Potassium Hydroxide Solution, 8M	P4494-50ML	–
Tris 1M, pH 7.0, RNase-free	Thermo Fisher Scientific/AM9850G	–
KAPA SYBR FAST qPCR Master Mix	Millipore Sigma/KK4600	–
Agilent High Sensitivity DNA Kit	Agilent/5067-4626	–
Visium Accessory Kit	10× Genomics/PN-1000194	–
Equipment	**Brand/Cat. No.**	**Notes**
Real-Time qPCR System	Bio-Rad/CFX96 Real-time System	–
Bio-Rad T100 thermocycler	Bio-Rad/1861096	–
2100 Bioanalyzer Instrument	Agilent/G2939BA	–

Table 11
FFPE: Visium spatial gene expression library construction

Visium spatial gene expression library construction materials		
Reagents and materials	**Brand/Cat. No.**	**Notes**
Library Construction Kit	10× Genomics/PN-1000190	–
Dual Index Kit TT Set A, 96 rxns	PN-1000215	–
Nuclease-free water (NFW)	Invitrogen™/AM9932	–
Buffer EB	Qiagen/19086	–
Visium Accessory Kit	10× Genomics/PN-1000194	–

3 Procedure

3.1 Part I: Fresh Frozen

3.1.1 Tissue Cryosectioning and Section Placement: Equipment Listed in Table 2

1. Pre-chill cryostat to −20°C for at least 12 h.
2. Wipe inner surfaces of the cryostat including the stage, chuck holder, chucks, and all utensils with RNAse Away reagent, followed by 70% ethanol.
3. Place all utensils, cryomolds, and Visium Slides into the cryostat and allow them to equilibrate at −20°C for at least 30 min (*see* **Note 1**).
4. Place OCT compound bottle on ice to pre-chill for at least 15 min. Place in an inverted position.
5. Place cryovials containing tissue samples (from liquid nitrogen or in −80°C storage) in the cryostat to equilibrate for at least 30 min.
6. Label cryomolds with sample IDs.
7. Fill a cryomold with cold OCT compound just enough to cover the base and allow the OCT to begin freezing—i.e., when OCT starts to turn opaque. At this point, place tissue sample into the cryomold with a pair of clean forceps.
8. Immediately fill the cryomold with cold OCT to cover the entire tissue.
9. Immediately transfer the cryomold with the OCT-embedded tissue onto dry ice to speed up the freezing process. Allow the OCT-embedded tissue to freeze completely (OCT turns opaque completely).
10. Repeat Steps 6 to 9 for all samples (*see* **Note 2**).
11. Transfer cryomold containing OCT-embedded tissue from dry ice into the cryostat.
12. Invert cryomold and press down on its base to dislodge the OCT-embedded tissue block.
13. Apply OCT to a chuck just enough to cover its surface. Immediately place the OCT-embedded tissue block onto the chuck to let it adhere fully. A conductor may be used to help in leveling the block surface. Let the tissue chuck equilibrate for at least 30 min.
14. Place the chuck onto the chuck holder and lock firmly.
15. Load a new microtome blade into blade holder.
16. Proceed to trim the block until tissue is fully exposed. Trimming may be performed at thickness of the user's preference (*see* **Note 3**).

17. Using a microtome blade, carefully nick a 6 × 6 mm area of interest on the tissue block.
18. Proceed to section the tissue in a smooth and controlled motion at 10 μm using a clean part of the blade.
19. Using clean brushes, gently unroll to flatten the section when needed. Ensure that there are no folds, cracks or tears present on the sections.
20. Remove a Visium slide from its container and warm up a frame (capture area) by placing your finger on the underside of the slide beneath the frame. Keep the slide in the cryostat at all times.
21. Carefully place the section onto the frame, ensuring that the section, including its surrounding OCT, fits fully within the frame. Warm the underside of the frame again to allow the section to fully adhere to the slide (*see* **Note 4**).
22. Repeat Steps 11 to 21 until all fiducial frames on the Visium Slide are filled. Fill the frames in an orderly manner from the top to the bottom of the slide (*see* **Note 5**).
23. Place the completed Visium slide back into its container and store at −80°C. The slide can be stored for up to 2 weeks. Proceed to Visium Tissue Optimization or Gene Expression as soon as possible to avoid mRNA degradation.

3.1.2 H&E Staining: Equipment listed in Table 3

Before you begin—H&E staining			
Reagent/reagent kit	**10× PN**	**Prep and Handling**	**Storage**
Prepare and equilibrate to 37°C			
VISIUM slide adapter	3000380	Gently clean with an RNase decontamination solution of choice, then with 70% ethanol before placing into the thermocycler	–
Obtain			
Pre-chilled Methanol	–	Maintain fresh aliquot for assay at −20°C for at least 30 min.	−20°C
2-Propanol (Isopropanol), ≥99.5%	–	–	Ambient
Dako Mayer's Hematoxylin (Lillie's Modification)	–	–	Ambient
Dako Eosin	–	–	Ambient

Before you begin—H&E staining			
Reagent/reagent kit	**10× PN**	**Prep and Handling**	**Storage**
Dako Bluing Buffer	–	–	Ambient
Tris-Acetic Acid buffer (0.45 M, pH 6.0)	–	Prepared ahead of time. Check pH on the day of assay. Adjust to pH 6.0 if necessary	Ambient
Milli-Q® EQ 7000 ultrapure water or equivalent	–	–	Ambient
KimWipes™ Delicate Task Wipes	–	–	–
Staining tray	–	–	Ambient
Bio-Rad T100 thermocycler	–	–	–
50 ml Sterile Polypropylene Centrifuge Tube	–	Fill with 45 ml Milli-Q water.	Ambient
Four 1 l glass beakers	–	Fill each beaker with at least 600 ml Milli-Q water. Label 1–4	Ambient
Glycerol	Merck/G5516-100ML	–	Ambient

1. Pre-heat VISIUM slide adapter to 37°C for at least 10 min.
2. Remove VISIUM Gene Expression slide from dry ice containment and quickly transfer onto the VISIUM slide adapter. Incubate slide at 37°C for 1 min.
3. Remove slide and gently immerse into pre-chilled (*see* **Note 6**) methanol in falcon tube. Store in –20°C in an upright position for 30 min.
4. After 30 min, remove slide gently and wipe excess methanol off the back of the slide and the surrounding areas of the frames with a laboratory wipe.
5. Add 500 μl 2-propanol dropwise (*see* **Note** 7) to the slide and incubate 1 min.
6. Drain off excess 2-propanol and gently wipe the back of the slide with a laboratory wipe.
7. Air dry slide for not more than 5 min.
8. Add 1 ml Dako Hematoxylin dropwise to cover tissues. Incubate 7 min (*see* **Note 8**).
9. Prepare eosin mix:
   Add 900 μl Tris-Acetic Acid buffer (0.45 M, pH 6.0) to 100 μl Dako Eosin. Mix well by pipetting and maintain at room temperature until ready to be used.

10. Drain off excess hematoxylin into the tray and onto a laboratory wipe.
11. Dip slide into 50 ml falcon tube containing 45 ml MilliQ water, five times gently.
12. Dip slide into Beaker 1, 15 times gently and then into Beaker 2, 15 times gently. Drain off (*see* **Note 9**) excess water onto a laboratory wipe.
13. Add 1 ml Dako Bluing Buffer dropwise to cover the tissues. Incubate 2 min.
14. Drain off excess Bluing Buffer into the tray and onto a laboratory wipe.
15. Dip slide into Beaker 2, five times gently. Drain off (*see* **Note 10**) excess water onto a laboratory wipe.
16. Add 1 ml eosin mix dropwise to cover the tissues. Incubate 2 min (*see* **Note 11**).
17. Drain off the excess eosin mix into the tray and onto a laboratory wipe.
18. Dip the slide into Beaker 3, 10 times (*see* **Note 12**) gently. Drain off excess water onto a laboratory wipe.
19. Air-dry the slide until the tissues turn opaque. Place slide on the thermocycler adapter and incubate for 5 min at 37°C. Ensure that tissue is completely dry before proceeding to mounting step.

3.1.3 Tissue Imaging

1. Using a pipette with a wide-bore tip, gently pipette 150 μl 100% Glycerol onto the Visium Gene Expression Slide. Avoid introducing air bubbles (*see* **Note 13**). Ensure that the pipette tip does not come into direct contact with the slide.
2. Gently lower a coverslip over the Visium slide, starting from the bottom of the slide. Avoid pressing down on the slide.
3. Allow the glycerol to spread and cover the slide fully. Carefully wick excess glycerol off from the edges of the slide (*see* **Note 14**).
4. Secure the Visium slide onto a slide rack and load it into the slide scanner.
5. Scan the Visium Tissue Optimization Slides using the brightfield and TRITC fluorescent protocols, respectively, and Brightfield channel protocol for Visium Gene Expression Slides using an appropriate exposure time and settings.
6. Ensure that the tissue morphology and fiducial frames are sharp and clear in the scanned images.
7. For Visium Tissue Optimization Slides, assess the fluorescent images to select an appropriate tissue permeabilization timing with a good balance of strong signal intensity and clarity of tissue morphology (*see* **Note 15**).

3.1.4 Tissue Optimization Assay

Note: To be done after fixation, staining, and imaging

Before you begin—Permeabilization and cDNA synthesis			
Reagent/reagent kit	**10× PN**	**Prep and handling**	**Storage**
Prepare and equilibrate to 37°C			
♦ Permeabilization Enzyme	2000214	Centrifuge briefly and resuspend in 1.2 ml HCl (0.1N). Pipette mix, centrifuge briefly, verify no precipitate. Equilibrate to 37°C for 15 min prior to Step 3 of *Permeabilization.* **DO NOT** exceed 20 min of preheating. Permeabilization enzyme will be kept at 37°C throughout Steps 3–7 of *Permeabilization.* Store unused resuspended enzyme at −20°C **immediately** after Tissue Permeabilization. DO NOT freeze-thaw more than 3×. DO NOT keep at 37°C for extended periods	−20°C
Equilibrate to room temperature			
♦ RT Reagent C Minimize light exposure	2000215/ 2000377	Thaw, vortex, centrifuge briefly	−20°C
♦ Template Switch Oligo	3000228	Centrifuge briefly, resuspend in 80 μl Low TE Buffer. Vortex 15 s at maximum speed, centrifuge briefly, leave at room temperature for ≥30 min. After resuspension, store at −80°C	−20°C
♦ Reducing Agent B	2000087	Thaw, vortex, verify no precipitate, centrifuge briefly	−20°C
Place on ice			
♦ RT Enzyme D	2000216/ 2000227	Pipette mix, centrifuge briefly	−20°C

Before you begin—Permeabilization and cDNA synthesis			
Reagent/reagent kit	**10× PN**	**Prep and handling**	**Storage**
Obtain			
NFW	–	–	Ambient
20× SSC	–	For preparation of 3× and 0.1× SSC Shake well before using.	Ambient
Visium Slide Cassette	3000406	–	Ambient
Visium Slide Seals	3000279	–	Ambient
Low TE Buffer	–	–	–
Hydrochloric Acid Solution (HCl), 0.1N	–	–	–
Reference RNA	–	Human or mouse RNA, RIN ≥7, ≥500 ng/μl	−20°C
800 ml Glass Beaker	–	Ensure beaker is sterile	–

1. Prepare 600 ml 3× SSC buffer:
   Add 90 ml 20× SSC buffer to 510 ml MilliQ water in a clean glass beaker. Mix well.
2. Once imaging is complete, gently immerse slide in 3× SSC buffer and hold it still in a horizontal position until coverslip slides off.
3. Dip slide into 3× SSC buffer 15 times to wash any remaining glycerol off.
4. Wipe the back off the slide and any excess SSC buffer gently with a laboratory wipe before proceeding to tissue permeabilization step.
5. Assemble slide into Visium Slide Cassette.
6. Indicate the appropriate Permeabilization timings (min) on the cassette next to each well, the corners where there is no tissue (for easier pipetting), and the Positive and Negative controls as such:
   a. Positive Control well: Add 2 μl RNA (≥500 ng/μl) to the center of the dry well. DO NOT add Permeabilization Enzyme.
   b. Negative Control well: DO NOT add Permeabilization Enzyme.

3.1.5 Permeabilization

1. Prepare 0.1× SSC buffer (from 20× SSC buffer):
   Add 250 μl of 20× SSC buffer to 49.75 ml of MilliQ water in a 50 ml falcon tube. Mix well and keep at room temperature.

2. Place a Thermocycler Adaptor in the thermal cycler. Prepare a thermal cycler with the following incubation protocol and start the program.

Lid temperature: 37°C or 50°C	Reaction volume: 100 μl	Run time: N/A
Step	**Temperature**	**Time**
Pre-equilibrate	37°C	∞
Permeabilization	37°C	∞

3. Add 70 μl Permeabilization Enzyme along the side of the "30 min" well and tap cassette.
4. Apply Slide Seal to the Slide Cassette and place on the Thermocycler Adaptor at 37°C. Close lid and start the timer, counting down from 30 min.
5. After 6 min, remove the Slide Cassette from Thermocycler Adaptor and remove seal.
6. Add 70 μl Permeabilization Enzyme along the side of the well to "24 min" well, reapply the seal, and incubate on the Thermocycler Adaptor at 37°C with the lid closed.
7. Repeat process, working backwards to the shortest incubation time (3 min).
8. Remove Slide Cassette from the Thermocycler Adaptor after time course completion.
9. Using a pipette, remove reagents from each well except the positive control well without touching the tissue sections.
10. Add 100 μl 0.1x SSC to all wells except the positive control.

3.1.6 Fluorescent cDNA Synthesis

1. Prepare a thermal cycler with the following incubation protocol and start the program.

Lid temperature: 53°C	Reaction volume: 100 μl	Run time: 45 min
Step	**Temperature**	**Time**
Pre-equilibrate	53°C	∞
cDNA Synthesis	53°C	00:45:00
Hold	4°C	∞

2. Prepare Fluorescent RT Master Mix on ice. Pipette mix 10x and centrifuge briefly. Keep away from light and keep on ice.

RT master mix *Add reagents in order listed. Maintain on ice.*	10× PN	Volume/slide + 10% (μl)
Nuclease-free Water	–	221.8
♦ RT Reagent C Minimize light exposure	2000215/2000377	110.0
♦ Template Switch Oligo	3000228	30.8
♦ Reducing Agent B	2000087	8.8
♦ RT Enzyme D	2000216/2000227	68.6
Total	–	440

3. Using a pipette, remove 0.1× SSC from each well.
4. Add 50 μl Fluorescent RT Master Mix to each well, ensuring that the well surface is uniformly covered with the Master Mix.
5. Apply Slide Seal on the Slide Cassette firmly and place on the Thermocycler Adaptor on the pre-heated thermal cycler. Close thermal cycler lid.
6. Skip Pre-equilibrate to initiate cDNA Synthesis.

3.1.7 Tissue Removal

Before you begin—Permeabilization and cDNA synthesis			
Reagent/reagent kit	**10× PN**	**Prep & Handling**	**Storage**
Equilibrate to room temperature			
Tissue Removal Buffer	2000221/2000378	Pipette mix, verify no precipitate. If necessary, heat at 50°C for 5 min to remove precipitate	Ambient
Tissue Removal Enzyme	3000387	Vortex, centrifuge briefly	Ambient
Obtain			
Thermocycler Adaptor	3000380	–	Ambient
Slide Seals	3000279	–	Ambient
2× SSC/0.1%- SDS (can be prepared ahead of time)	-	See below. Pre-warm to 50°C for at least 30 min prior to step 16 of Tissue Removal. Store at room temperature	Ambient
0.2× SSC (can be prepared ahead of time)	-	See below	Ambient
0.1× SSC (can be prepared ahead of time)	-	Prepared in Step 1 of *Permeabilization*	Ambient

1. Prepare 2× SSC/0.1%-SDS. Invert to mix and pre-warm to 50°C in a water bath for at least 30 min prior to use.

2× SSC/0.1% SDS Pre-warm to 50°C for at least 30 min prior to step 2.1n. Store at room temperature	**Stock**	**Final**	**45 ml (2 slides)**
SSC	20×	2×	4.5 ml
SDS	10%	0.1%	450 μl
Water (Ultrapure/Milli-Q)	–	–	40.05 ml

2. Prepare 0.2× SSC buffer. Mix well and store at room temperature until ready to use.

0.2× SSC store at room temperature	**Stock**	**Final**	**45 mL (2 slides)**
SSC	20×	0.2×	4.5 ml
Water (Ultrapure/Milli-Q)	–	–	44.55 ml

3. Prepare a thermocycler with the following incubation protocol and start the program.

Lid temperature: 56°C	**Reaction volume: 100 μl**	**Run time: 60 min**
Step	**Temperature**	**Time**
Pre-equilibrate	53°C	∞
Tissue Removal	56°C	00:60:00
Hold	22°C	up to 24:00:00

4. Prepare Tissue Removal Mix. Pipette mix gently 10× (pipette set to 600 μl), centrifuge briefly, and maintain at room temperature (*see* **Note 16**).

Tissue removal mix ***Prepare Fresh. Add reagents in the order listed***	**10× PN**	**Volume/slide + 10% (μl)**
Tissue Removal Buffer	2000221/2000378	539
Tissue Removal Enzyme	3000387	77
Total	–	616

5. Remove the Slide Cassette from the Thermocycler Adaptor and place on a flat, clean work surface.
6. Remove the Slide Seal and using a pipette, remove Fluorescent RT Master Mix from the wells.
7. Add 100 μl 0.1× SSC to each well.
8. Using a pipette, remove 0.1× SSC from each well.
9. Add 70 μl Tissue Removal Mix to each well without introducing bubbles. Ensure uniform tissue coverage.
10. Apply Slide Seal on the Slide Cassette and place on the Thermocycler Adaptor. Close lid.
11. Skip Pre-equilibrate step to initiate Tissue Removal.
12. Dispense 45 ml 2× SSC-0.1% SDS in a 50-ml centrifuge tube and pre-warm to 50°C in a water bath or heat block for at least 30 min.
13. Dispense 45 ml 0.2× SSC, and 45 ml 0.1× SSC buffer in two separate 50-ml centrifuge tubes and maintain at room temperature.
14. At the end of incubation, remove the Slide Seal and using a pipette, remove Tissue Removal Mix from wells.
15. Remove the slide from the Slide Cassette.
16. Immerse the slide 15× in the pre-warmed 2× SSC-0.1% SDS.
17. Immerse the slide 15× in the 0.2× SSC.
18. Immerse the slide 15× in the 0.1× SSC.
19. Wipe the back of the slide with a laboratory wipe.
20. Centrifuge for 30 s in a slide spinner, or in a 50-ml centrifuge tube in a swinging bucket centrifuge. Spin at 250 rcf for 30 s. DO NOT exceed 250 rcf, as slides may break at higher speeds.
21. Verify that there is no remaining tissue (*see* **Note 17**) on the slide. Proceed to imaging.

3.1.8 Imaging

1. Follow Tissue Imaging protocol.

3.2 Visium Gene Expression Assay (GEX Assay)

Note: To be done after TO assay to determine the best optimal permeabilization timing for each tissue sample.

Before you begin—Permeabilization and reverse transcription			
Reagents and materials	**10× PN**	**Prep and handling**	**Storage**
Prepare and equilibrate to 37°C			
◆ Permeabilization Enzyme	2000214	Centrifuge briefly and resuspend in 1.2 ml HCl (0.1N), pipettemix, centrifuge briefly, verify no precipitate. Equilibrate to 37°C for 15 min prior to Step 2 of *Permeabilization*. DO NOT exceed 20 min of preheating. Permeabilization enzyme will be kept at 37°C throughout Steps 2–3 of *Permeabilization*. Store unused resuspended enzyme at −20°C immediately after Tissue Permeabilization. DO NOT freeze-thaw more than 3×. DO NOT keep at 37°C for extended periods.	−20°C
Equilibrate to room temperature			
◆ RT Reagent	2000086	Thaw, vortex, verify no precipitate, centrifuge briefly	−20°C
◆ Template Switch Oligo	3000228	Centrifuge briefly, resuspend in 80 μl Low TE Buffer. Vortex 15 s at maximum speed, centrifuge briefly, leave at room temperature for ≥30 min. After resuspension, store at −80°C	−20°C
◆ Reducing Agent B	2000087	Thaw, vortex, verify no precipitate, centrifuge briefly	−20°C
Place on ice			
◆ RT Enzyme D	2000216/2000227	Pipette mix, centrifuge briefly	−20°C
Obtain			
NFW	–	–	Ambient
0.1× SSC	–	Refer to Step 1 of TO: Permeabilization for protocol.	Ambient
Visium Slide Cassette and Gasket	2000281/2000282	–	Ambient
Visium Slide Seals	2000283/2000284/ 3000279	–	Ambient
Low TE Buffer	–	–	Ambient
Hydrochloric Acid Solution (HCl), 0.1N	–	–	Ambient

3.2.1 Permeabilization

1. After imaging, remove coverslip by performing Steps 1 to 5 in Tissue Optimization Assay protocol.
2. Set the thermocycler to the following:

Lid temperature: 37°C or 50°C	Reaction volume: 100 μl	Run time: N/A
Step	**Temperature**	**Time**
Hold	37°C	∞
Permeabilization	37°C	Determined by TO assay
Hold	4°C	∞

3. Add 70 μl to of pre-heated (*see* **Note 18**) Permeabilization (Perm) Enzyme to the corner of the well with the longest permeabilization duration (determined by TO assay).
   Example:
4. Gently tap to ensure the reagent evenly covers the tissues. Apply Visium seal, place on adapter in thermocycler. Incubate with lid closed for the pre-determined permeabilization time (refer to TO assay results). Start timer, counting down to the next Permeabilization Time.
5. Remove cassette from thermocycler and gently peel off seal. Repeat Steps 3 to 4 to the next well with the next longest permeabilization duration.
6. Repeat Steps 3 to 5 until Permeabilization Enzyme has been added to all 4 wells.
7. Once permeabilization is complete, remove Permeabilization Enyzme (*see* **Note 19**) from corner of each well and add 100 μl 0.1× SSC buffer.

3.2.2 Reverse Transcription

1. Prepare Reverse Transcription (RT) Master Mix on ice. Pipette mix 10×, centrifuge briefly and keep on ice.

RT master mix *Add reagents in order listed. Maintain on ice.*	10× PN	1× (μl)	4× + 10% (μl)
Nuclease-free Water	–	37.84	166.50
◆ RT Reagent	2000086	18.75	82.50
◆ Template Switch Oligo	3000228	5.22	23.00
◆ Reducing Agent B	2000087	1.50	6.60
◆ RT Enzyme D	2000216/2000227	11.69	51.40
Total	–	75.0	330.0

2. Set the thermocycler to the following:

Lid temperature: 53°C	Reaction volume: 100 μl	Run time: 45 min
Step	**Temperature**	**Time**
Hold	53°C	∞
RT	53°C	00:45:00
Hold	4°C	∞

3. Remove all 0.1× SSC buffer from the wells. Go in with a P10 pipette to remove any excess quickly.
4. Add 75 μl RT Master Mix to the corner of each well, gently tap to ensure tissues are evenly covered. Apply the seal, place the cassette into the thermocycler, close the lid and start incubation after skipping the hold step.

3.2.3 Second Strand Synthesis

Before you begin—Second strand synthesis			
Reagent/ reagent kit	**10× PN**	**Prep and handling**	**Storage**
Equilibrate to room temperature			
◆ Second Strand Reagent	2000219	Thaw, vortex, centrifuge briefly	−20°C
◆ Second Strand Primer	2000217	Thaw, vortex, centrifuge briefly	−20°C
Place on ice			
◆ Second Strand Enzyme	2000218/ 2000183	Pipette mix, centrifuge briefly	−20°C
Obtain			
NFW	–	–	Ambient
Qiagen Buffer EB	–	Manufacturer's recommendations	Ambient
Tris 1 M, pH 7.0 (Tris-HCl)	2000281/ 2000282	Manufacturer's recommendations	Ambient
Visium Slide Seals	2000283/ 2000284/ 3000279	–	Ambient
8 M KOH	–	Manufacturer's recommendations	Ambient

1. Prepare 0.08M KOH:
   Add 5 μl 8 M KOH (*see* **Note 20**) to 495 μl of NFW. Vortex to mix and centrifuge briefly. Maintain at room temperature until ready to use in Step 3.
2. Remove all RT Master Mix from the wells after RT incubation. Go in with a P10 pipette to remove any excess quickly.
3. Add 75 μl 0.08 M KOH to the corner of each well. Gently tap to ensure tissues are evenly covered. Incubate 5 min at room temperature.
4. Remove all 0.08 M KOH from the wells and add 100 μl Buffer EB to the corners of each well.
5. Prepare Second Strand Master Mix on ice. Vortex to mix, centrifuge briefly, and keep on ice.

Second strand mix ****Add reagents in order listed. Maintain on ice.***	**10× PN**	**1× (μl)**	**4× + 10% (μl)**
◆ Second Strand Reagent	2000219	69.5	305.8
◆ Second Strand Primer	2000217	4.0	17.6
◆ Second Strand Enzyme	2000218/ 2000183	1.50	6.60
Total	–	75.0	330.0

6. Set the thermocycler to the following:

Lid temperature: 65°C	**Reaction volume: 100 μl**	**Run time: 15 min**
Step	**Temperature**	**Time**
Hold	65°C	∞
Second strand synthesis	65°C	00:15:00
Hold	4°C	∞

7. Remove all EB buffer from the wells. Go in with a P10 pipette to remove any excess quickly.
8. Add 75 μl Second Strand Mix to the corner of each well, gently tap to ensure tissues are evenly covered. Apply the seal, place the cassette into the thermocycler, close the lid and start incubation after skipping the hold step.

3.2.4 Denaturation

1. Remove all Second Strand Master Mix from the wells after incubation. Go in with a P10 pipette to remove any excess quickly.
2. Add 100 μl Buffer EB to each well, then remove the Buffer EB from the wells.
3. Add 35 μl 0.08 M KOH to each well, gently tap to ensure tissues are evenly covered. Incubate 10 min.
4. Add 5 μl Tris (1 M, pH 7.0) to up to four tubes in an eight-tube strip.
5. After 10 min incubation, transfer ~35 μl sample from each well to a corresponding tube containing Tris.
6. Vortex to mix, briefly centrifuge and place on ice (*see* **Note 21**).

Before you begin—cDNA amplification and QC			
Reagents and materials	**10× PN**	**Prep and handling**	**Storage**
Equilibrate to room temperature			
♦ cDNA Primers	2000089	Thaw, vortex, centrifuge briefly	−20°C
Beckman Coulter SPRIselect Reagent	–	Manufacturer's recommendations	–
Agilent Bioanalyzer High Sensitivity kit	–	Manufacturer's recommendations	–
Place on ice			
KAPA SYBR FAST qPCR Master Mix *Minimize light exposure*	–	Vortex, centrifuge briefly	−20°C
♦ Amp Mix	2000047/2000103	Vortex, centrifuge briefly	−20°C
Obtain			
NFW	–	–	Ambient
Qiagen Buffer EB	–	Manufacturer's recommendations	Ambient
qPCR Plate	–	–	–
10× Magnetic Separator	230003	–	Ambient
80% Ethanol	–	Prepare fresh	Ambient
Special Equipment			
Real-Time qPCR system			

3.2.5 qPCR

1. Prepare qPCR Mix on ice. Vortex and centrifuge briefly, then maintain on ice and away from light.

qPCR mix ****Add reagents in order listed. Maintain on ice.***	**10× PN**	**Vol. for 5 rxn (+ 10%) (µl) *Includes 1 negative ctrl**	**Vol. for 9 rxn (+ 10%) (µl) *Includes 1 negative ctrl**
NFW	–	20.4	36.6
KAPA SYBR FAST qPCR Master Mix	–	27.5	49.5
♦ cDNA Primers	2000089	1.7	3.0
Total	–	49.6	89.1

1. Prepare a qPCR system with the following protocol:

Lid temperature: 105°C	**Reaction volume: 10 µl**	**Run time: 35 min**
Step	**Temperature**	**Time**
1	98°C	00:03:00
2	98°C	00:00:05
3	63°C (READ SIGNAL)	00:00:30
4	Go to Step 2, for 30 cycles (*see* **Note 22**) total	–

2. Add 1 µl sample to a qPCR plate. For negative control, add 1 µl of nuclease-free water in place of sample.
3. Add 9 µl qPCR Mix to each of the sample well and pipette mix. Seal plate and centrifuge briefly. Place the plate into the qPCR system and start the program.
4. Once the run is complete, record the Cq value of each sample:

   I. Ensure y-axis is on the linear scale.

   II. Enable the viewing of point values. Find the peak fluorescence value point value and calculate for 25% of it.

   III. Set the baseline threshold value as the value calculated in Step II and record the Cq Value for each sample (*see* **Note 23**).

3.2.6 cDNA Amplification

1. Prepare cDNA mix on ice. Vortex and centrifuge briefly, then maintain on ice.

cDNA amplification mix ***Add reagents in order listed.*** ***Maintain on ice.***	**10× PN**	**1× (μl)**	**4× + 10% (μl)**
◆ Amp Mix	2000047/2000103	50	220
◆ cDNA Primers	2000089	15	66
Total	–	65	286

2. Add 65 μl of cDNA amplification mix to the remaining ~35 μl of sample step 6 of *Denaturation*. Pipette mix 15×, with pipette set to 90 μl. Centrifuge briefly and maintain on ice until next step is ready.
3. Prepare thermocycler with the following protocol:

Lid temperature: 105°C	**Reaction volume: 100 μl**	**Run time: ~45–60 min**
Step	**Temperature**	**Time**
1	98°C	∞
2	98°C	00:03:00
3	98°C	00:00:15
4	63°C	00:00:20
5	72°C	00:01:00
6	Repeat Steps 3–5 for # of cycles determined by Cq Value.	
7	72°C	00:01:00
8	4°C	∞

4. Place samples in thermocycler when ready and skip Step 1 to initiate cDNA amplification.
5. If not proceeding to next step, store samples at 4°C for up to 72 h or at −20°C for up to 1 week.

3.2.7 cDNA Amplification Clean Up

1. Vortex to resuspend the SPRIselect reagent. Add 60 μl SPRIselect reagent (0.6×) to each sample (100 μl) and pipette mix 15× (pipette set to 150 μl) (*see* **Note 24**).
2. Incubate 5 min at room temperature.
3. Place on 10× magnet on HIGH for 1 min or until the solution clears.
4. Remove supernatant (*see* **Note 25**).
5. Add 200 μl 80% ethanol to the pellet. Wait 30 s. Remove the ethanol.

6. Repeat Step 5 for a total of 2 washes,
7. Centrifuge briefly and place on 10× magnet on LOW for 1 min or until the solution clears.
8. Remove any remaining ethanol with a P10 pipette and air dry for 2 min (*see* **Note 26**).
9. Remove tube strip from magnet and add 42.5 μl Buffer EB. Pipette mix 15× (pipette set to 40 μl).
10. Incubate 5 min at room temperature.
11. Place on 10× magnet on LOW for 1 min or until the solution clears.
12. Transfer 40 μl sample to a new tube strip.
13. If not proceeding to next step, store samples at 4°C for up to 72 h or at −20°C for up to 4 weeks in DNA LoBind tubes.

3.2.8 cDNA QC and Quantification

1. Run 1 μl of sample on an Agilent Bioanalyzer High Sensitivity chip.
2. Perform calculations for quantification as shown in the example below:

   I. Perform region gating with a range from 200 to 9000 bp and record concentration.

   II. Multiply the concentration with the dilution factor, and then divide by 1000 to obtain the cDNA concentration in ng/μl.

   III. For the total cDNA yield, multiple the value in II by the total volume of sample post-cleanup (40 μl).

   Example:

3.3 Library Construction

3.3.1 Fragmentation, End Repair, and A-tailing

Before you begin—Library construction			
Reagent/reagent kit	**10× PN**	**Prep and handling**	**Storage**
Equilibrate to room temperature			
♦ Fragmentation Buffer	2000091	Vortex, verify no precipitate, centrifuge briefly	−20°C
♦ Adaptor Oligos	2000094	Vortex, centrifuge briefly	−20°C
♦ Ligation Buffer	2000092	Vortex, verify no precipitate, centrifuge briefly.	−20°C
Dual Index Plate TT Set A	3000431	–	−20°C
Beckman Coulter SPRIselect Reagent	–	Manufacturer's recommendations	–

Before you begin—Library construction			
Reagent/reagent kit	**10× PN**	**Prep and handling**	**Storage**
Agilent Bioanalyzer High Sensitivity kit	–	Manufacturer's recommendations	–
Place on ice			
♦ Fragmentation Enzyme	2000090/ 2000104	Pipette mix, centrifuge briefly before using	−20°C
♦ DNA Ligase	220110/ 220131	Pipette mix, centrifuge briefly before using	−20°C
♦ Amp Mix	2000047/ 2000103	Vortex, centrifuge briefly.	−20°C
Obtain			
Qiagen Buffer EB	–	Manufacturer's recommendations	Ambient
10× Magnetic Separator	230003	–	Ambient
80% Ethanol	–	Prepare fresh	Ambient

1. Prepare thermocycler with the following protocol:

Lid temperature: 65°C	Reaction volume: 50 μl	Run time: ~35 min
Step	**Temperature**	**Time**
Hold	4°C	∞
Fragmentation	32°C	00:05:00
End Repair and A-tailing	65°C	00:30:00
Hold	4°C	∞

2. Prepare Fragmentation Mix on ice. Pipette mix and centrifuge briefly and maintain on ice.

Fragmentation mix ****Add reagents in order listed. Maintain on ice.***	**10× PN**	**1× (μl)**	**4× + 10% (μl)**
♦ Fragmentation Buffer	2000091	5	22
♦ Fragmentation Enzyme	2000090/ 2000104	10	44
Total	–	15	66

3. Transfer 10 μl of purified cDNA sample to a clean tube strip and maintain on ice. Top up with 25 μl Buffer EB for each sample (*see* **Note 27**).
4. Add 15 μl Fragmentation Mix to each sample and pipette mix 15× (pipette set to 35 μl) on ice. Centrifuge briefly.
5. Transfer strip into the pre-cooled thermocycler and skip Hold Step to initiate Fragmentation.

3.3.2 Post–Fragmentation, End Repair, and A-tailing Double Sized Size Selection

1. Vortex to resuspend the SPRIselect reagent. Add 30 μl SPRIselect reagent (0.6×) to each sample (50 μl) and pipette mix 15× (pipette set to 75 μl) (*see* **Note 28**).
2. Incubate 5 min at room temperature.
3. Place on 10× magnet on HIGH for 1 min or until the solution clears. KEEP supernatant.
4. Transfer 75 μl supernatant to a new tube strip.
5. Vortex to resuspend SPRIselect reagent. Add 10 μl SPRIselect reagent (0.8×) to each sample. Pipette mix 15× (pipette set to 80 μl).
6. Incubate 5 min at room temperature.
7. Place on 10× magnet on HIGH for 1 min or until the solution clears.
8. Remove 80 μl supernatant and retain the beads (*see* **Note 29**).
9. Add 125 μl 80% ethanol to the pellet. Wait 30 s. Remove the ethanol.
10. Repeat Step 9 for a total of 2 washes.
11. Centrifuge briefly and place on 10× magnet on LOW for 1 min or until the solution clears.
12. Remove any remaining ethanol with a P10 pipette and air dry (*see* **Note 30**).
13. Remove from the magnet and add 52.5 μl Buffer EB to each sample. Pipette mix 15× (pipette set to 50 μl).
14. Incubate 5 min at room temperature.
15. Place on 10× magnet on HIGH for 1 min or until the solution clears.
16. Transfer 50 μl sample to a new tube strip.

3.3.3 Adapter Ligation and Cleanup

1. Prepare Adaptor Ligation Mix. Pipette mix and centrifuge briefly.

Adaptor ligation mix **Add reagents in order listed.*	**10× PN**	**1× (μl)**	**4× + 10% (μl)**
◆ Ligation Buffer	2000092	20	88
◆ DNA Ligase	220110/2000094	10	44
◆ Adaptor Oligos	2000094	20	88
Total	–	50	220

2. Add 50 μl Adaptor Ligation Mix to 50 μl sample. Pipette mix 15× (pipette set to 90 μl). Centrifuge briefly.
3. Prepare thermocycler with the following protocol:

Lid temperature: 30°C	**Reaction volume: 100 μl**	**Run time: 15 min**
Step	**Temperature**	**Time**
Hold	20°C	∞
Ligation	20°C	00:15:00
Hold	4°C	∞

4. Transfer strip into the thermocycler and skip Hold Step to initiate Ligation (*see* **Note 31**).
5. Vortex to resuspend SPRIselect Reagent. Add 80 μl SPRIselect Reagent (0.8×) to each sample. Pipette mix 15× (pipette set to 150 μl).
6. Incubate 5 min at room temperature.
7. Place on 10× magnet on HIGH for 1 min or until the solution clears.
8. Remove supernatant (*see* **Note 32**).
9. Add 200 μl 80% ethanol to the pellet. Wait 30 s. Remove the ethanol.
10. Repeat Step 5 for a total of two washes,
11. Centrifuge briefly and place on 10× magnet on LOW for 1 min or until the solution clears.
12. Remove any remaining ethanol with a P10 pipette and air dry for 2 min (*see* **Note 33**).

13. Remove tube strip from magnet and add 32.5 μl Buffer EB. Pipette mix 15× (pipette set to 30 μl).
14. Incubate 5 min at room temperature.
15. Place on 10× magnet on LOW for 1 min or until the solution clears.
16. Transfer 30 μl sample to a new tube strip.

3.3.4 Sample Index PCR, Cleanup, and QC

1. Add 50 μl Amp Mix (PN-2000047 or 2000103) to 30 μl sample.
2. Add 20 μl of an individual Dual Index TT Set A to each well and record the well ID used. Pipette mix 5× (pipette set to 90 μl). Centrifuge briefly (*see* **Note 34**).
3. Prepare a thermocycler with the following protocol:

Lid temperature: 105°C	**Reaction volume: 100 μl**	**Run time: ~25–40 min**
Step	**Temperature**	**Time**
1	98°C	∞
2	98°C	00:00:45
3	98°C	00:00:20
4	63°C	00:00:30
5	72°C	00:00:20
6	Repeat steps 3–5 # of cycles determined by cDNA input	
7	72°C	00:01:00
8	4°C	∞

Recommended cycle numbers

cDNA input	Total cycles
0.25–25 ng	17–19
25–150 ng	15–17
150–500 ng	13–15
500–1000 ng	11–13
1000–1500 ng	9–11
>1500 ng	8

4. Place samples in thermocycler when ready and skip Step 1 to initiate PCR.
5. If not proceeding to next step, store samples at 4°C for up to 72 h.

6. Vortex to resuspend the SPRIselect reagent. Add 60 μl SPRIselect Reagent (0.6×) to each sample. Pipette mix 15× (pipette set to 150 μl) (*see* **Note 35**).
7. Incubate 5 min at room temperature.
8. Place on 10× magnet on HIGH for 1 min or until the solution clears. KEEP supernatant.
9. Transfer 150 μl supernatant to a new tube strip.
10. Vortex to resuspend SPRIselect reagent. Add 20 μl SPRIselect reagent (0.8×) to each sample. Pipette mix 15× (pipette set to 150 μl).
11. Incubate 5 min at room temperature.
12. Place on 10× magnet on HIGH for 1 min or until the solution clears.
13. Remove 165 μl supernatant and retain the beads (*see* **Note 36**).
14. Add 200 μl 80% ethanol to the pellet. Wait 30 s. Remove the ethanol.
15. Repeat Step 9 for a total of two washes.
16. Centrifuge briefly and place on 10× magnet on LOW for 1 min or until the solution clears.
17. Remove any remaining ethanol with a P10 pipette and air dry (*see* **Note 37**).
18. Remove from the magnet and add 37.5 μl Buffer EB to each sample. Pipette mix 15× (pipette set to 35 μl).
19. Incubate 5 min at room temperature.
20. Place on 10× magnet on LOW for 1 min or until the solution clears.
21. Transfer 35 μl sample to a new tube strip.
22. Store at 4°C for up to 72 h or at −20°C for long-term storage.
23. Run 1 μl of sample (1:10 dilution) on an Agilent Bioanalyzer High Sensitivity chip.
24. Determine the average fragment size and molarity from the Bioanalyzer trace.

3.3.5 Sequencing

1. Open the Visium Manual Alignment Wizard in Loupe Browser and select Visium fiducial alignment.
2. Upload scanned H&E image with fiducial frames and enter slide information.
3. Identify fiducials on the slide, adjust alignment and proceed to select spots covered by tissue. Record the number of spots selected.
4. Export JSON file for Space Ranger analysis. Repeat for each Frame.

5. Sequencing Depth/spot is recommended as a minimum of 50000 read pairs per tissue covered spot on Capture Area. Calculate the sequencing depth required by calculating Capture Area (%) covered by tissue.
   Calculations based on given example (Figs. 13–17) above:
   % Capture area = 2064/5000 × 100% = 41.28 %
   Total sequencing depth/sample = (0.4128 × 5000 total spots) × 50000 read pairs/spot = 103200000 total read pairs for that sample
6. Calculate the sequencing depths required for each of the four samples. Determine if samples can be pooled to fit into partial sequencing lane.
7. If samples can be pooled, calculate the pooling ratio. The sample with the lowest sequencing requirement can be used as the denominator:
   Example:

Sample	Sequencing depth required	Pooling ratio
A	77000000	3.48 (A/C)
B	105500000	4.76 (B/C)
C	22150000	1.00 (C/C)
D	42350000	1.91 (D/C)

8. Calculate the volumes required for pooling based on the molarity (nM) determined at the final library QC step. Store pooled/individual libraries at −20°C until ready to be sent for sequencing.

3.4 Part II: FFPE

3.4.1 FFPE Tissue Sectioning and Section Placement

Cryosectioning materials		
Reagent/reagent kit	**Brand/Cat. No.**	**Notes**
Microscope slide	Thermo Scientific Mensel-Glaser AGAA000001##12E	For H&E QC
Microtome blade	Leica 818 High Profile Microtome Blades	–
RNase Away Reagent	Invitrogen #10328-011	–
Absolute ethanol	Chemtech H/G ETHANOL 99.9%	–
Visium Spatial Gene Expression Slide	10× Genomics/2000233	–
Desiccant Drying Beads	–	–

Cryosectioning materials		
Reagent/reagent kit	**Brand/Cat. No.**	**Notes**
Equipment	**Brand/Cat. No.**	**Notes**
Microtome	Leica RM2265	–
Leica Histocore Water Bath	Leica #140607020C0	–
Leica Histocore Slide Dryer	Leica#140607010C0	–
Histo-Tek Coolier Paraffin Block Cooling Plate	Histo-Tek REI-202	–
Room temperature water bath	–	Any container/ dish can be used
Brightfield upright microscope	Olympus BX41	–
Biorad T100 Thermal cycler	Biorad #1861096	–

1. Clean the microtome surfaces and all utensils with RNase Away Reagent followed by 70% Ethanol.
2. Fill up the Leica Histocore Water Bath with DI water and warm the water to 42°C.
3. Prepare a room temperature water bath (use any nuclease-free container/dish) with DI water.
4. Chill FFPE blocks on Paraffin Block Cooling Plate at −4°C.
5. Load a FFPE block onto the microtome clamp and secure it.
6. Trim the block using a fresh microtome blade until the tissue is fully exposed. Trimming may be performed at thickness (*see* **Note 38**) of the user's preference.
7. Remove the block from the microtome clamp. Using a microtome blade, carefully nick a 6 mm x 6 mm area of interest on the block.
8. Return the nicked block onto the Paraffin Block Colling Plate for chilling.
9. Repeat steps 5 to 8 for all the FFPE blocks to prepare.
10. Load a FFPE block back onto the microtome clamp and secure it.
11. Section the block in a smooth and controlled motion at 5 μm using a clean part of the blade.
12. Transfer the sectioned ribbon (*see* **Note 39**) into the room temperature water bath and separate the individual sections using clean forceps.

13. Select a section and transfer it into the Leica Histocore Water Bath. Ensure that the section has no folds, tears, or cracks.
14. Float the section on Leica Histocore Water Bath for 1 min to allow it to flatten completely.
15. Fish the section onto a microscope slide and examine it under the microscope, ensure that no folds, tears, or cracks are present.
16. Transfer the section back onto the room temperature water bath.
17. Remove a Visium Gene Expression Slide from its container.
18. Carefully guide the tissue section using a brush onto a capture area (frame) of the Visium slide. Ensure that the section fits fully within the capture area and avoid covering the fiducial frame with the tissue or surrounding wax.
19. Repeat Step 10 to 18 for all FFPE blocks (*see* **Note 40**).
20. Allow the completed Visium slide to air dry for at least 30 min. Place the Visium Slide Adaptor into the thermal cycler and set it to 42°C. Allow it to equilibrate.
21. Heat the Visium slide on the thermal cycler at 42°C for 3 h. Keep the lid open at all times.
22. Remove the Visium slide from thermal cycler and allow it to cool down to room temperature for 5 min.
23. Store the Visium slide in its container and place it in a box of desiccant. The slide can be stored for up to 2 weeks at room temperature. Proceed on to the Visium Gene Expression Assay as soon as possible to avoid mRNA degradation.

3.5 Deparaffinization

1. Prepare five varying concentrations of ethanol in five separate tubes according to the table below:

% Ethanol	Vol. of 100% ethanol	Vol. of NFW	Total Vol.
Tube 1: 96% Ethanol	4.8 ml	0.20 ml	5.0 ml
Tube 2: 85% Ethanol	4.25 ml	0.75 ml	5.0 ml
Tube 3: 70% Ethanol	3.5 ml	1.5 ml	5.0 ml
Tube 4: 50% Ethanol	2.5 ml	2.5 ml	5.0 ml
Tube 5: 30% Ethanol	1.5 ml	3.5 ml	5.0 ml

2. According to the order below, pipette the reagents dropwise on to non-tissue areas (make sure slide is evenly and fully covered) (*see* **Note 41**).
   1) Pipette 1 ml of xylene onto slide. Incubate for 10 min.
   2) Discard xylene by tilting and draining into an appropriate waste container and dry the back of the slide with Kimwipes.
   3) Repeat Steps 1 to 2, two more times (total of three xylene washes).
   4) Pipette 1 ml of 100% EtOH onto slide. Incubate for 3 min.
   5) Discard 100% EtOH and dry the back of the slide with Kimwipes.
   6) Repeat Steps 4 to 5, two more times (total of three 100% EtOH washes).
   7) Pipette 1 ml of 96% EtOH onto slide. Incubate for 3 min.
   8) Discard 96% EtOH by tilting and draining into an appropriate waste container and dry the back of the slide with Kimwipes.
   9) Repeat Steps 7 to 8 once (total of two 96% EtOH washes).
   10) Pipette 1 ml of 85% EtOH onto slide. Incubate for 3 min.
   11) Discard 85% EtOH by tilting and draining into an appropriate waste container and dry the back of the slide with Kimwipes.
   12) Pipette 1 ml of 70% EtOH onto slide. Incubate for 3 min.
   13) Discard 70% EtOH by tilting and draining into an appropriate waste container and dry the back of the slide with Kimwipes.
   14) Pipette 1 ml of 50% EtOH onto slide. Incubate for 3 min.
   15) Discard 50% EtOH by tilting and draining into an appropriate waste container and dry the back of the slide with Kimwipes.
   16) Pipette 1 ml of 30% EtOH onto slide. Incubate for 3 min.
   17) Discard 30% EtOH by tilting and draining into an appropriate waste container and dry the back of the slide with Kimwipes.
   18) Gently immerse slide into 45 ml of MilliQ water in falcon tube and hold for 20 s. Wipe excess MilliQ water off back of slide and around frames. Proceed immediately to H&E staining.

3.6 H&E Staining

Before you begin—H&E Staining			
Reagent/reagent kit	**10× PN**	**Prep and Handling**	**Storage**
Prepare and equilibrate to 37°C			
VISIUM slide adapter	3000380	Gently clean with an RNase decontamination solution of choice, then with 70% ethanol before placing into the thermocycler	–
Obtain			
Xylene	Millipore Sigma/ 214736	Work with chemical in the fume hood	Ambient
Dako Mayer's Hematoxylin (Lillie's Modification)	Dako/ S3309	–	Ambient
Eosin Y-solution, Alcoholic	Millipore Sigma/ HT110116	–	Ambient
Dako Bluing Buffer	Dako/ CS702	-	Ambient
Milli-Q® EQ 7000 ultrapure water or equivalent	–	–	Ambient
KimWipes™ Delicate Task Wipes	–	–	–
Staining tray	–	–	Ambient
Bio-Rad T100 thermocycler	–	–	–
50 ml Sterile Polypropylene Centrifuge Tube	–	Fill with 45 ml Milli-Q water	Ambient
Four 1 l glass beakers	–	Fill each beaker with at least 600 ml Milli-Q water. Label 1–4	Ambient
Glycerol	Merck/ G5516-100ML	–	Ambient

1. Pipette reagents dropwise on to non-tissue areas (make sure slide is evenly covered (*see* **Note 42**)).
   1) Pipette 1 ml hematoxylin onto slide. Incubate for 3 min.
   2) Tilt slide to discard hematoxylin into staining tray.
   3) Gently immerse slide into MilliQ Beaker 1. Hold for 20 s.
   4) Gently immerse slide into MilliQ Beaker 2. Hold for 10 s. Wipe off excess liquid from the back of the slide and around the frames.

5) Pipette 1 ml Bluing Buffer onto slide. Incubate for 1 min.
6) Tilt slide to discard hematoxylin into staining tray.
7) Gently dunk slide into MilliQ Beaker 3, five times, then immerse for 20 s. Wipe off excess liquid from the back of the slide and around the frames.
8) Immerse slide in 30 ml alcoholic eosin in 50 ml falcon tube for 1 min. Drain excess alcoholic eosin off.
9) Gently dunk slide into MilliQ Beaker 4, five times, then immerse for 20 s. Wipe off excess liquid from the back of the slide and around the frames. Proceed to imaging step immediately.

3.7 Tissue Imaging

1. Using a pipette with a wide-bore tip, gently pipette 150 μl of 100% Glycerol (*see* **Note 43**) onto the Visium Gene Expression Slide while avoiding the introduction of air bubbles (*see* **Note 44**). Ensure that the pipette tip does not come into direct contact with the slide. Refer to Fig. 1 for illustration.
2. Allow the glycerol to spread and cover the slide fully. Carefully wick off the excess glycerol from the edges of the slide (*see* **Note 45**) Refer to Fig. 2 for illustration.
3. Secure the Visium slide onto a slide rack and load it into the imaging system (*see* **Note 46**) Refer to Fig. 3 for illustration.
4. Scan the Visium Gene Expression Slide using the brightfield protocol. Refer to Fig. 4 for illustration.

Fig. 1 H&E staining procedures performed on a nonabsorbent surface

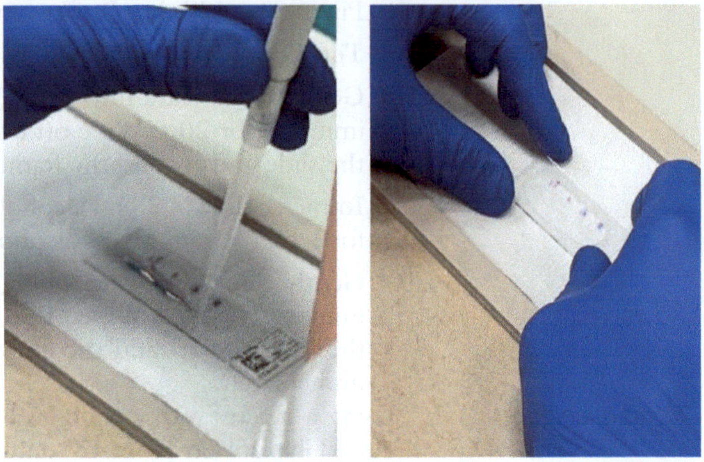

Step 1: Addition of glycerol Step 2: Gentle mounting of coverslip

Fig. 2 Mounting of coverslip onto slide

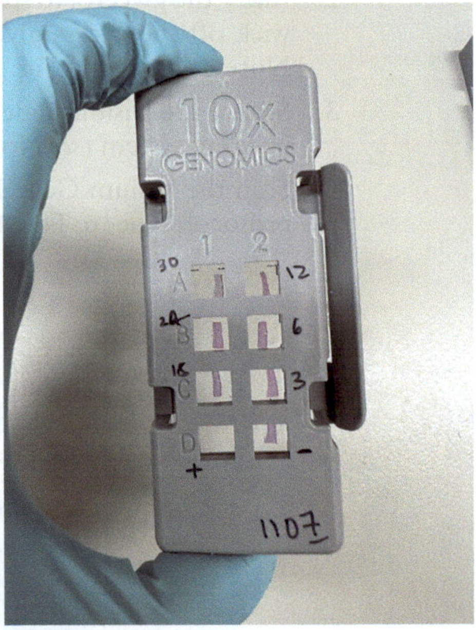

Fig. 3 Optimized permeabilization durations are indicated on the cassette for clarity

5. Ensure that the tissue morphology and fiducial frames are sharp and clear in the scanned images.
6. Remove coverslip by immersing slide into beaker containing 500 ml MilliQ and hold horizontally until coverslip slides off. Gently dunk slide 15 times to wash (*see* **Note 47**).
7. Assemble the slide into the cassette with gasket provided.
8. Using an alcohol-resistant marker, make a mark on the cassette at the corners of the wells (*see* **Note 48**) in which there

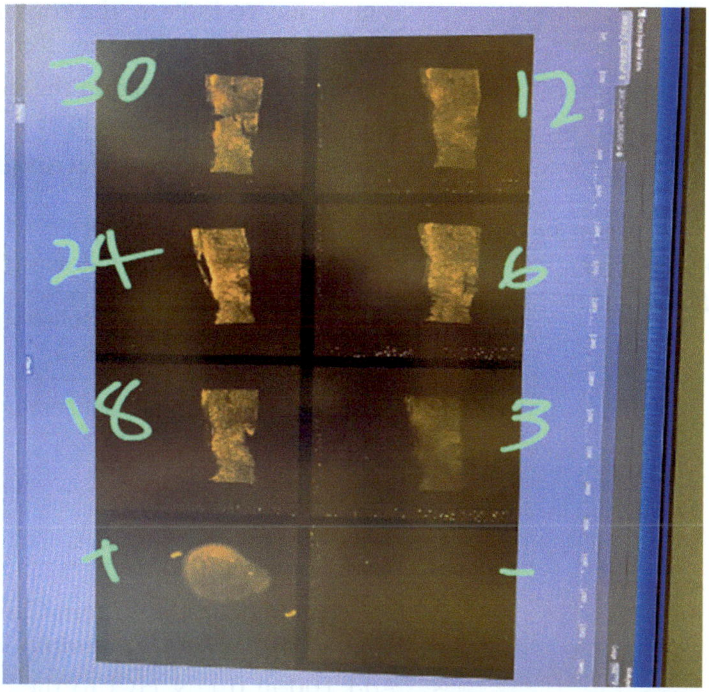

Fig. 4 Fluorescence image captured from Tissue Optimization. Select the optimized permeabilization timing that gives strong fluorescence intensity and clarity of tissue morphology. In this particular example, 6 min was the best duration

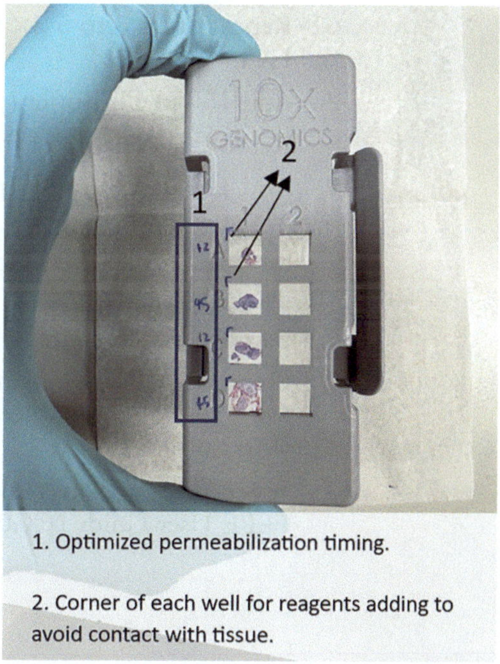

Fig. 5 Recommendations for annotating on the Visium cassette to ensure an error-free workflow

is no tissue, to indicate the corners where the pipette tips can touch throughout the assay. Refer to Fig. 5 for illustration.

9. Dry slide by incubating on the slide adapter in the thermocycler with lid open for 3 min at 37°C.
10. Proceed immediately to decrosslinking.

3.8 Decrosslinking for H&E Stained Sections

1. Pre-equilibrate thermocycler adapter in thermocycler with the program set to the following (maintain on hold):

Lid temperature: 70°C	Reaction volume: 100 μl	Run time: 60 min
Step	**Temperature**	**Time**
Pre-equilibrate	70°C	∞
Decrosslinking	70°C	00:60:00
Hold	22°C	∞

2. Place the slide in the Visium Cassette.
   Practice assembly with a dummy slide.
3. Add 100 μl 0.1 N HCl to the corners of each well and tap cassette gently to uniformly cover the tissue sections, without introducing bubbles.
4. Incubate for 1 min at room temperature.
5. Using a pipette, remove all the HCl from the well corners.
6. Repeat Steps 3 to 5 2× for a total of three washes with 0.1N HCl.
7. Add 150 μl TE Buffer (pH 9.0) to the corners of each well.
8. Remove all TE Buffer from the wells.
9. Add 100 μl TE Buffer (pH 9.0) to the corners of each well.
10. Apply Visium Slide Seal on the Visium Cassette and place the cassette on the Thermocycler Adaptor at 70°C.
11. Close the thermal cycler lid. Skip Pre-equilibrate step and initiate Decrosslinking.
12. Once the Decrosslinking is complete, remove the cassette from the Thermocycler Adaptor and place on a flat, clean work surface.
13. Proceed immediately to Visium Spatial Gene Expression for FFPE User Guide (CG000407).

3.9 Probe Hybridization

Before you begin—probe hybridization			
Reagent/reagent kit	**10× PN**	**Prep and handling**	**Storage**
Equilibrate to room temperature			
FFPE Hyb Buffer	2000423	Thaw at room temperature. If precipitate persists, heat at 37°C until dissolved. Avoid vortexing to prevent bubble formation. Keep the buffer at room temperature after thawing. Store at −20°C when not in use	−20°C
Place on ice			
Perm Enzyme B	3000602/ 3000553	Pipette mix, centrifuge briefly. Maintain on ice until ready to use. Dilute 200× by adding 1 μl Perm Enzyme B in 199 μl Buffer EB	−20°C
Probes for human samples			
♦ Human WT Probes - RHS	2000453/ 2000449	Thaw on ice. Vortex and centrifuge briefly. Maintain on ice until ready to use	−20°C
♦ Human WT Probes - LHS	2000454/ 2000450	Thaw on ice. Vortex and centrifuge briefly. Maintain on ice until ready to use	−20°C
Probes for mouse samples			
♦ Mouse WT Probes - RHS	2000457/ 2000455	Thaw on ice. Vortex and centrifuge briefly. Maintain on ice until ready to use	−20°C
♦ Mouse WT Probes - LHS	2000458/ 2000456	Thaw on ice. Vortex and centrifuge briefly. Maintain on ice until ready to use	−20°C
Other reagents/consumables			
Nuclease-free water	–	–	Ambient
Visium Casette and Gasket Assembly	2000282/ 2000281	–	Ambient
Visium Slide Seals	2000284/ 2000283	–	Ambient
Buffer EB	–	–	Ambient
10% Tween-20	–	–	Ambient
10× PBS	–	–	Ambient

1. Prepare Pre-hybridization Mix shortly before using and keep at room temperature. Pipette mix 10× and centrifuge briefly.

Pre-hybridization mix ***Add reagents in order listed. Maintain at room temperature***	**10× PN**	**1× (μl)**	**4X + 10% (μl)**
Nuclease-free Water	–	89.0	391.6
10× PBS	–	10.0	44
Diluted Perm Enzyme B *Dilute Perm Enzyme B 200× in Buffer EB before using. DO NOT use concentrated stock directly.*	3000602/ 3000553	0.5	2.2
10% Tween-20	–	0.5	2.2
Total	–	100.0	440.0

2. Retrieve the Visium Cassette containing H&E stained or IF stained sections and remove the Visium Slide Seal.
3. Using a pipette, remove all buffer from the well corners. For H&E stained slide, remove all TE buffer.
4. Add 100 μl Pre-hybridization Mix at the well corners and tap cassette gently to uniformly cover the tissue sections, without introducing bubbles.
5. Apply Visium Slide Seal on the cassette and incubate for 15 min at room temperature.
6. Prepare a thermal cycler with the following incubation protocol and start the program.

Lid temperature: 50°C	**Reaction volume: 100 μl**	**Run time: -**
Step	**Temperature**	**Time**
Pre-equilibrate	50°C	∞
Hybridization	50°C	Overnight (16–24 h)
Post-Hybridization Wash	50°C	∞

7. Prepare Probe Hybridization Mix shortly before using and keep at room temperature. Pipette mix 10× and centrifuge briefly.

Probe hybridization mix ****Add reagents in order listed. Maintain at room temperature***	**10× PN**	**1× (μl)**	**4× + 10% (μl)**	**8× + 10% (μl)**
Nuclease-free Water	–	10.0	44.0	88.0
FFPE Hyb Buffer	–	70.0	308.0	616.0
♦ **Human WT Probes –RHS Or Mouse WT Probes – RHS**	2000453/ 2000449 Or 2000457/ 2000455	10.0	44.0	4.4
♦ **Human WT Probes –LHS Or Mouse WT Probes – LHS**	2000454/ 2000450 Or 2000458/ 2000456	10.0	44.0	4.4
Total	–	100.0	440.0	880.0

8. Remove all Pre-hybridization Mix from the well corners.
9. Add 100 μl room temperature Probe Hybridization Mix to the well corners and tap cassette gently to uniformly cover the tissue sections, without introducing bubbles.
10. Apply a new Visium Slide Seal on the cassette and place on the Thermocycler Adaptor on the pre-heated thermal cycler. Close the thermal cycler lid.
11. Skip Pre-equilibrate step to initiate Hybridization.

3.10 Probe Ligation

Before you begin—Probe ligation			
Reagent/reagent kit	**10× PN**	**Prep and handling**	**Storage**
Equilibrate to room temperature			
FFPE Post-Hyb Wash Buffer	2000424	Thaw at room temperature. If precipitate persists, heat at 37°C until dissolved. Vortex and centrifuge briefly	−20°C
♦ 2X Probe Ligation Buffer	2000446/2000445	Thaw at room temperature. Vortex and centrifuge briefly	−20°C

Before you begin—Probe ligation			
Reagent/reagent kit	**10× PN**	**Prep and handling**	**Storage**
Post Ligation Wash Buffer	2000420/2000419	Thaw at room temperature. If precipitate persists, heat at 37°C until dissolved. Vortex and centrifuge briefly. The tube is filled to the top. Pipette carefully	−20°C
Place on ice			
♦ Probe Ligation Enzyme	2000426/2000425	Thaw on ice. Centrifuge briefly	−20°C
Other reagents/ consumables			
Nuclease-free water	–	–	Ambient
20× SSC Buffer	–	–	Ambient

3.10.1 Post-Hybridization Wash

1. Pre-heat FFPE Post-Hyb Wash Buffer (495 μl/per sample) to 50°C.
2. Prepare 2× SSC Buffer.

SSC buffer *Add reagents in order listed. Maintain at room temperature*	Stock	Final	1× (μl)	4× + 10% (μl)
SSC	20×	2×	120.0	528.0
Nuclease-free Water	–	–	1080.0	4752.0
Total	–	–	1200.0*	5280.0*

789 *This volume of 2× SSC Buffer is sufficient for washes in all subsequent steps.

3. Remove the Visium Cassette from the Thermocycler Adaptor and place on a flat, clean work surface.
4. Remove the Visium Slide Seal and using a pipette, remove all Probe Hybridization Mix from the well corners.
5. Immediately add 150 μl pre-heated FFPE Post-Hyb Wash Buffer to each well. Avoid well drying or cooling to room temperature (*see* **Note 49**). Removal and addition of buffers should be done quickly.
6. Apply Visium Slide Seal on the cassette and place on the Thermocycler Adaptor on the pre-heated thermal cycler. Close the thermal cycler lid.
7. Skip the Hybridization step and initiate Post-Hybridization Wash. Incubate in the thermal cycler at 50°C for 5 min.

8. Remove the Visium Cassette from the Thermocycler Adaptor and place on a flat, clean work surface.
9. Remove the Visium Slide Seal and using a pipette, remove all FFPE Post-Hyb Wash Buffer from the well corners.
10. Repeat Step 5 to 9 two more times.
11. Add 150 μl 2× SSC Buffer to each well.
12. Let the cassette cool to room temperature (~3 min) before proceeding to the next step.

3.10.2 Probe Ligation

1. Prepare a thermal cycler with the following incubation protocol and start the program.

Lid temperature: 37°C (lid may be turned off if the instrument does not enable 37°C)	**Reaction volume: 100 μl**	**Run time: 1 h**
Step	**Temperature**	**Time**
Pre-equilibrate	37°C	∞
Ligation	37°C	01:00:00
Hold	4°C	∞

2. Prepare Probe Ligation Mix shortly before using. Pipette mix 10× and centrifuge briefly.

Probe Ligation Mix ****Add reagents in order listed. Maintain at room temperature***	**10× PN**	**1× (μl)**	**4× + 10% (μl)**
Nuclease-free Water	–	24.0	105.6
◆ 2× Probe Ligation Buffer	2000446/2000445	30.0	132.0
◆ Probe Ligation Enzyme	2000426/2000425	6.0	26.4
Total	–	60.0	264.0

3. Remove all 2× SSC Buffer from all wells.
4. Add 60 μl Probe Ligation Mix to the well corners and tap the cassette gently to uniformly cover the tissue sections, without introducing bubbles.
5. Apply a new Visium Slide Seal on the Visium Cassette and place on the Thermocycler Adaptor on the pre-heated thermal cycler. Close the thermal cycler lid. Discard old slide seals.
6. Skip Pre-equilibrate step to initiate Ligation.

3.10.3 Post-Ligation Wash

1. Pre-heat Post Ligation Wash Buffer (110 μl/sample) to 57°C. Only 100 μl per sample is needed.
2. Remove the Visium Cassette from the Thermocycler Adaptor and place on a flat, clean work surface.
3. Prepare a thermal cycler with the following incubation protocol and start the program.

Lid temperature: 57°C	**Reaction volume: 100 μl**	**Run time: -**
Step	**Temperature**	**Time**
Incubate	57°C	∞

4. Remove the Visium Slide Seal and using a pipette, remove all Probe Ligation Mix from all wells.
5. Immediately add 100 μl room temperature Post Ligation Wash Buffer to each well. The Post Ligation Wash Buffer should be at room temperature. Avoid well drying.
6. Apply Visium Slide Seal on the Visium Cassette and place on the Thermocycler Adaptor on the pre-heated thermal cycler. Close the thermal cycler lid.
7. Incubate at 57°C for 5 min.
8. Remove the Visium Cassette from the Thermocycler Adaptor and place on a flat, clean work surface.
9. Remove the Visium Slide Seal and using a pipette, remove all Post Ligation Wash Buffer.
10. Add 100 μl pre-heated Post Ligation Wash Buffer to each well.
11. Apply Visium Slide Seal on the Visium Cassette and place on the Thermocycler Adaptor on the pre-heated thermal cycler. Close the thermal cycler lid.
12. Incubate at 57°C for 5 min.
13. Remove the Visium Cassette from the Thermocycler Adaptor and place on a flat, clean work surface.
14. Remove the Visium Slide Seal and using a pipette, remove all Post Ligation Wash Buffer.
15. Add 150 μl 2× SSC Buffer prepared at step 2.1b to each well.
16. Remove all 2× SSC buffer.
17. Add 150 μl 2× SSC Buffer to each well.
18. Let the slides cool to room temperature and proceed to next step or apply Visium Slide Seal on the Visium Cassette and store the slides in 2× SSC Buffer at 4°C for up to 24 h.

3.11 Probe Release and Extension

3.11.1 RNA Digestion and Probe Release

Before you begin—RNA digestion & probe release			
Reagent/reagent kit	**10× PN**	**Prep and handling**	**Storage**
Equilibrate to room temperature			
Extension Buffer	2000409/ 2000408	Thaw at room temperature. Vortex and centrifuge briefly	−20°C
♦ 2× RNase Buffer	2000411/ 2000410	Thaw at room temperature. Vortex and centrifuge briefly	−20°C
♦ Perm Buffer B	2000413/ 2000412	Thaw at room temperature. DO NOT vortex	−20°C
Place on ice			
Extension Enzyme	2000427/ 2000389	Pipette mix, centrifuge briefly. Maintain on ice until ready to use	−20°C
♦ Perm Enzyme B	3000602/ 3000553	Pipette mix, centrifuge briefly. Maintain on ice until ready to use	−20°C
♦ RNase Enzyme	3000605/ 3000593	Pipette mix, centrifuge briefly. Maintain on ice until ready to use	−20°C
Other reagents/consumables			
Nuclease-free water	–	–	Ambient
Tris 1 M, pH 7.0	–	Manufacturer's recommendations	Ambient
2× SSC Buffer	–	Prepared at step 2	Ambient
8 M KOH Solution	–	Manufacturer's recommendations	Ambient
Visium Slide Seals	2000284/ 2000283	–	Ambient

3.11.2 RNA Digestion and Probe Release

1. Place a Thermocycler Adaptor in the thermal cycler. Prepare the thermal cycler with the following incubation protocol and start the program.

Lid temperature: 37°C (Lid may be turned off if the instrument does not enable 37°C)	Reaction volume: 100 μl	Run time: ~70 min
Step	**Temperature**	**Time**
Pre-equilibrate	37°C	∞
RNA Digestion	37°C	00:30:00
Hold	37°C	∞
Permeabilization	37°C	00:40:00

2. Prepare RNase Mix shortly before using. Vortex and centrifuge briefly.

RNase mix *Maintain on ice*	10× PN	1× (μl)	4× + 10% (μl)
Nuclease-free Water	–	33.0	145.2
♦ 2X RNase Buffer	2000411/2000410	37.5	165.0
♦ RNase Enzyme	3000605/3000593	4.5	19.8
Total	–	75.0	330.0

3. Using a pipette, remove all 2× SSC Buffer from the well corners. If the slide was stored overnight, remove the Visium Slide Seal before removing the 2× SSC Buffer.
4. Add 75 μl RNase Mix to corners of each well. Gently tap the cassette to ensure uniform coverage of the Capture Area.
5. Apply a new Visium Slide Seal on the Visium Cassette and place on the Thermocycler Adaptor on the pre-heated thermal cycler. Close the thermal cycler lid. Discard old slide seals.
6. Skip Pre-equilibrate step to initiate RNA Digestion.
7. Prepare Permeabilization Mix shortly before using and pipette mix 10×. DO NOT vortex.

Permeabilization Mix *Maintain at room temperature*	10× PN	1× (μl)	4× + 10% (μl)
♦ Perm Buffer B	2000413/2000412	70.3	309.4
♦ Perm Enzyme B	3000602/3000553	4.7	20.6
Total	–	75.0	330.0

8. After the RNA Digestion is complete, remove the Visium Cassette from the Thermocycler Adaptor and place on a flat, clean work surface.
9. Remove the Visium Slide Seal and using a pipette, remove all RNase Mix from the wells.
10. Add 75 µl Permeabilization Mix to corners of each well. Gently tap the cassette to ensure uniform coverage of the Capture Area.
11. Apply a new Visium Slide Seal on the Visium Cassette and place on the Thermocycler Adaptor on the pre-heated thermal cycler. Close the thermal cycler lid. Discard old slide seals.
12. Skip Hold step to initiate Permeabilization.
13. After the permeabilization is complete, remove the Visium Cassette from the Thermocycler Adaptor and place on a flat, clean work surface.
14. Remove the Visium Slide Seal and using a pipette, remove all Permeabilization Mix from the well corners (*see* **Note 50**).
15. Add 175 µl 2× SSC Buffer prepared at step 2.1b to each well.
16. Remove all 2× SSC Buffer from the wells.
17. Repeat Steps 15 to 16 one more time.
18. Add 175 µl 2× SSC Buffer to each well and proceed immediately to Probe Extension.

3.11.3 Probe Extension

1. Prepare the thermal cycler with the following incubation protocol and start the program.

Lid temperature: 45°C (lid may be turned off if the instrument does not enable 45°C)	Reaction volume: 100 µl	Run time: 15 min
Step	**Temperature**	**Time**
Pre-equilibrate	45°C	∞
Probe Extension	45°C	00:15:00
Hold	4°C	∞

2. Prepare Probe Extension Mix shortly before using. Vortex and centrifuge briefly.

Probe Extension Mix *Maintain on ice	10× PN	1× (μl)	4× + 10% (μl)
◆ Extension Buffer	2000409/200008	73.5	323.4
◆ Extension Enzyme	2000427/2000389	1.5	6.6
Total	–	75.0	330.0

3. Remove all 2× SSC Buffer from the wells.
4. Add 75 μl Probe Extension Mix to corners of each well. Gently tap the cassette to ensure uniform coverage of the Capture Area.
5. Apply a new Visium Slide Seal on the Visium Cassette and place on the Thermocycler Adaptor on the pre-heated thermal cycler. Close the thermal cycler lid. Discard old slide seals.
6. Skip Pre-equilibrate step to initiate Probe Extension.
7. After the Probe Extension is complete, immediately proceed to next step or store slides at 4°C for up to 72 h. DO NOT remove the Visium Slide Seal during storage.

3.11.4 Probe Elution

1. Prepare 0.08 M KOH Mix. Vortex and centrifuge briefly (*see* **Note 51**).

KOH Mix *Maintain at room temperature	Stock	Final	1× (μl)	4× + 10% (μl)
KOH	8M	0.08M	0.4	1.8
Nuclease-free Water	–	–	39.6	174.2
Total	–	–	40.0	176.0

2. Remove the Visium Cassette from the Thermocycler Adaptor and place on a flat, clean work surface, after the Probe Extension is complete.
3. Remove the Visium Slide Seal and using a pipette, remove all Probe Extension Mix from the wells.
4. Add 100 μl 2× SSC Buffer prepared at step 2.1b to each well.
5. Remove all 2× SSC Buffer from the wells.
6. Add 40 μl 0.08 M KOH Mix to corners of each well. Gently tap the cassette to ensure uniform coverage of the Capture Area.
7. Incubate at room temperature for 10 min.

8. Transfer all solutions containing the ligation product to a fresh 8-tube strip. DO NOT leave behind any solution in the wells. The solution might contain tissue pieces. Transfer all the solution even if there is tissue.
9. Add 5 μl 1 M Tris-HCl pH 7.0 to the solution in the eight-tube strip. Vortex briefly, centrifuge briefly, and place on ice.
10. Proceed to library preparation or store at −20°C for up to 72 h.

3.12 Visium Spatial Gene Expression FFPE Library Construction

Before you begin—Visium spatial gene expression FFPE library construction

Reagent/reagent kit	10× PN	Prep and handling	Storage
Equilibrate to room temperature			
Dual Index Plate TS Set A	3000511	Thaw at room temperature. Vortex and centrifuge briefly	−20°C
♦ TS Primer Mix A	2000447	Thaw at room temperature. Vortex and centrifuge briefly	−20°C
Beckman Coulter SPRIselect Reagent	–	Vortex well before use	Ambient
Agilent BioAnalyzer High Sensitivity Kit	–	Equilibrate gel to room temperature for at least 30 min before use	4°C
Place on ice			
Amp Mix	2000047/ 2000113	Vortex, centrifuge briefly. Maintain on ice until ready to use	−20°C
KAPA SYBR FAST qPCR Master Mix	–	Vortex, centrifuge briefly. Maintain on ice until ready to use. Minimize light exposure	−20°C
Other reagents/consumables			
Nuclease-free water	–	–	Ambient
Qiagen Buffer EB	–	–	Ambient
80% Ethanol	–	Prepare fresh	Ambient
10× Magnetic Separator	230003	–	Ambient

3.12.1 Cycle Number Determination: qPCR

1. Prepare qPCR Mix on ice. Vortex and centrifuge briefly.

qPCR Mix ***Add reagents in the order listed. Maintain on ice.***	**Stock**	**Final**	**1× (μl)**	**5×* + 10% (μl)** ***Includes 1 negative control***
Nuclease-free Water	–	–	4.0	22.0
KAPA SYBR FAST qPCR Master Mix Minimize light exposure	2×	1×	5.0	27.5
◆ TS Primer Mix A (PN-2000447)	–	–	1.0	5.5
Total	–	–	10.0	55.0

2. Add 9 μl qPCR Mix to each well in a qPCR plate (a well for negative control may be included).
3. Transfer 1 μl sample to the qPCR plate well containing the qPCR Mix. Pipette mix, centrifuge briefly. If using a negative control, add 1 μl nuclease-free water to the corresponding well. Briefly centrifuge.
4. Prepare a qPCR system with the following protocol, place the plate on the thermal cycler, and start the program.

Lid temperature: 105°C (Lid may be turned off if the instrument does not enable 45°C)	**Reaction volume: 10 μl**	**Run time: 35 min**
Step	**Temperature**	**Time**
1	98°C	00:03:00
2	98°C	00:00:05
3	63°C	00:00:30
	Read signal	
4	Go to step 2, 24× (total 25 cycles)	

5. Record the Cq Value for each sample. The threshold for determining the Cq Value should be set along the exponential phase of the amplification plot, at ~25% of the peak fluorescence value (*see* **Note 52**). Refer to Figs. 6–10 for illustration.

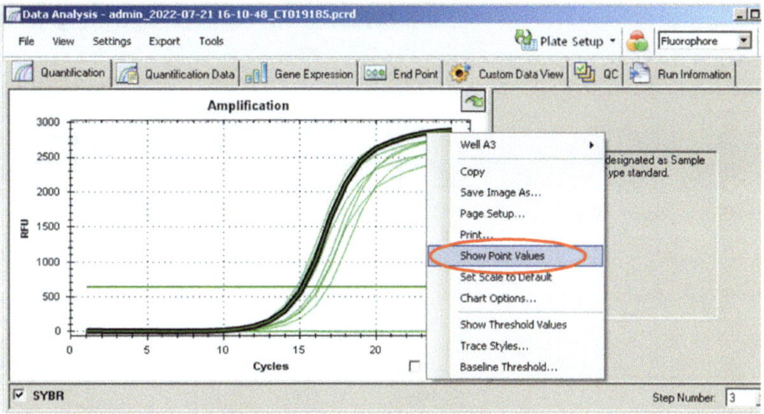

Fig. 6 Right click on plot to enable viewing of point values

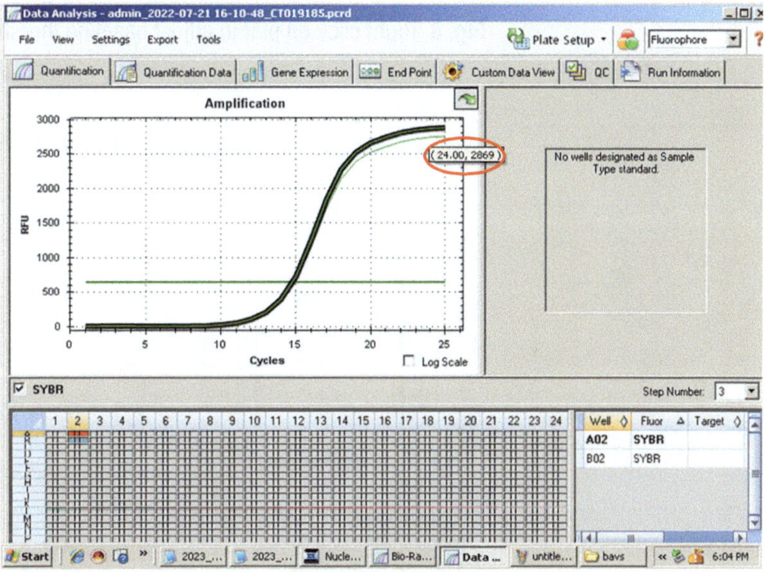

Fig. 7 Record 100% RFU value of sample/replicate (e.g., 2869)

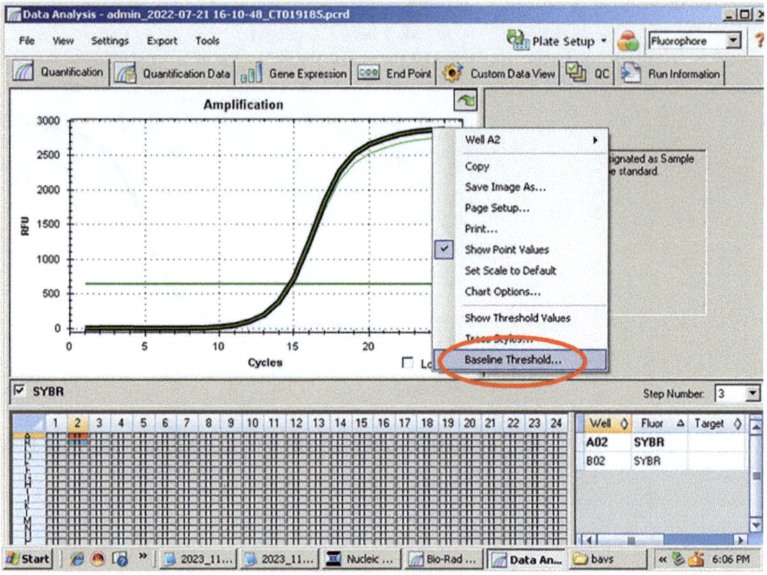

Fig. 8 Right click on plot to adjust baseline threshold

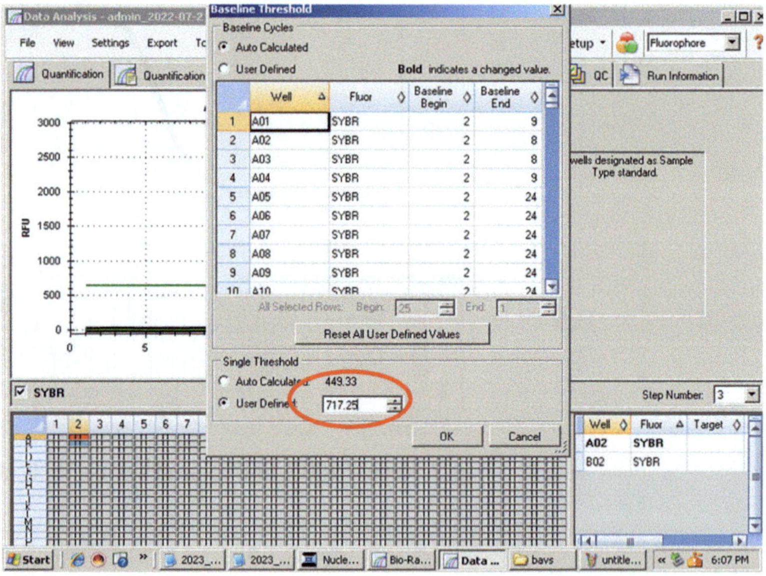

Fig. 9 Select "User Define" and enter calculated 25% RFU value (e.g., 25% of 2869 = 717.25)

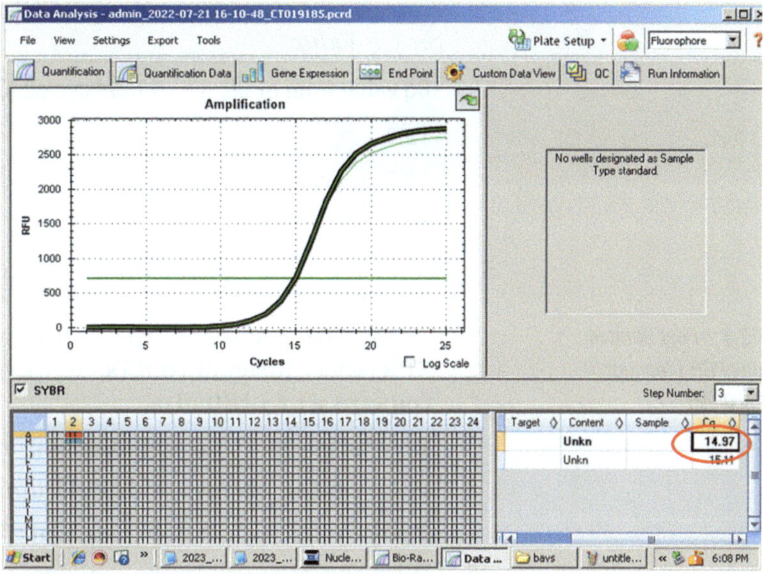

Fig. 10 Record Cq value. For duplicates, repeat Step 4 by refering to Figs. 6–10 for the other replicate. Take the average Cq to determine cDNA amplification cycle #

3.12.2 Sample Index PCR

1. Choose the appropriate sample index sets to ensure that no sample indices overlap in a multiplexed sequencing run. Record the 10× Sample Index name (PN-1000251/PN-3000511 Dual Index Kit/Plate TS Set A well ID) used.
2. Add 50 μl Amp Mix (PN-2000047 or 2000131) to ~45 μl sample.
3. Add 5 μl of an individual Dual Index TS Set A to each well and record the well ID used. Pipette mix 5× (pipette set to 90 μl). Centrifuge briefly.
4. Incubate in a thermal cycler with the following protocol.

Lid temperature: 105°C	**Reaction volume: 100 μl**	**Run time: ~25–40 min**
Step	**Temperature**	**Time**
1	98°C	00:01:00
2	98°C	00:00:15
3	63°C	00:00:20
4	72°C	00:00:30
5	Go to step 2, use the Cq+2 Value as the total # of cycles. See the table below for total # of cycle examples.	
6	72°C	00:01:00
7	4°C	∞

Example: Cycle number examples determined based on rounding the Cq Value

Cq value from qPCR	Total cycles (Cq+2)
12.2	14
13.5	16
19.7	22

5. Store at 4°C for up to 24 h or proceed to the next step.

3.12.3 Post Sample Index PCR Cleanup: SPRIselect

1. Vortex to resuspend the SPRIselect reagent. Add 85 μl SPRIselect Reagent (0.85×) to each sample. Pipette mix 15× (pipette set to 180 μl).
2. Incubate 5 min at room temperature.
3. Place on the magnet on HIGH until the solution clears.
4. Remove the supernatant (*see* **Note 53**).
5. With the tube still in the magnet, add 200 μl 80% ethanol to the pellet.
6. Remove the ethanol.
7. Repeat steps 5 and 6 for a total of two washes.
8. Centrifuge briefly. Place on the magnet on LOW for 1 min or until solution clears.
9. Remove any remaining ethanol with a P10 pipette and air dry for 2 min (*see* **Note 54**).
10. Remove tube-strip from the magnet. Add 27.5 μl Buffer EB. Pipette mix 15×.
11. Incubate 5 min at room temperature.
12. Place on the magnet on LOW until the solution clears.
13. Transfer 25 μl to a new tube strip.
14. Store at −20°C for long-term storage

3.12.4 Post Library Construction QC

1. Run 1 μl of sample (1:5 dilution) on an Agilent Bioanalyzer DNA High Sensitivity chip (*see* **Note 55**).
2. Determine the average fragment size from the Bioanalyzer trace. This will be used as the insert size for library quantification. Refer to Fig. 11 for an example Bioanalyzer trace of the generated cDNA.

Refer to Fig. 12 for an example Bioanalyzer trace of the final library.

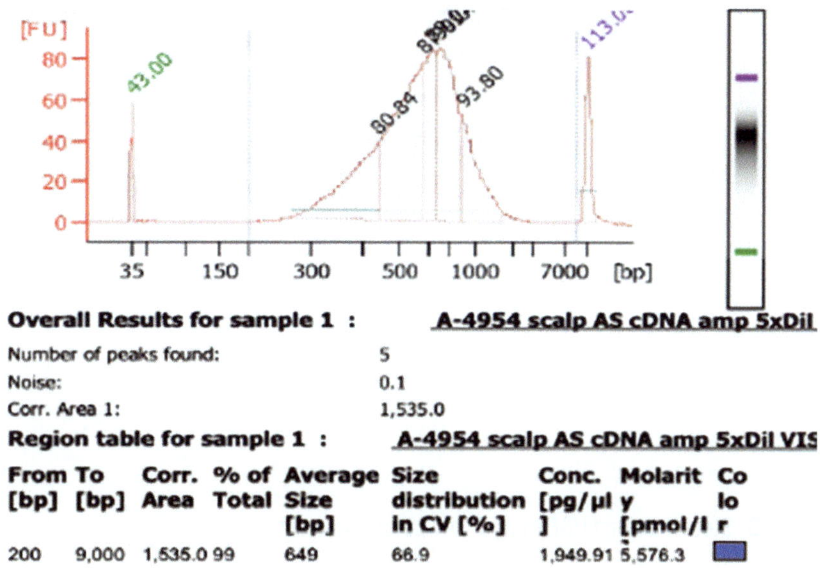

Fig. 11 BioAnalyzer QC electrogram example

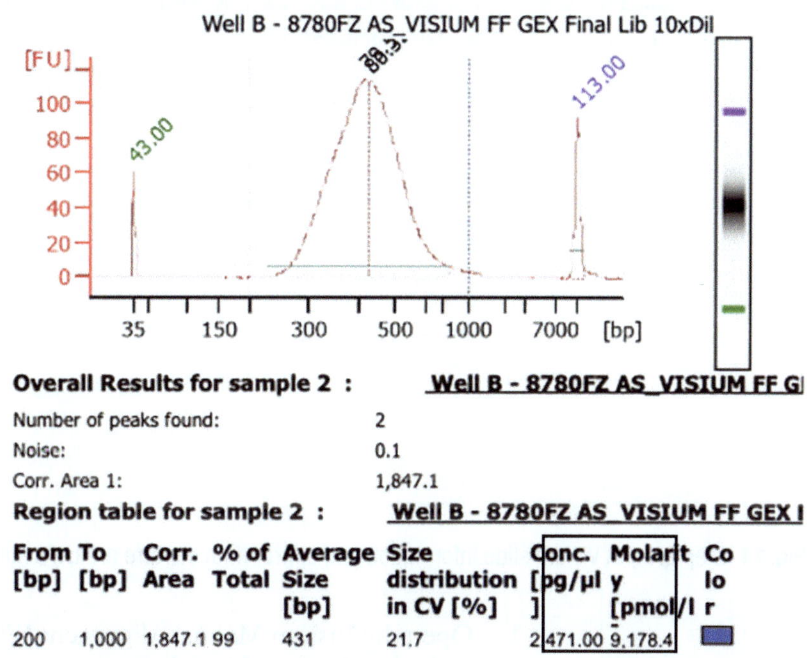

Fig. 12 Determining molarity (pmol/l) and average fragment size (bp) from BioAnalyzer QC results

3.13 Sequencing

Refer to Figs. 13–17 for reference.

Refer to Fig. 18 for an overview of the workflow.

Note that recommended sequencing depth for FFPE tissues half of that of Fresh Frozen tissues.

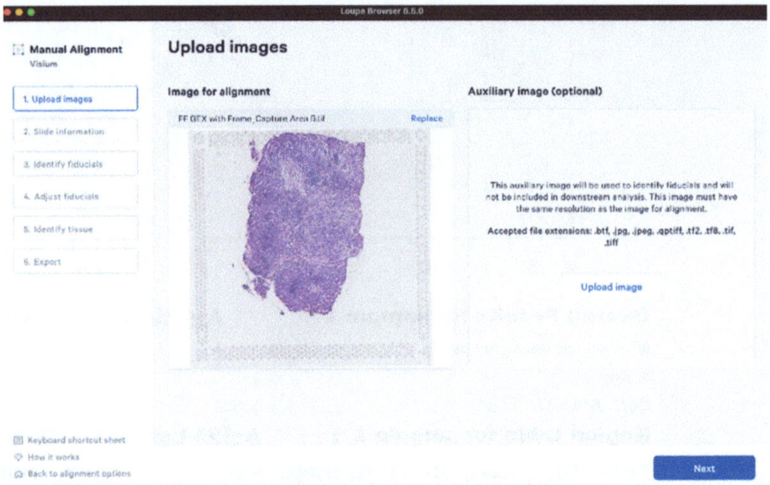

Fig. 13 Step 1: Upload H&E Image onto Loupe Browser

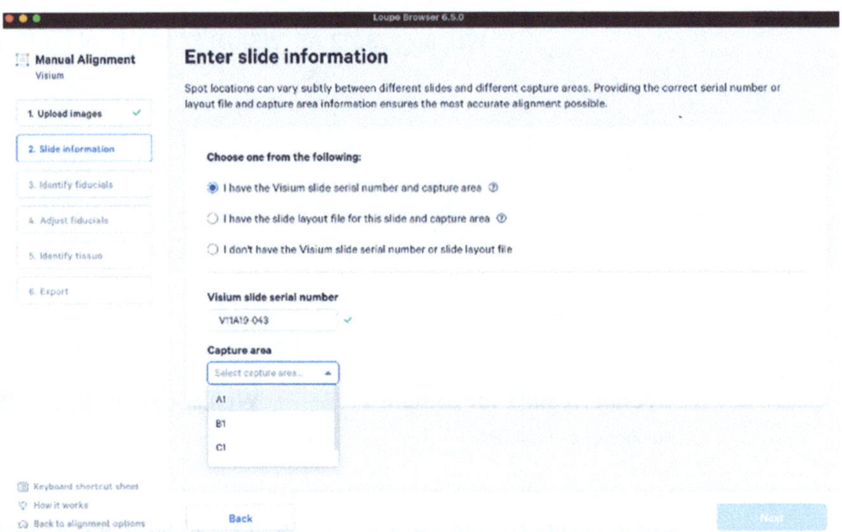

Fig. 14 Step 2: Input Visium slide information and appropriate capture area, if available

1. Open the Visium Manual Alignment Wizard in Loupe Browser and select Visium fiducial alignment.
2. Upload scanned H&E image with fiducial frames and enter slide information.
3. Identify fiducials on the slide, adjust alignment and proceed to select spots covered by tissue. Record the number of spots selected.

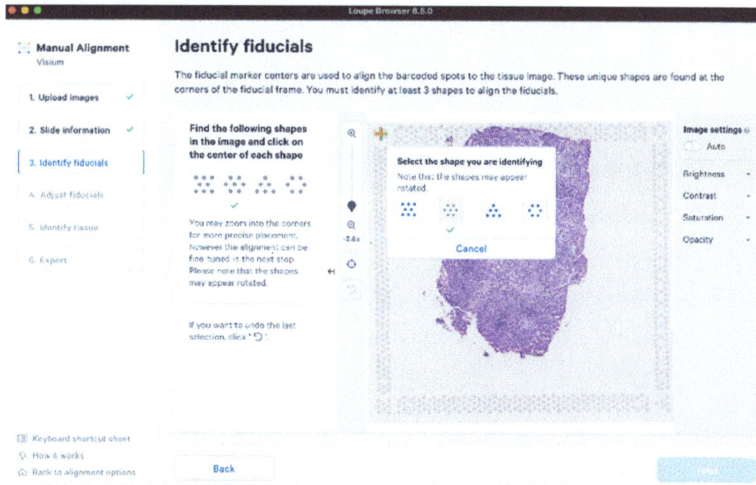

Fig. 15 Steps 3 and 4: Align the four unique fiducial markers to each corner of the fiducial frame, such that the spots overlay nicely onto the spots captured in the image

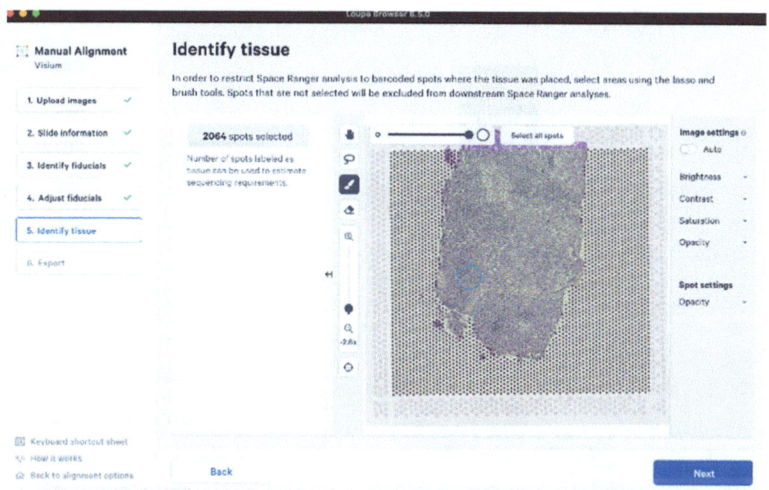

Fig. 16 Step 5: Highlight portions where tissues overlay the printed spots within the fiducial frame to determine number of spots covered by tissue

4. Export JSON file for Space Ranger analysis. Repeat for each Frame.
5. Sequencing Depth/spot is recommended as a minimum of 25 000 read pairs per tissue covered spot on Capture Area. Calculate the sequencing depth required by calculating Capture Area (%) covered by tissue.

   Calculations based on given example (Figs. 13–17) above:

   % Capture area = 2064/5000 × 100% = 41.28 %

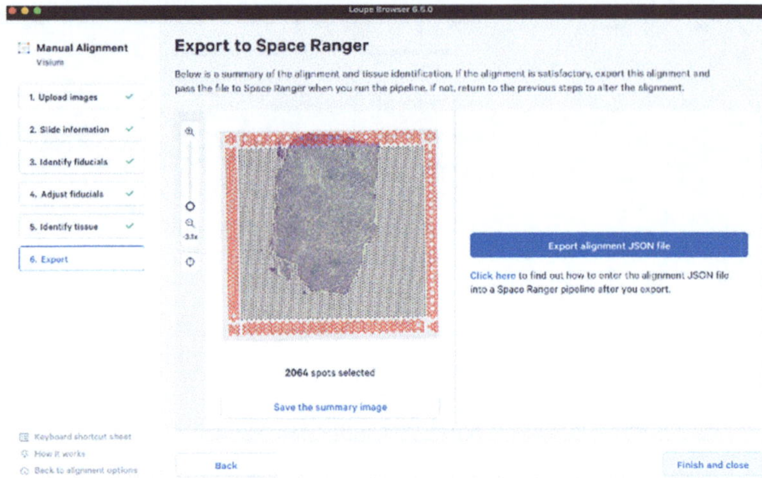

Fig. 17 Step 6: Export file (JSON) which will be required for analysis

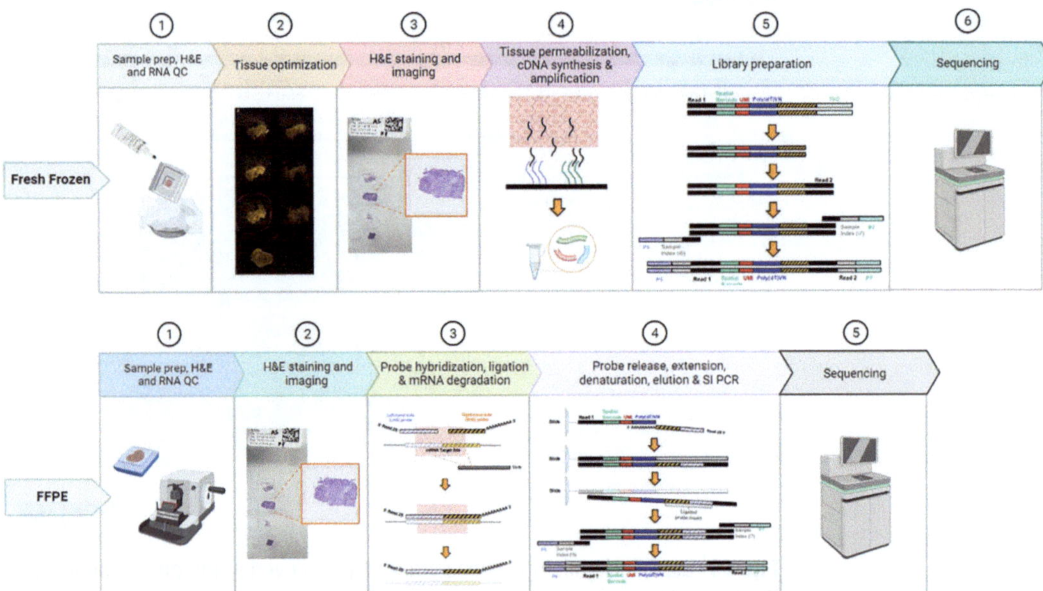

Fig. 18 Workflow overview

Total sequencing depth/sample = (0.4128 × 5000 total spots) × 25 000 read pairs/spot
= 51 600 000 total read pairs for that sample

6. Calculate the sequencing depths required for each of the four samples. Determine if samples can be pooled to fit into partial sequencing lane.
7. If samples can be pooled, calculate the pooling ratio. The sample with the lowest sequencing requirement can be used as the denominator:

Example:

Sample	Sequencing depth required	Pooling ratio
A	38500000	3.48 (A/C)
B	52750000	4.76 (B/C)
C	11075000	1.00 (C/C)
D	21175000	1.91 (D/C)

8. Calculate the volumes required for pooling based on the molarity (nM) determined at the final library QC step. Store pooled/individual libraries at −20°C until ready to be sent for sequencing.

4 Notes

1. It is advisable to keep the Visium slides in their original container(s) to avoid accidental damage.
2. It is advisable to perform the embedding process one sample at a time to avoid mixing up samples.
3. For small biopsy samples, it is advisable to perform trimming at a low thickness setting, e.g., 5 μm, to avoid depleting the sample.
4. It is strongly advisable not to cover the fiducial frame with the tissue section or OCT to avoid potential tissue detachment downstream.
5. When sectioning for Visium Spatial Gene Expression Slides, it is advisable to use a fresh part of the blade for each sample to avoid cross-contamination. Cryostat surfaces and utensils should also be cleaned with RNAse Away Reagent and 70% Ethanol between each sample.
6. Best to aliquot methanol fresh on the day of the procedure. Methanol must be pre-chilled for at least 20 min.
7. Do not add directly to tissues. Add to the areas surrounding the tissues dropwise and ensure that tissues are covered completely in a "bubble." See picture in Step 11 as an example. Follow this manner throughout the staining protocol.
8. Prepare the eosin mix while waiting here.
9. Ensure that most of the excess water has been drained off. Use a laboratory wipe to gently touch the edges of the frames to absorb the excess.

10. For even eosin staining, ensure that most of the excess water has been drained off at this step. Use a laboratory wipe to gently touch the edges of the frames to absorb the excess.
11. 10× Genomics recommends 1 min. For some tissues, this might not be enough. Two minutes is sufficient for most tissues tested.
12. 10× Genomics recommends 15 washes. For some tissues, this might wash the eosin off. Ten washes are sufficient for most tissues tested.
13. Should air bubbles be present, use a small pipette to gently suck them out.
14. When mounting the Visium Gene Expression Slide, it is advised to screen the slide under the microscope to check for air bubbles before proceeding on. If tiny air bubbles are present, it is recommended to remove the coverslip and remount the Visium slide. This is done by using a clean scalpel blade to gently lift the coverslip off the slide. Proceed to reapply an appropriate amount of glycerol and mount the slide using a new coverslip.
15. Avoid selecting a condition with high signal saturation and/or poor contrast with diffused signal.
16. Ensure little to no bubbles are present.
17. Any remaining tissue would cause auto-fluorescence and will affect the choice of an optimal permeabilization timing.
18. Perm enzyme needs to be pre-heated to 37°C for at least 15 min. Mark the corners of each well where there is NO tissue. Aim to pipette against that corner. This helps to prevent scratching the tissue. Indicate the timings next to well.
19. Removing all the Perm Enzyme is crucial to prevent any carry-over that might affect the next step of the protocol. After removing once with P200 pipette, use a P10 pipette to remove remaining reagent.
20. Prepare the 0.08M KOH fresh and ensure accurate dilution.
21. Ensure slide serial number has been recorded prior to discarding the slide.
22. 10× Genomics recommends 25 cycles total. For samples with lower DV200% values, 30 cycles can be set to ensure the exponential phase, peak value, and plateau can be observed in the amplification plot.
23. Technical duplicates recommended. If technical duplicates are performed, take the average Cq value of the replicates at this step.
24. Ensure accurate volumes of SPRI beads and sample for this step. E.g. Top sample up with NFW if 100 μl cannot be achieved.

25. Keep supernatant in clean tubes until QC is completed.
26. Air dry duration is dependent on ambient temperature and humidity. Shorten duration if necessary to prevent over drying. When beads have a glossy sheen and there are no surrounding ethanol droplets, proceed to the next step.
27. 10× Genomics recommends using only 10 μl (25%) cDNA for library construction as adding more would not result in higher library complexity. However, if cDNA yield is extremely low (e.g., for poorer quality tissues), use a higher volume of up to the maximum volume of cDNA (35 μl).
28. Ensure accurate volumes of SPRI beads and sample for this step. E.g., Top sample up with NFW if 50 μl cannot be achieved.
29. Keep supernatant in clean tubes until library QC is completed.
30. Air dry duration is dependent on ambient temperature and humidity. Shorten duration if necessary to prevent over drying. When beads have a glossy sheen and there are no surrounding ethanol droplets, proceed to the next step.
31. Immediately proceed on to the next step once Ligation is complete to minimize adapter-dimer formation.
32. Keep supernatant in clean tubes until QC is completed.
33. Air dry duration is dependent on ambient temperature and humidity. Shorten duration if necessary to prevent over drying. When beads have a glossy sheen and there are no surrounding ethanol droplets, proceed to the next step.
34. Ensure that no sample indices overlap in a multiplexed sequencing run.
35. Ensure accurate volumes of SPRI beads and sample for this step. E.g., Top sample up with NFW if 100 μl cannot be achieved.
36. Keep supernatant in clean tubes until library QC is completed.
37. Air dry duration is dependent on ambient temperature and humidity. Shorten duration if necessary to prevent over drying. When beads have a glossy sheen and there are no surrounding ethanol droplets, proceed to the next step.
38. For small biopsy samples, it is advisable to perform trimming at a low thickness setting, e.g., 5 μm, to avoid depleting the sample.
39. It is advised to section a ribbon of at least three consecutive sections and to avoid using the first section of the ribbon.
40. It is advisable to fill up the capture areas (frames) from the top to bottom of the Visium slide to avoid damaging the prior adhered section(s) at the lower frame(s).

41. Perform this step in the fume hood. Pipetting on reagents, instead of dunking the slide into Coplin jars, may be a better alternative for tissues with lower DV200% values to ensure the tissues remained adhered. Be gentle when drying the slide with Kimwipes to avoid scratching the slide.
42. Uneven coverage will result in uneven staining.
43. 10× Genomics recommends a glycerol mix (200 μl consisting of 10 μl RNase Inhibitor, 20 μl NFW and 170 μl glycerol. The presence of NFW might cause the eosin to leech for some tissues. One hundred percent glycerol is a more suitable option for these tissues. Optimization to find the best glycerol mix for each tissue sample before conducting the actual experiment is recommended.
44. Should air bubbles be present, use a small pipette to gently suck them out.
45. It is advised to visualize the slide under the microscope to check for air bubbles before proceeding on to the next step. If many air bubbles are present, it is recommended to remove the coverslip and remount the Visium slide. This is done by using a clean scalpel blade to gently lift the coverslip off the slide. Proceed to reapply an appropriate amount of glycerol and mount the slide using a new coverslip.
46. There are multiple imaging systems compatible with this application. Our preferred model is indicated under the list of materials and equipment required at the beginning of the protocol.
47. If coverslip does not slide off on its own after 5 min of immersion, try dunking a few times.
48. Refer to Fig. 5 for tips on marking the well corners on the Visium Casette to avoid contact with the tissue during pipetting.
49. Cooling of the well or Post-Hyb Wash Buffer may cause non-specific hybridization.
50. The tissue might disintegrate during Permeabilization. This is normal and does not affect performance.
51. Prepare the 0.08M KOH fresh every run and ensure accurate dilution.
52. Refer to Figs. 6–10 for an illustrated example.
53. Keep supernatant in clean tubes until library QC is completed.
54. Air dry duration is dependent on ambient temperature and humidity. Shorten duration if necessary to prevent over drying. When beads have a glossy sheen and there are no surrounding ethanol droplets, proceed to the next step.
55. If high yield is expected, perform 10× dilution for QC.

Conflict of Interest

The authors declare no competing interests.

References

1. Boyd DF, Allen EK, Randolph AG, Guo XJ, Weng Y, Sanders CJ, Bajracharya R, Lee NK, Guy CS, Vogel P, Guan W, Li Y, Liu X, Novak T, Newhams MM, Fabrizio TP, Wohlgemuth N, Mourani PM, Wight TN et al (2020) Exuberant fibroblast activity compromises lung function via ADAMTS4. Nature **587**(7834):466–471. https://doi.org/10.1038/s41586-020-2877-5
2. Cassier PA, Navaridas R, Bellina M, Rama N, Ducarouge B, Hernandez-Vargas H, Delord J-P, Lengrand J, Paradisi A, Fattet L, Garin G, Gheit H, Dalban C, Pastushenko I, Neves D, Jelin R, Gadot N, Braissand N, Léon S et al (2023) Netrin-1 blockade inhibits tumour growth and EMT features in endometrial cancer. Nature **620**(7973):409–416. https://doi.org/10.1038/s41586-023-06367-z
3. Hwang WL, Jagadeesh KA, Guo JA, Hoffman HI, Yadollahpour P, Reeves JW, Mohan R, Drokhlyansky E, Van Wittenberghe N, Ashenberg O, Farhi SL, Schapiro D, Divakar P, Miller E, Zollinger DR, Eng G, Schenkel JM, Su J, Shiau C et al (2022) Single-nucleus and spatial transcriptome profiling of pancreatic cancer identifies multicellular dynamics associated with neoadjuvant treatment. Nat Genet **54**(8):1178–1191. https://doi.org/10.1038/s41588-022-01134-8
4. Karras P, Bordeu I, Pozniak J, Nowosad A, Pazzi C, Van Raemdonck N, Landeloos E, Van Herck Y, Pedri D, Bervoets G, Makhzami S, Khoo JH, Pavie B, Lamote J, Marin-Bejar O, Dewaele M, Liang H, Zhang X, Hua Y et al (2022) A cellular hierarchy in melanoma uncouples growth and metastasis. Nature **610**(7930):190–198. https://doi.org/10.1038/s41586-022-05242-7
5. Lee JY, Kannan B, Lim BY, Li Z, Lim AH, Loh JW, Ko TK, Ng CC-Y, Chan JY (2022) The multi-dimensional biomarker landscape in cancer immunotherapy. Int J Mol Sci **23**(14):7839. https://doi.org/10.3390/ijms23147839
6. Loh JW, Lee JY, Lim AH, Guan P, Lim BY, Kannan B, Lee ECY, Gu NX, Ko TK, Ng CC-Y, Lim JCT, Yeong J, Lim JQ, Ong CK, Teh BT, Chan JY (2023) Spatial transcriptomics reveal topological immune landscapes of Asian head and neck angiosarcoma. Commun Biol **6**(1):461. https://doi.org/10.1038/s42003-023-04856-5
7. Ståhl PL, Salmén F, Vickovic S, Lundmark A, Navarro JF, Magnusson J, Giacomello S, Asp M, Westholm JO, Huss M, Mollbrink A, Linnarsson S, Codeluppi S, Borg Å, Pontén F, Costea PI, Sahlén P, Mulder J, Bergmann O et al (2016) Visualization and analysis of gene expression in tissue sections by spatial transcriptomics. Science **353**(6294):78–82. https://doi.org/10.1126/science.aaf2403

Chapter 11

Highly Multiplexed Single-Cell In Situ RNA and DNA Analysis by Consecutive Hybridization

Lu Xiao and Jia Guo

Abstract

Knowledge of the copy numbers of transcripts and genomic loci in their natural spatial contexts plays an important role in our understanding of biology and medicine. Fluorescent hybridization probes have emerged as a powerful tool to profile transcripts and genomic loci in single cells in situ. However, the number of different nucleic acid species that can be quantified by fluorescence imaging-based methods is limited. Here, we report a highly multiplexed in situ hybridization approach for spatial transcriptomics and genomics analysis. In this approach, each nucleic acid molecule is visualized as a fluorescent spot at its natural cellular context throughout the consecutive cycles of fluorescence in situ hybridization. In each analysis cycle, fluorescent oligonucleotide probes stain the nucleic acid targets by hybridizing to the probes applied in the previous cycle. And these probes also introduce the binding sites for the next cycle probes. Through reiterative cycles of hybridization, imaging, and photobleaching, unique color sequences are generated as barcodes for varied nucleic acids. With multi-color staining and reiterative cycles, tens of thousands of different transcripts or genomic loci could be precisely profiled in individual cells in situ.

Keywords In situ hybridization, Fluorescent probes, Nucleic acids, Transcripts, Genomic loci, Spatial omics

1 Introduction

Comprehensive analyses of transcripts and genomic loci in single cells in situ promise to advance our understanding of many complex biological systems, such as solid tumors, brain tissues, and developing embryos [1]. Fluorescence In situ hybridization has proven to be a promising tool to study nucleic acids in their natural spatial contexts [2–4]. However, the multiplexing capacity of this fluorescence imaging-based method is limited. To enable multiplexed in situ nucleic acids analysis, combinatorial labeling [5–7], reiterative hybridization [8–12], sequential hybridization [13, 14], in situ sequencing [15, 16], and multiplexed error-robust fluorescence in situ hybridization (MER-FISH) [17–19] have been developed recently. Although these methods enable multiplexed nucleic acids profiling at the

Timothy L. Frankel and Arvind Rao (eds.), *Cellular Spatial Characterization and Analysis*, Methods in Molecular Biology, vol. 2995, https://doi.org/10.1007/978-1-0716-5027-1_11,

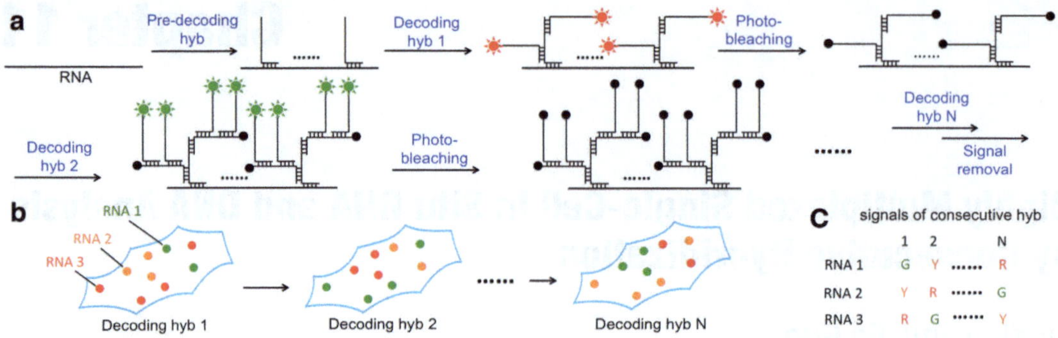

Fig. 1 Highly multiplexed single-cell in situ RNA and DNA analysis using C-FISH. (**a**) In every hybridization cycle, the nucleic acids targets are stained by decoding probe hybridization. Following image capture, the staining signals are photobleached to initiate the next cycle. (**b**) Under a fluorescence microscope, each target molecule is detected as a fluorescent spot. (**c**) As the spot locations remain in each cycle, the varied nucleic acids can be identified by a unique color barcode. Reproduced with permission from Ref. [20] from MDPI

subcellular resolution, further improvements on analysis accuracy, detection sensitivity, and multiplexing capacity are still required.

Here, we describe a novel spatial transcriptomics and genomics approach with super high analysis accuracy. In this method (Fig. 1), each nucleic acid molecule is stained via consecutive fluorescence In situ hybridization (C-FISH) [20]. Specifically, each individual transcript or genomic locus is first hybridized with a set of non-fluorescently labeled pre-decoding probes. In each of the following C-FISH cycles, these transcripts or genomic locus are detected as fluorescent spots under a fluorescence microscope via decoding probe hybridization. Each of these decoding probes introduces multiple binding sites for the probes in the next cycle. By amplifying the staining signals cycle by cycle and also avoiding the probe dehybridization, the high signal-to-noise ratio is maintained throughout all the analysis cycles. As a result, without any complicated error correction, extremely high analysis accuracy is obtained using the image raw data. Following image capture, all of the fluorescence signals are removed by photobleaching. By consecutive cycles of target staining, imaging, and signal removal, a unique color sequence barcode is generated to decipher the identity of the nucleic acids. The multiplexing capacity of this approach is determined by the number of distinct color barcodes, which increases exponentially with the number of analysis cycles. Thus, with just a small number of C-FISH cycles, our approach could allow single-cell spatial transcriptomic and genomic analysis.

2 Materials

All the decoding probes are 70 nt long composed of three 20 nt sequences separated by two 5T spacers. The first 20 nt sequence hybridize to the target or the probes in the previous cycle, while the second and third 20 nt share the sequence to recruit the probes in the next cycle. The 45 nt pre-decoding probes include a 20 nt target-binding sequence and 20 nt probe-binding sequence, separated by a 5T spacer. The established probe design programs are used to design the probe sequences [2]. All the solutions are prepared with nuclease-free water.

2.1 Probe Preparation

1. Pre-decoding probes library: 10 nmol/μl pre-decoding probes, 1% Tris-EDTA, pH 8.0. Combine and dissolve over 30 pre-decoding probes for the same nucleic acid target.
2. 3′ Amino-modified decoding probes: 1 nmol/μl decoding probe in nuclease-free water.
3. Qusar 570 *N*-hydroxysuccinimide: 20 mM Qusar 570 in anhydrous DMF.
4. Cy5 *N*-hydroxysuccinimide: 20 mM Cy5 in anhydrous DMF.
5. Alexa 488 *N*-hydroxysuccinimide: 20 mM Alexa 488 in anhydrous DMF.
6. $NaHCO_3$: 1 M in nuclease-free water.
7. Nucleotide removal kit (Qiagen)
8. High-performance liquid chromatography (HPLC) C18 column (Agilent)
9. HPLC buffer A: 0.1 M triethyl ammonium bicarbonate in water, pH 8.0.
10. HPLC buffer B: acetonitrile.

2.2 Cell Culture and Fixation

1. Cell culture medium: 10% fetal bovine serum, 100 g/ml streptomycin, 100 U/ml penicillin in Dulbelcco's modified Eagle's Medium (DMEM).
2. Fixation solution (4% formaldehyde in nuclease-free 1× PBS).
3. Chambered coverglass.

2.3 RNA Pre-decoding Hybridization

1. Wash buffer: 10% formamide, 2 mM vanadyl ribonucleoside complex in 2× SSC.
2. RNA pre-decoding hybridization buffer: 100 mg/ml dextran sulfate, 1 mg/ml *Escherichia coli* tRNA, 2 mM vanadyl ribonucleoside complex, 20 μg/ml bovine serum albumin, and 10% formamide in 2× SSC.
3. Decoding hybridization buffer: 100 mg/ml dextran sulfate, 2 mM vanadyl ribonucleoside complex and 10% formamide in 2× SSC.
4. GLOX buffer: 0.4% glucose, 10 mM Tris HCl in 2× SSC.
5. GLOX solution: 0.37 mg/ml glucose oxidase, 1% catalase, 0.4% glucose in GLOX buffer.
6. Photobleaching buffer: 2 mM vanadyl ribonucleoside complex in 2× SSC.

7. 4',6-diamidino-2-phenylindole (DAPI): 5 ng/ml in wash buffer.

2.4 DNA Pre-decoding Hybridization

1. 2× SSCT: 0.1% Tween-20 in 2× SSC.
2. 1× PBST: 0.1% Tween-20 in 1× PBS.
3. DNA pre-decoding hybridization buffer: 100 mg/ml dextran sulfate, 50% formamide in 2× SSCT.
4. DNA denaturing buffer: 70% formamide in 2× SSCT.

2.5 Consecutive RNA and DNA FISH

1. Wash buffer: 10% formamide, 2 mM vanadyl ribonucleoside complex in 2× SSC.
2. Decoding hybridization buffer: 100 mg/ml dextran sulfate, 2 mM vanadyl ribonucleoside complex, and 10% formamide in 2× SSC.
3. GLOX buffer: 0.4% glucose, 10 mM Tris HCl in 2× SSC.
4. GLOX solution: 0.37 mg/ml glucose oxidase, 1% catalase, 0.4% glucose in GLOX buffer.
5. Photobleaching buffer: 2 mM vanadyl ribonucleoside complex in 2× SSC.
6. 4',6-diamidino-2-phenylindole (DAPI) solution: 5 ng/ml in wash buffer.

3 Methods

All the steps are performed at room temperature unless otherwise specified.

3.1 Synthesis of Fluorescent Decoding Probes

1. Mix 1 μl of 3' amino-modified decoding probe with 2 μl of nuclease-free water, 3 μl of 1 M $NaHCO_3$ and 5 μl of Alexa 488, Quasar 570 or Cy5 NHS ester (20 mM).
2. Incubate the solutions at room temperature in dark for 2 h.
3. Purify the reaction mixture with nucleotide removal kit according to vendor protocol.
4. Purify the product from the last step with HPLC equipped with a C18 column. HPLC is set to detect DNA absorption (260 nm) as well as the absorption of the fluorophore (e.g., 550 nm for Quasar 570). Buffer B is increased from 7% to 30% over the course of 30 min. Then run buffer B at 70% for 10 min, followed by 7% for another 10 min. The flow rate is 1 ml/min.
5. Dry the product after HPLC in a lyophilizer.
6. Dissolve the dried product with 100 μl 1% 1× Tris-EDTA, pH 8.0, as decoding probe stock solution and store at 4°C.

3.2 Cell Culture and Fixation

1. Maintain Hela CCL-2 cells in Dulbelcco's modified Eagle's Medium (DMEM) supplemented with 10% fetal bovine serum, 10 g/ml streptomycin, and 10 U/ml penicillin in a humidified atmosphere at 37°C with 5% CO_2.
2. Plate cells on chambered coverglass (0.2 ml medium/chamber) and maintain the cells in the incubator for 2 to 3 days to reach 60% confluency.
3. Wash cells with 1× PBS at room temperature for 5 min.
4. Add fixation solution and incubate at room temperature for 10 min.
5. Wash cells with 1× PBS twice, each for 5 min.
6. Add 70% EtOH and incubate at 4°C overnight to permeabilize the cells.

3.3 RNA Pre-decoding Hybridization

1. Add 1 μl of pre-decoding stock solution to 100 μl of RNA pre-decoding hybridization buffer (*see* **Note 1**), vortex, and centrifuge to obtain the direct staining hybridization solution.
2. Wash the fixed cells with wash buffer for 5 min.
3. Incubate the fixed cells with RNA pre-decoding hybridization solution for overnight at 37°C (*see* **Note 2**).
4. Wash the fixed cells three times with wash buffer at 37°C, each for 30 min.
5. Proceed to "3.5. Consecutive RNA and DNA FISH."

3.4 DNA Pre-decoding Hybridization

1. Add 1 μl of pre-decoding stock solution to 100 μl of RNA pre-decoding hybridization buffer, vortex, and centrifuge to obtain the DNA pre-decoding hybridization solution.
2. Wash the fixed cells with 1× PBS for 1 min.
3. Wash the fixed cells with 1× PBST for 1 min.
4. Incubate the fixed cells with 1× PBS + 0.5% (v/v) Triton-X 100 for 10 min.
5. Wash the fixed cells with 1× PBST for 2 min.
6. Incubate the fixed cells with 0.5 mg/ml RNase A in 1× PBST for 15 min at 37°C.
7. Wash the fixed cells with 1× PBS for 5 min.
8. Incubate the fixed cells with 0.1 M HCl for 5 min.
9. Wash the fixed cells three times with 2× SSCT, each for 2 min.
10. Wash the fixed cells with DNA denaturing buffer for 5 min.
11. Incubate the fixed cells with DNA denaturing buffer for 20 min at 78°C.

12. Incubate the fixed cells with DNA denaturing buffer for 20 min at 60°C.
13. Cool down the fixed cells to room temperature.
14. Incubate the fixed cells with DNA denaturing buffer for 15 min at 78°C.
15. Incubate the fixed cells with DNA pre-decoding hybridization solution for 10 min at 78°C.
16. Transfer the fixed cells to 37°C and incubate for overnight (*see* **Note 2**).
17. Wash the fixed cells with 2× SSC for 15 min at 60°C.
18. Wash the fixed cells with 2× SSC for 10 min.
19. Wash the fixed cells with 0.2× SSC for 10 min.

3.5 Consecutive RNA and DNA FISH

1. Add 5 μl of decoding probe stock solution to 100 μl of decoding hybridization buffer, vortex, and centrifuge to obtain the decoding hybridization solution.
2. Incubate the fixed cells with decoding hybridization solution for 30 min at 37°C.
3. Wash the fixed cells with wash buffer for 30 min at 37°C.
4. Incubate the fixed cells with DAPI solution for 30 min at 37°C.
5. Equilibrate the cells in GLOX buffer (*see* **Note 3**) for 2 min and image in fresh GLOX solution.
6. After imaging, photobleach the fluorescent signal (*see* **Note 4**).
7. Perform the next cycle of consecutive RNA and DNA FISH.

3.6 Imaging and Spot Identification

1. Image the stained cells under a fluorescence microscope (*see* **Note 5**).
2. Identify the fluorescent spots computationally using an image processing program [16].

4 Notes

1. Prepare the RNA-pre-decoding hybridization buffer at 10 ml scale, store the aliquot at −20°C to maintain the function of *Escherichia coli* tRNA and bovine serum albumin.
2. Four hours of incubation is enough for hybridization in this step and all the other steps where overnight incubation is mentioned. Researchers can arrange a more efficient experiment plan based on the schedule. We place the cells in a humidified chamber to prevent the solution drying.

3. GLOX buffer and solution need to be freshly prepared right before the imaging step.
4. We photobeach Alexa 488, Quasar 570 or Cy5 with their corresponding filters at each z-step for 60 s, 20 s, and 5 s, respectively. During the photobleaching, we incubate the cells in photobleaching buffer, and the buffer is changed every 3 min.
5. We image the stained cells under a Nikon Ti-E epifluorescence microscope equipped with a 100× objective, using a 5 μm Z-range and 0.3 μm Z-spacing. We capture images using a CoolSNAP HQ2 camera and analyzed with NIS-Elements Imaging software. We use Chroma filters 49011, 49004, and 49009 for Alexa 488, Quasar 570, and Cy5, respectively.

Acknowledgments

We are grateful for support from the National Institute of General Medical Sciences (1R01GM127633).

Conflict of Interest The authors have no conflicts of interest to declare that are relevant to the content of this chapter.

References

1. Crosetto N, Bienko M, Oudenaarden AV (2014) Spatially resolved transcriptomics and beyond. Nat Rev Genet 16:57–66
2. Raj A et al (2008) Imaging individual mRNA molecules using multiple singly labeled probes. Nat Methods 5:877–879
3. Franzini RM, Kool ET (2009) Efficient nucleic acid detection by templated reductive quencher release. J Am Chem Soc 131:16021–16023
4. Guo J, Ju J, Turro NJ (2012) Fluorescent hybridization probes for nucleic acid detection. Anal Bioanal Chem 402:3115–3125
5. Levesque MJ, Raj A (2013) Single-chromosome transcriptional profiling reveals chromosomal gene expression regulation. Nat Methods 10:246–248
6. Levsky JM, Shenoy SM, Pezo RC, Singer RH (2002) Single-cell gene expression profiling. Science 297:836–840
7. Lubeck E, Cai L (2012) Single-cell systems biology by super-resolution imaging and combinatorial labeling. Nat Methods 9:743–748
8. Xiao L, Guo J (2015) Multiplexed single-cell in situ RNA analysis by reiterative hybridization. Anal Methods 7:7290–7295
9. Xiao L, Guo J (2018) Single-cell in situ RNA analysis with switchable fluorescent oligonucleotides. Front Cell Dev Biol 6:1–9
10. Mondal M et al (2018) Highly multiplexed single-cell in situ RNA and DNA analysis with bioorthogonal cleavable fluorescent oligonucleotides. Chem Sci 9:2909–2917
11. Shaffer SM et al (2017) Rare cell variability and drug-induced reprogramming as a mode of cancer drug resistance. Nature 546:431–435
12. Xiao L, Labaer J, Guo J (2021) Highly sensitive and multiplexed in situ RNA profiling with cleavable fluorescent tyramide. Cells 10:1277
13. Eng C-HL et al (2019) Transcriptome-scale super-resolved imaging in tissues by RNA seqFISH+. Nature 568:235–239
14. Lubeck E et al (2014) Single-cell in situ RNA profiling by sequential hybridization. Nat Methods 11:360–361
15. Ke R et al (2013) In situ sequencing for RNA analysis in preserved tissue and cells. Nat Methods 10:857–860
16. Lee JH et al (2014) Highly multiplexed subcellular RNA sequencing in situ. Science 343:1360–1363

17. Chen KH et al (2015) Spatially resolved, highly multiplexed RNA profiling in single cells. Science 348:aaa6090
18. Moffitt JR et al (2016) High-performance multiplexed fluorescence in situ hybridization in culture and tissue with matrix imprinting and clearing. Proc Natl Acad Sci 113:14456–14461
19. Moffitt JR et al (2016) High-throughput single-cell gene-expression profiling with multiplexed error-robust fluorescence in situ hybridization. Proc Natl Acad Sci 113:11046–11051
20. Xiao L, Liao R, Guo J (2020) Highly multiplexed single-cell in situ RNA and DNA analysis by consecutive hybridization. Molecules 25:4900

Check for updates

Chapter 12

From Raw Data to Biological Insights: A Practical Guide for Spatial Transcriptomics Analysis in R and Python

Ahmed M. Elhossiny, Reva Kulkarni, Arvind Rao and Timothy L. Frankel

Abstract

Spatial transcriptomics has revolutionized molecular biology by enabling the capture of gene expression within intact tissue architecture, thereby preserving crucial spatial context often lost in traditional single-cell RNA-sequencing. This breakthrough allows for the study of cellular organization, neighborhood interactions, and functional niches, offering critical insights into complex biological processes. To effectively analyze this complex data, specialized data containers are employed, integrating spatial coordinates with molecular expression. Before extracting biological insights, rigorous preprocessing steps are essential to characterize the tissue accurately. These foundational steps are followed by downstream analyses, including deconvolution, spatial-domain identification, and advanced methods for cell-type-specific differential expression, cell–cell communication, and neighborhood analysis. This chapter provides detailed descriptions of major R and Python object classes tailored for spatial transcriptomics analysis, supporting comprehensive workflows from data management to the derivation of profound biological insights.

Keywords Spatial transcriptomics, R, Python, Data objects, Seurat, Squidpy, Spatial feature experiment, Giotto, Data analysis, Deconvolution, Clustering

1 Introduction

Spatial transcriptomics has emerged as a transformative technology in molecular biology, earning the title of "Method of the Year" in 2020 [1]. Unlike traditional RNA-sequencing approaches that dissociate cells and erase spatial context, spatial transcriptomics captures gene expression within intact tissue architecture. This breakthrough enables the study of cellular organization, neighborhood interactions, and functional niches within tissues—an especially powerful application in the tumor microenvironment, where spatial context shapes disease progression and therapeutic response. The ability to retain positional information adds complexity to data analysis, often requiring deconvolution to resolve cellular compositions within multicellular spots, spatially-aware clustering to identify different

Timothy L. Frankel and Arvind Rao (eds.), *Cellular Spatial Characterization and Analysis*, Methods in Molecular Biology, vol. 2995, https://doi.org/10.1007/978-1-0716-5027-1_12,

spatial domains and downstream analysis to account for the spatial relationships between the observations (cells/spots).

By preserving spatial coordinates, this technology allows researchers to examine not just what genes are expressed, but *where* and *in relation to what*, revealing critical insights into immune evasion, stromal remodeling, therapy resistance, and tumor heterogeneity. Cutting-edge platforms—ranging from 10× Visium to subcellular tools like MERFISH and 10x Xenium—offer varying resolution and throughput, supporting applications from microenvironmental mapping to subcellular RNA localization. As this field rapidly advances, spatial transcriptomics is evolving from a descriptive modality into a mechanistic tool driving precision oncology and biomarker discovery [2, 3].

2 Materials

2.1 Software

- R (https://www.r-project.org/): A programming language widely used for statistical computing and graphics [4]. The following R packages are also needed.
  a. Seurat V5 (https://satijalab.org/seurat/): An R package designed for quality control, analysis, and exploration of single-cell RNA-seq data, with extensions for spatial transcriptomics [5].
  b. SpatialFeatureExperiment (SFE) (https://www.bioconductor.org/packages/release/bioc/html/SpatialFeatureExperiment.html): An R package from Bioconductor for handling spatial omics data, integrating expression, spatial coordinates, and images [6].
  c. Giotto Suite (https://drieslab.github.io/Giotto_website/): A comprehensive R toolkit specifically designed for the analysis and visualization of spatial transcriptomics data [7].
  d. RCTD (Robust Cell Type Deconvolution) (https://github.com/dmcable/spacexr): An R package focused on deconvolution of spatial transcriptomics data to estimate cell type proportions and cell-type specific differential expression [8].
  e. C-SIDE (Cell-type Specific Inference of Differential Expression) (https://github.com/dmcable/spacexr): An R method within spaceXr for identifying differentially expressed genes within specific cell types in spatial transcriptomics data [9].
  f. BayesPrism (https://github.com/Danko-Lab/BayesPrism): An R package for Bayesian deconvolution of bulk and spatial transcriptomics data, capable of handling hierarchical cell type structures [10].

g. InstaPrism (https://github.com/humengying0907/InstaPrism): A faster implementation of the BayesPrism algorithm for deconvolution [11].
h. CARD (Cell-type Aware Resolution Deconvolution) (https://github.com/YMa-lab/CARD): An R method that incorporates spatial context to improve the accuracy of cell type deconvolution in spatial transcriptomics [12].
i. BayesSpace (https://www.bioconductor.org/packages/release/bioc/html/BayesSpace.html): An R package that uses a Bayesian statistical model to perform spatially-aware clustering of spatial transcriptomics data [13].
j. CellChat (https://github.com/jinworks/CellChat): An R package for inferring and visualizing cell-cell communication networks from single-cell RNA-seq data, with spatial context integration [14].
k. SPATA2 (https://themilolab.github.io/SPATA2/): An R package SPATA2 integrates spatial transcriptomics data analysis with advanced features like trajectory inference and gene module identification [15].
l. Semla (https://ludvigla.github.io/semla/): An R package designed for interactive processing, analysis, and visualization of spatially resolved transcriptomics data including image alignment, cell type mapping, spatial statistics, and web-based exploration tools [16].

- Python (https://www.python.org/): A programming language widely used for data science and machine learning. The following Python packages are also needed.

m. Scanpy (https://scanpy.readthedocs.io/en/stable/): A Python-based toolkit for single-cell gene expression data analysis, with functionalities relevant to spatial transcriptomics [17].
n. Squidpy (https://squidpy.readthedocs.io/en/stable/): A Python package that extends Scanpy for the spatial analysis of single-cell transcriptomics data [18].
o. AnnData (https://anndata.readthedocs.io/en/stable/): A Python package designed for quality control, analysis, and exploration of matrix-like data, especially RNA-seq, and is flexible for single-cell or spatial transcriptomics [19].
p. GraphST (https://deepst-tutorials.readthedocs.io/en/latest/index.html): An advanced clustering method that uses graph neural networks to integrate spatial and transcriptional information for spatial transcriptomics data [20].
q. LIANA+ (https://liana-py.readthedocs.io/en/latest/): A Python framework for ligand-receptor interaction

analysis in single-cell and spatial transcriptomics, using spatial autocorrelation metrics [21].

2.2 Datasets

1. **Spatial transcriptomics data:** generated by various platforms like 10× Visium, Visium HD, Xenium, and MERFISH, can be either imaging-based or sequencing-based. The analytical framework utilizes an input dataset consisting of an observation (cell/spot/pixel) by gene matrix, along with a corresponding spatial coordinate matrix that includes x and y coordinates for each observation. These are common outputs of the data processing pipelines such as SpaceRanger software from 10× Genomics.
2. **A single-cell RNA sequencing (scRNA-seq) dataset:** consisting of a cell-by-feature matrix of gene expression data, is required. This dataset should originate from the same tissue being analyzed with spatial transcriptomics. The purpose of incorporating the scRNA-seq data is to establish the transcriptomic profiles for each cell type, which will then be used for deconvolution in the spatial analysis.

3 Methods

3.1 Creating Data Objects for Spatial Transcriptomics Datasets

Several data objects are commonly employed in spatial transcriptomics data analysis and must be created to perform analysis. Here, we detail four primary R object types: Seurat, SpatialFeatureExperiment (SFE), Giotto, and specialized objects like spacexr as well as AnnData for Python. We also present interoperability between R and Python data objects, as switching between languages is often necessary for full use of spatial analysis tools.

3.1.1 Seurat Object

Seurat objects are widely used in both single-cell RNA-seq (scRNA-seq) and spatial transcriptomics analyses. They provide a comprehensive container that integrates spatial and gene expression data.

A Seurat object comprises several key slots:

- **Assays:** Stores multiple assay types (e.g., raw counts, normalized expression data, and deconvolution outputs, … etc.).
- **Metadata:** Contains detailed information for each observation (cell/spot), such as sample identifiers, experimental conditions, patient information, and cluster assignments.
- **Reductions:** Holds dimensionally reduced representations of the data, like PCA, UMAP, or integrated embeddings.
- **Neighbors and Graphs:** Maintains graph structures and neighborhood information, crucial for clustering methods like Leiden or Louvain.

- **Image Data:** Accommodates both low- and high-resolution histological images (e.g., H&E-stained tissue sections) along with corresponding spatial coordinates of spots.
- **Miscellaneous:** Provides storage for additional unstructured data or annotations.
- **Version and Commands**: Tracks the version of Seurat used and the commands executed, ensuring reproducibility.

Seurat offers a suite of wrapper functions that streamline data processing. These include methods for normalization, data scaling, dimensionality reduction, multi-dataset integration, and visualization, enabling effective interpretation of spatial transcriptomics data.

3.1.2 SpatialFeature Experiment (SFE)

SpatialFeatureExperiment (SFE) extends the Bioconductor SpatialExperiment framework, offering robust integration of spatial metadata with expression data beside key features including:

- **Spatial Data Integration:** Combines gene expression, spatial coordinates, and image data.
- **Compatibility:** Integrates seamlessly with spatial statistics packages like "spdep" and "sf", facilitating advanced geospatial analysis.

SFE objects provide a standardized structure for handling spatial transcriptomics data within the Bioconductor ecosystem.

3.1.3 Giotto Object

Giotto is a specialized suite designed specifically for spatial transcriptomics, supporting a wide range of spatial analyses, platforms and technologies. Salient features of Giotto objects are:

- **Data Storage and Flexibility:** Handles diverse data types, including expression matrices, spatial coordinates, and cell annotations.
- **Spatial Analysis:** Provides comprehensive tools for spatial clustering, differential expression, and interactive visualization.

Giotto's design emphasizes comprehensive spatial analysis, making it a powerful tool for researchers focused on spatial transcriptomics.

3.1.4 Additional Specialized Objects

In addition to the primary objects mentioned above, several other specialized R objects are used for specific spatial transcriptomics analyses:

- **spaceXr (spatialRNA):** Tailored for RCTD deconvolution, estimating cellular composition from spatial transcriptomics data.
- **SPATA2:** Integrates spatial transcriptomics data analysis with advanced features like trajectory inference and gene module identification.

These specialized objects address specific analytical needs within the broader field of spatial transcriptomics.

3.1.5 Interoperability Between Objects

Efficient data analysis often requires the use of multiple software tools. While we focus on R objects in this protocol, there are many Python packages providing key spatial transcriptomics analyses, including LIANA+ for cell communication, and Scanpy for domain identification and visualization as detailed in a later section. The main Python object used to contain gene expression counts, spatial coordinates, and any additional spot-level or gene-level variables is an AnnData object. Once the cell/spot-by-gene matrix X, cell/spot coordinate matrix Y, and corresponding H&E image pixel values along with pixel to micron conversions are obtained, an AnnData object can be created. This object can be saved as an *h5ad* file, which can be read and accessed in R using the same functions as in Python after installing the "anndata" and "reticulate" packages. This allows conversion between AnnData and Seurat objects, enabling the downstream use of multiple tools across programming languages.

Additionally, interconversion between different R object frameworks enhances flexibility and supports diverse analytical pipelines. Key conversion functions in R include:

- as.Seurat(): Converts Giotto or SpatialFeatureExperiment objects to Seurat objects.
- as.SpatialExperiment(): Converts Seurat objects to SpatialFeatureExperiment objects.
- Export/import functionalities: Support standard formats like .h5, .csv, and .rds for smooth integration with other software.

These conversion capabilities ensure that researchers can leverage the strengths of different packages and workflows.

3.2 Quality Control (QC) and Sample Preprocessing

3.2.1 Spatially-Aware QC and Spot-Swapping Correction

Before any downstream analyses, the sample must undergo rigorous QC to remove overly sparse genes and cells/spots. Common filters include excluding spots or cells with high mitochondrial gene counts, which often signal low quality. Tools like the R package "SpotSweeper" offer spatially-aware QC: they compute local (nearest-neighbor) metrics (e.g., library size, unique genes, mitochondrial read percentage) to detect both isolated low-quality spots and larger technical artifacts—ensuring spatial continuity while removing noise [22]. Another prevalent artifact in spatial transcriptomics is "spot-swapping," where transcripts bleed into neighboring spots, skewing gene expression profiles. The R package "SpotClean" addresses this by estimating a contamination rate and then probabilistically adjusting gene-specific UMI counts. This improves accuracy in tasks like marker gene detection, clustering, and tissue annotation. However, SpotClean assumes at least ~25% of the slide is empty (no tissue), which is critical for distinguishing contamination from signal [23].

3.2.2 Normalization

Normalization remains an active area of research. While methods from scRNA-seq (like log-normalization or SCTransform) are still widely used, they may inadvertently remove genuine spatial biology. Indeed, studies show library size correlates with tissue structure, and naive normalization can degrade spatial domain detection. To address this, the new "SpaNorm" method uses spatially-aware normalization: it jointly models library size and biological variability via spatially smoothed functions, then subtracts only the technical component. Benchmarks across 27 samples from six platforms show SpaNorm retains spatial domains and variable genes more effectively than popular scRNA-seq methods [24, 25].

3.2.3 Batch Effects and Samples Integration

Batch-effect correction is often done implicitly, especially during normalization and modelling steps like deconvolution, however, an independent batch-effect correction method is usually needed when integrating multiple heterogeneous datasets. Although approaches like MNN or scVI (borrowed from scRNA-seq) work for integrating multiple samples, spatial-specific tools are emerging [26, 27]. For example, "GraphST" supports vertical integration across serial sections and horizontal integration of adjacent sections, preserving spatial structure [20].

3.3 Deconvolution Methods in Spatial Transcriptomics

Deconvolution is a critical step in spatial transcriptomics data analysis. It aims to quantify the proportions of different cell types within each spatially resolved spot or pixel. While reference-free methods exist, the accuracy of deconvolution is significantly enhanced by using gene expression references from known cell types, typically derived from single-cell RNA-seq datasets. Various computational methods are available, each employing distinct statistical models, but all seek to output a matrix of spots/pixels by cell-type fractions. Some methods, such as "BayesPrism" and "DestVI", also estimate cell-type-specific gene expression [28].

3.3.1 RCTD (spaceXr)

spaceXr is a flexible toolkit designed explicitly for spatial transcriptomics data. It offers robust cell-type deconvolution (RCTD) and cell-type-specific differential expression analysis (C-SIDE). spaceXr accommodates varying spatial resolutions, with modes tailored for single-cell resolution, dual-cell mixtures, or multicellular spots.

3.3.2 BayesPrism

BayesPrism, originally developed for bulk RNA-seq deconvolution, has been adapted for spatial transcriptomics. Its strength lies in its probabilistic framework, which allows for nuanced inference by handling hierarchical cell-type structures. BayesPrism can differentiate between general cell types (e.g., T-cells) and specific subtypes or states (e.g., CD8+ T-cells, CD4+ T-cells). It also predicts cell-type-specific expression profiles, enabling further single-cell analytical techniques. A primary limitation of BayesPrism is its computational demand, which requires substantial runtime. "InstaPrism" has been developed to address this, providing faster performance while maintaining accuracy.

3.3.3 CARD

CARD (Conditional AutoRegressive model-based Deconvolution) incorporates spatial context into cell-type deconvolution. It explicitly models spatial autocorrelation to leverage the spatial arrangement of cells, improving the accuracy and biological relevance of cell-type distribution estimates across tissue sections. CARD is particularly suitable for analyzing spatially structured tissues, where neighboring cells influence gene expression patterns.

3.4 Spatially-Aware Clustering

Clustering is a fundamental step in characterizing and interpreting spatial transcriptomics data. While numerous clustering algorithms exist, spatially-informed methods have shown superior performance in defining distinct cell types or spatial domains within samples. Graph-based methods like Louvain or Leiden, commonly used in single-cell RNA sequencing, are less effective in spatially resolved transcriptomics due to their inability to capture spatial context. Methods that explicitly incorporate the spatial coordinates of spots or pixels have therefore gained prominence [29].

Spatially-aware clustering categorizes each spot, pixel, or cell into groups based on similarities in their gene expression profiles and spatial context. This differs from deconvolution, which estimates the proportions of different cell types within a single spatial data point. Spatially-aware clustering excels at identifying complex spatial domains, including mixtures of multiple cell types that form biologically meaningful structures, such as tertiary lymphoid structures, which deconvolution methods may not resolve.

3.4.1 BayesSpace

BayesSpace employs a Bayesian statistical approach using a Potts model to capture spatial dependencies alongside gene expression data. The Potts model enables the algorithm to respect spatial contiguity, resulting in clusters that reflect biologically meaningful spatial domains. BayesSpace includes a method to determine the optimal number of clusters using an elbow plot of the negative log-likelihood against the number of clusters. It also supports joint clustering of multiple samples using integrated dimension reduction methods like Canonical Correlation Analysis (CCA), Harmony, or robust Principal Component Analysis (rPCA). However, BayesSpace can face limitations in computational scalability, particularly with large numbers of samples or very large spatial datasets.

3.4.2 GraphST

GraphST is an advanced clustering method that uses graph neural networks (GNNs) to integrate spatial and transcriptional information. It models the spatial relationships of spots or pixels as nodes in a graph structure. By propagating information across graph edges, GraphST effectively incorporates spatial adjacency and gene expression similarity to identify meaningful clusters. Benchmarking studies have shown GraphST's superior performance compared to traditional methods, with improved scalability relative to BayesSpace. GraphST is optimized for integrating serial (vertical integration) or side-by-side tissue sections (horizontal integration), enhancing the comparison of spatially correlated samples. However, it may be less effective for integrating unrelated spatial transcriptomics samples or datasets with substantial biological variance between samples.

3.4.3 SpaGCN (Histology Integration)

SpaGCN is a clustering method that incorporates spatial coordinates and histology imaging with gene expression to identify spatial domains. Specifically, this tool creates a network for each sample, where every node represents a spot, node features are gene expression vectors, and node vertices incorporate both spatial distance and histological RGB pixel value similarity. Then, graph convolutional layers along with unsupervised clustering identify spatially and histologically informed transcriptomic domains which can be further investigated for specific functional programs. While SpaGCN uses the raw RGB values from the histology image, recent tools use foundation model-based morphological features integrated with gene expression and spatial coordinates such as ResST [30].

3.5 Downstream Analyses: Differential Expression, Cell Communication, and Neighborhood Analysis

3.5.1 Cell-Type Specific Differential Expression (C-SIDE)

C-SIDE (Cell-type Specific Inference of Differential Expression) identifies differentially expressed genes within individual cell types. This method allows researchers to model differential expression as a function of biologically relevant covariates, such as spatial proximity to other cell types, pathological state, interactions between neighboring cell types, or localization within specific tissue niches. Users can define these variables in the model formula, enabling tailored and context-aware analysis of the spatial transcriptomic landscape.

3.5.2 Spatially-Aware Cell–Cell Communication (CCC)

CellChat is a widely used tool for modeling cell-cell communication based on known ligand-receptor (LR) interactions. While originally designed for single-cell RNA-seq data, CellChat includes a spatial module that incorporates the physical proximity of cell types to modulate interaction probabilities. This allows for a more realistic estimation of communication strength by accounting for spatial adjacency between sender and receiver cell populations.

LIANA+ offers an alternative approach for scenarios where direct cell-type annotations are unavailable or less reliable. It performs ligand-receptor interaction analysis independently of predefined cell-type pairs by using bivariate spatial autocorrelation metrics. LIANA+ quantifies both global and local spatial interaction scores, enabling the identification and mapping of signaling hotspots regardless of explicit sender-receiver identities.

3.5.3 Neighborhood Analysis

Neighborhood analysis quantifies the spatial arrangement and co-localization patterns of cell types within tissues, providing insights into tissue architecture and cellular niches. While similar to spatially-aware clustering with the goal of identifying domains, the following methods identify neighborhoods defined by cell type proximity and thus work best for single cell resolution spatial data:

- **Giotto**: Provides a framework for defining spatial neighborhoods and quantifying interactions across spatial domains, enabling the identification of spatial domains enriched in specific cell types or interaction motifs.

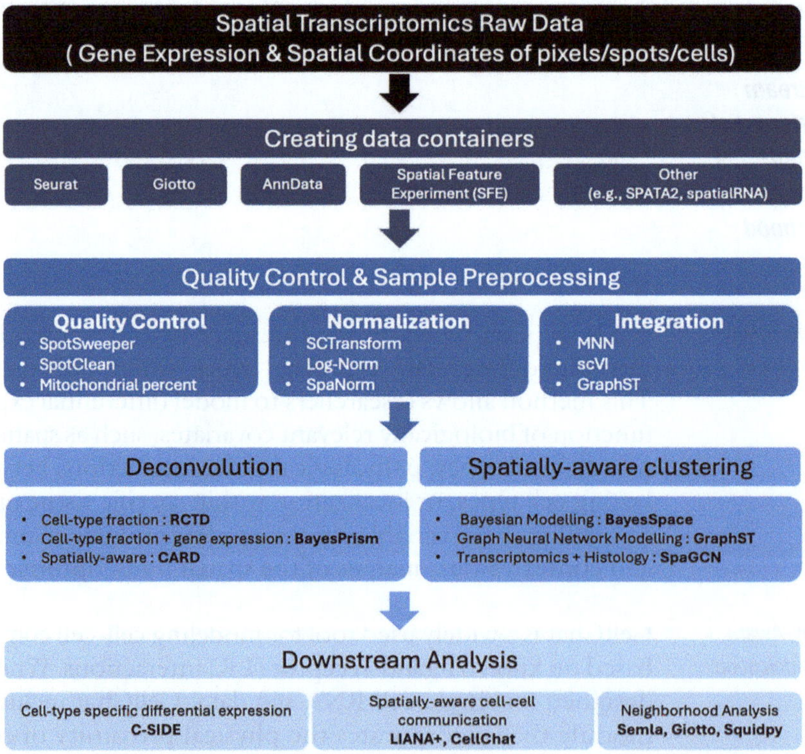

Fig. 1 Workflow for spatial transcriptomics analysis. From raw spatial data to insights: key steps include data structuring, quality control, deconvolution or clustering, and downstream analyses like differential expression, cell–cell communication, and neighborhood mapping

- **semla**: Implements methods for computing cell-cell proximity scores and neighborhood compositions, facilitating niche definition and comparative spatial analysis.
- **Scanpy and Squidpy**: These Python-based toolkits support neighborhood enrichment analysis and co-occurrence probability scores, offering flexible and scalable pipelines for quantifying spatial associations in large datasets.

Neighborhood-based approaches are crucial for uncovering spatial cellular ecosystems and defining biologically relevant microenvironments, particularly in the context of disease progression and treatment response (see Fig. 1).

Conflict of Interest

The authors have no conflicts of interest to declare that are relevant to the content of this chapter.

References

1. Marx V (2021) Method of the year: spatially resolved transcriptomics. Nat Methods 18:9–14
2. Williams CG, Lee HJ, Asatsuma T, Vento-Tormo R, Haque A (2022) An introduction to spatial transcriptomics for biomedical research. Genome Med 14:68.
3. Danishuddin Khan S, Kim JJ (2024) Spatial transcriptomics data and analytical methods: an updated perspective. Drug Discov Today 29:103889
4. R: The R project for statistical computing. https://www.r-project.org/.
5. Hao Y et al (2024) Dictionary learning for integrative, multimodal and scalable single-cell analysis. Nat Biotechnol 42:293–304
6. Moses L, et al (2023) Voyager: exploratory single-cell genomics data analysis with geospatial statistics. BioRxiv Prepr Serv Biol 2023:549945. https://doi.org/10.1101/2023.07.20.549945
7. Chen JG, et al (2023) Giotto Suite: a multi-scale and technology-agnostic spatial multi-omics analysis ecosystem. bioRxiv 2023:568752. https://doi.org/10.1101/2023.11.26.568752
8. Cable DM et al (2022) Robust decomposition of cell type mixtures in spatial transcriptomics. Nat Biotechnol 40:517–526
9. Cable DM et al (2022) Cell type-specific inference of differential expression in spatial transcriptomics. Nat Methods 19:1076–1087
10. Chu T, Wang Z, Pe'er D, Danko CG (2022) Cell type and gene expression deconvolution with BayesPrism enables Bayesian integrative analysis across bulk and single-cell RNA sequencing in oncology. Nat Cancer 3(4):505–517. https://doi.org/10.1038/s43018-022-00356-3
11. Hu M, Chikina M (2024) InstaPrism: an R package for fast implementation of BayesPrism. Bioinformatics 40:btae440. https://doi.org/10.1093/bioinformatics/btae440
12. Ma Y, Zhou X (2022) Spatially informed cell-type deconvolution for spatial transcriptomics. Nat Biotechnol 40:1349–1359
13. Zhao E, Stone MR, Ren X, Guenthoer J, Smythe KS, Pulliam T et al (2021) Spatial transcriptomics at subspot resolution with BayesSpace. Nat Biotechnol 39:1375–1384. https://doi.org/10.1038/s41587-021-00935-2
14. Jin S, Plikus MV, Nie Q (2025) CellChat for systematic analysis of cell–cell communication from single-cell transcriptomics. Nat Protoc 20:180–219
15. Kueckelhaus J et al (2024) Inferring histology-associated gene expression gradients in spatial transcriptomic studies. Nat Commun 15:7280.
16. Larsson L, Franzén L, Ståhl PL, Lundeberg J (2023) Semla: a versatile toolkit for spatially resolved transcriptomics analysis and visualization. Bioinformatics 39:btad626
17. Wolf FA, Angerer P, Theis FJ (2018) SCANPY: large-scale single-cell gene expression data analysis. Genome Biol 19:15.
18. Palla G et al (2022) Squidpy: a scalable framework for spatial omics analysis. Nat Methods 19:171–178

19. Virshup I, Rybakov S, Theis FJ, Angerer P, Wolf FA (2024) anndata: Access and store annotated data matrices. J Open Source Softw 9:4371
20. Long Y, Ang KS, Li M, Chong KLK, Sethi R, Zhong C et al (2023) Spatially informed clustering, integration, and deconvolution of spatial transcriptomics with GraphST. Nat Commun 14:1155. https://doi.org/10.1038/s41467-023-36796-3
21. Dimitrov D et al (2024) LIANA+ provides an all-in-one framework for cell–cell communication inference. Nat Cell Biol 26:1613–1622
22. Totty M, Hicks SC, Guo B (2025) SpotSweeper: spatially aware quality control for spatial transcriptomics. Nat Methods 22:1520–1530. https://doi.org/10.1038/s41592-025-02713-3
23. Ni Z et al (2022) SpotClean adjusts for spot swapping in spatial transcriptomics data. Nat Commun 13:2971.
24. Bhuva DD et al (2024) Library size confounds biology in spatial transcriptomics data. Genome Biol 25:99.
25. Salim A et al (2025) SpaNorm: spatially-aware normalization for spatial transcriptomics data. Genome Biol 26:109.
26. Haghverdi L, Lun ATL, Morgan MD, Marioni JC (2018) Batch effects in single-cell RNA-sequencing data are corrected by matching mutual nearest neighbors. Nat Biotechnol 36:421–427
27. Lopez R, Regier J, Cole MB, Jordan MI, Yosef N (2018) Deep generative modeling for single-cell transcriptomics. Nat Methods 15:1053–1058
28. Li H et al (2023) A comprehensive benchmarking with practical guidelines for cellular deconvolution of spatial transcriptomics. Nat Commun 14:1548.
29. Yuan Z et al (2024) Benchmarking spatial clustering methods with spatially resolved transcriptomics data. Nat Methods 21:712–722
30. Huang J, Fu X, Zhang Z, Xie Y, Liu S, Wang Y, Zhao Z, Peng Y (2024) A graph self-supervised residual learning framework for domain identification and data integration of spatial transcriptomics. Commun Biol 7(1). https://doi.org/10.1038/s42003-024-06814-1

Subject Index

Timothy L. Frankel and Arvind Rao (eds.), *Cellular Spatial Characterization and Analysis*, Methods in Molecular Biology, vol. 2995, https://doi.org/10.1007/978-1-0716-5027-1,

MIX
Papier aus verantwortungsvollen Quellen
Paper from responsible sources
FSC® C105338

If you have any concerns about our products,
you can contact us on
ProductSafety@springernature.com

In case Publisher is established outside the EU,
the EU authorized representative is:
Springer Nature Customer Service Center GmbH
Europaplatz 3, 69115 Heidelberg, Germany

Printed by Libri Plureos GmbH
in Hamburg, Germany